Modern Language Association of America

Approaches to Teaching
World Literature

Joseph Gibaldi, Series Editor

1. Joseph Gibaldi, ed. *Approaches to Teaching Chaucer's* Canterbury Tales. 1980.
2. Carole Slade, ed. *Approaches to Teaching Dante's* Divine Comedy. 1982.
3. Richard Bjornson, ed. *Approaches to Teaching Cervantes'* Don Quixote. 1984.
4. Jess B. Bessinger, Jr., and Robert F. Yeager, eds. *Approaches to Teaching* Beowulf. 1984.
5. Richard J. Dunn, ed. *Approaches to Teaching Dickens'* David Copperfield. 1984.
6. Steven G. Kellman, ed. *Approaches to Teaching Camus's* The Plague. 1985.
7. Yvonne Shafer, ed. *Approaches to Teaching Ibsen's* A Doll House. 1985.
8. Martin Bickman, ed. *Approaches to Teaching Melville's* Moby-Dick. 1985.
9. Miriam Youngerman Miller and Jane Chance, eds. *Approaches to Teaching* Sir Gawain and the Green Knight. 1986.
10. Galbraith M. Crump, ed. *Approaches to Teaching Milton's* Paradise Lost. 1986.
11. Spencer Hall, with Jonathan Ramsey, eds. *Approaches to Teaching Wordsworth's Poetry.* 1986.
12. Robert H. Ray, ed. *Approaches to Teaching Shakespeare's* King Lear. 1986.
13. Kostas Myrsiades, ed. *Approaches to Teaching Homer's* Iliad *and* Odyssey. 1987.
14. Douglas J. McMillan, ed. *Approaches to Teaching Goethe's* Faust. 1987.
15. Renée Waldinger, ed. *Approaches to Teaching Voltaire's* Candide. 1987.
16. Bernard Koloski, ed. *Approaches to Teaching Chopin's* The Awakening. 1988.
17. Kenneth M. Roemer, ed. *Approaches to Teaching Momaday's* The Way to Rainy Mountain. 1988.
18. Edward J. Rielly, ed. *Approaches to Teaching Swift's* Gulliver's Travels. 1988.
19. Jewel Spears Brooker, ed. *Approaches to Teaching Eliot's Poetry and Plays.* 1988.
20. Melvyn New, ed. *Approaches to Teaching Sterne's* Tristram Shandy. 1989.
21. Robert F. Gleckner and Mark L. Greenberg, eds. *Approaches to Teaching Blake's* Songs of Innocence and of Experience. 1989.
22. Susan J. Rosowski, ed. *Approaches to Teaching Cather's* My Ántonia. 1989.
23. Carey Kaplan and Ellen Cronan Rose, eds. *Approaches to Teaching Lessing's* The Golden Notebook. 1989.
24. Susan Resneck Parr and Pancho Savery, eds. *Approaches to Teaching Ellison's* Invisible Man. 1989.
25. Barry N. Olshen and Yael S. Feldman, eds. *Approaches to Teaching the Hebrew Bible as Literature in Translation.* 1989.
26. Robin Riley Fast and Christine Mack Gordon, eds. *Approaches to Teaching Dickinson's Poetry.* 1989.
27. Spencer Hall, ed. *Approaches to Teaching Shelley's Poetry.* 1990.

28. Sidney Gottlieb, ed. *Approaches to Teaching the Metaphysical Poets*. 1990.

29. Richard K. Emmerson, ed. *Approaches to Teaching Medieval English Drama*. 1990.

30. Kathleen Blake, ed. *Approaches to Teaching Eliot's* Middlemarch. 1990.

31. María Elena de Valdés and Mario J. Valdés, eds. *Approaches to Teaching García Márquez's* One Hundred Years of Solitude. 1990.

32. Donald D. Kummings, ed. *Approaches to Teaching Whitman's* Leaves of Grass. 1990.

33. Stephen C. Behrendt, ed. *Approaches to Teaching Shelley's* Frankenstein. 1990.

34. June Schlueter and Enoch Brater, eds. *Approaches to Teaching Beckett's* Waiting for Godot. 1991.

35. Walter H. Evert and Jack W. Rhodes, eds. *Approaches to Teaching Keats's Poetry*. 1991.

36. Frederick W. Shilstone, ed. *Approaches to Teaching Byron's Poetry*. 1991.

37. Bernth Lindfors, ed. *Approaches to Teaching Achebe's* Things Fall Apart. 1991.

38. Richard E. Matlak, ed. *Approaches to Teaching Coleridge's Poetry and Prose*. 1991.

39. Shirley Geok-lin Lim, ed. *Approaches to Teaching Kingston's* The Woman Warrior. 1991.

40. Maureen Fries and Jeanie Watson, eds. *Approaches to Teaching the Arthurian Tradition*. 1992.

41. Maurice Hunt, ed. *Approaches to Teaching Shakespeare's* The Tempest *and Other Late Romances*. 1992.

42. Diane Long Hoeveler and Beth Lau, eds. *Approaches to Teaching Brontë's* Jane Eyre. 1993.

43. Jeffrey B. Berlin, ed. *Approaches to Teaching Mann's* Death in Venice *and Other Short Fiction*. 1992.

44. Kathleen McCormick and Erwin R. Steinberg, eds. *Approaches to Teaching Joyce's* Ulysses. 1993.

45. Marcia McClintock Folsom, ed. *Approaches to Teaching Austen's* Pride and Prejudice. 1993.

46. Wallace Jackson and R. Paul Yoder, eds. *Approaches to Teaching Pope's Poetry*. 1993.

Approaches to Teaching Pope's Poetry

Edited by
Wallace Jackson
and
R. Paul Yoder

Modern Language Association of America
New York   1993

Library of Congress Cataloging-in-Publication Data

Approaches to teaching Pope's poetry / edited by Wallace Jackson and
  R. Paul Yoder
    p. cm. — (Approaches to teaching world literature ; 46)
  Includes bibliographical references and indexes.
  ISBN 0-87352-715-1 (hard) ISBN 0-87352-716-X (pbk.)
  1. Pope, Alexander, 1688–1744 — Study and teaching. I. Jackson,
Wallace, 1930–   . II. Yoder, R. Paul. III. Series.
PR3637.S78A67 1993
821'.5 — dc20   93-24854

Cover illustration of the paperback edition: Aubrey Beardsley, "The Battle of the
Beaux and Belles," illustration for *The Rape of the Lock* (1896), photo engraving.

Published by The Modern Language Association of America
10 Astor Place, New York, New York 10003-6981

Printed on recycled paper

CONTENTS

PREFACE TO THE SERIES

In *The Art of Teaching* Gilbert Highet wrote, "Bad teaching wastes a great deal of effort, and spoils many lives which might have been full of energy and happiness." All too many teachers have failed in their work, Highet argued, simply "because they have not thought about it." We hope that the Approaches to Teaching World Literature series, sponsored by the Modern Language Association's Publications Committee, will not only improve the craft — as well as the art — of teaching but also encourage serious and continuing discussion of the aims and methods of teaching literature.

The principal objective of the series is to collect within each volume different points of view on teaching a specific literary work, a literary tradition, or a writer widely taught at the undergraduate level. The preparation of each volume begins with a wide-ranging survey of instructors, thus enabling us to include in the volume the philosophies and approaches, thoughts and methods of scores of experienced teachers. The result is a sourcebook of material, information, and ideas on teaching the subject of the volume to undergraduates.

The series is intended to serve nonspecialists as well as specialists, inexperienced as well as experienced teachers, graduate students who wish to learn effective ways of teaching as well as senior professors who wish to compare their own approaches with the approaches of colleagues in other schools. Of course, no volume in the series can ever substitute for erudition, intelligence, creativity, and sensitivity in teaching. We hope merely that each book will point readers in useful directions; at most each will offer only a first step in the long journey to successful teaching.

Joseph Gibaldi
Series Editor

PREFACE TO THE VOLUME

Pope began writing poetry as a very young man, at an age, in fact, when he was hardly more than a boy, and he continued in a full life of original composition, translation, and editing until his death in 1744. He was during his lifetime and, for many, still is today the most important poet of the eighteenth century writing poetry in any Western language. Between Dryden, who died in 1700, and Blake and Wordsworth, who began writing in the late years of the eighteenth century, there were few English and European poets to rival him. Pope remains for us not only a writer of infinite skill and address but a touchstone to that "excellent and indispensable eighteenth century," as Matthew Arnold referred to it (40). His poetry provides, therefore, the acknowledged index to social criticism, to enlightened religious belief, to witty and vivacious writing, and to the bearing of much of the Western literary tradition on the eighteenth-century mind. If the eighteenth century is excellent and indispensable, Pope is one of the main occasions for its being so.

In these pages we have gathered together essays by a number of eminent scholars and teachers who have endeavored to make their understanding available to students. The burden and purpose of the volume is the art of teaching Pope, of knowing what needs to be known within traditional and modern contexts to enable that teaching. The essays are only less various and multisided than Pope himself, for his brilliance and versatility can hardly be matched anywhere. We are tempted to say that Pope is an intellectual's poet, though strictly speaking he is not a great creator of ideas and his deployment of philosophical concepts has always seemed to some a weakness of his purportedly philosophical verse, the *Essay on Man*, for example. It may be safer, and closer to the mark, to say that he is a writer of unusual sophistication, a term implying the exacting harmony of metropolitan virtues: urbanity, wit, craft, knowingness, an eye for what is in and what is out of place. He has been called a poet of civilization, his poetry has been styled a poetry of allusion, he has been reckoned a superb technician. Each of these efforts to distill an essence is in its own way accurate, for each tries to summarize a writer who seems especially alert and responsively aggressive. Pope's poetry often adjudicates, exonerates, convicts, or praises. So deeply is it given to such actions that Eloisa's own epistle is both a subtle indictment and a defense of the sexual passion motivating her love for Abelard, is both love poetry of a high order and a criticism of passion that sets its own standards of conduct. The poetry is thus commonly disposed to evaluate the subjects and objects of its discourse.

Appraisal may be carried out on various levels, it may be evoked in different ways, and it may of course reach varying degrees of intensity, but it is always—or almost always—present, and its very presentness is inescapable. These essays help bring this activity into focus for modern students by grounding it in the intricacies of thought and vision that inform the poetry; they allow us to see what regulates and necessitates the adjudicatory mode, even complicates that mode by, as Fredric Bogel points out in his contribution to this volume, ensnaring the arbiter in the arbitration. Condemnation and praise may therefore turn out to be more powerfully and humanly operative than they at first seem, and the act of judgment itself complicated by the network of allusions in which it appears.

Something of the same sort may be said about Pope's meditations on his role as writer and his response across the centuries to Horace, a distant predecessor enabling the vocational self-consciousness that so deeply informs the *Imitations of Horace*. The adjudicatory mode bears on Pope's imitations of Horace insofar as imitation itself provides the occasion for differing from and commenting on a predecessor, and Pope excels at this technique. Adjudication may extend even to Pope's appraisal of a nobleman's park, and his evaluation, which may initially seem a matter of taste, soon comes to appear a matter of civilized style, of the play of mind on nature and on the disposition of prospect and vision, order and design. Before long the adjudicatory mode reveals the pressure of values that lie behind it, motivate it, and define its urgency. We believe that a poetry so situated culturally is the one students must encounter, though everything depends on how the introductions are managed. It is therefore not surprising that many essays here are directed toward controverting first impressions, while acknowledging that Pope is a "difficult" poet. The very first essay in the "Approaches" section begins, "Although he may seem at times among the most artificial or old-fashioned of poets, Pope speaks our language." The very last starts out, "Teaching *The Dunciad* can be a daunting prospect."

Indeed. But *The Dunciad* is a work of passionate indictments and defenses, the adjudicatory mode in its highest and most prophetic manifestation, and thus part satire, part epic poem, part sublime ode—a voluminous farrago of genres brought to bear on an idea of civilization, a work designed to baffle and confound opponents. The *Moral Essays* are concerned with usage (of riches) and with the characters of men and women; *The Rape of the Lock* arbitrates (and satirizes) relations between the sexes; the *Essay on Criticism* condemns bad literary judgment. And so it goes through an extraordinary range of tones and voices, arguments and counterarguments, exhortation and rebuke. The energy of Pope's engagement is alone compelling, as adversaries and interlocutors within (and outside) the poems often discover (note, in particular, *An Essay on Man*). Readers of this volume will find many essays under one rubric or another, in large or in little, inevitably responsive to this characteristic feature of his verse, but whatever the specific utility of this book, we think there is much utility here. The "Course Survey" and "Bibliographic Essay" should serve as guides to teaching practices and to the recent history of Pope scholarship. We therefore commend to you the collective knowledge and wisdom of the many scholar-teachers who have participated in the making of this work, and we trust that their experience will enrich yours. The Publications Committee of the Modern Language Association — particularly the series editor, Joseph Gibaldi, and his former associate, Adrienne Marie Ward — have contributed enormously to the making of this work, as have the various editorial readers and consultants who have guided our progress from beginning to end.

Part One

MATERIALS

A Course Survey

'Tis with teachers as with watches, none go just alike. Therefore, I do not intend to propose a single course description for teaching Alexander Pope. Instead, using the surveys sent out by the MLA when this volume was announced, I here provide information on what poems we teachers of Pope are teaching, what texts we are using in the classroom, and what we hope to accomplish with our students by reading these works. Of the approximately three hundred surveys distributed to MLA members officially listing an interest in eighteenth-century English literature, a disappointing twenty-three were returned, a number that suggests that the teachers may be suffering from the apathy toward Pope they fear in their students. (Not even all of our own contributors completed the survey.) Nevertheless, the respondents did include one retired professor, several well-known scholars from well-known universities, and a variety of both new and more experienced teachers at different levels in other universities and in two- and four-year colleges. Though few in number, these surveys provide an interesting and readily manageable "database" from which we may begin to describe the community of teachers of Alexander Pope's poetry.

What are we teaching? Of the twenty-five poems mentioned, the vast majority were listed by only one or two teachers. A few, however, were mentioned often. I suppose it will come as no surprise that *The Rape of the Lock* is by far the most commonly taught of Pope's poems. Nineteen out of twenty-three teach it in at least one class, many in several different classes. The *Rape* shows up in classes on courtship in the English tradition and on Greek and Roman mythology, in introductory survey courses and graduate seminars. Second only to the *Rape*, interestingly enough, is *The Dunciad*, although often only parts and, of those parts, often only book 4. Following these two, the four poems most frequently taught are, in order, the *Essay on Man* (usually only parts), the *Epistle to Dr. Arbuthnot*, the *Essay on Criticism*, and the *Epistle to a Lady*. Less frequently than these, the *Epistle to Burlington*, *Windsor-Forest*, and the *Epilogue to the Satires* are all taught in the same number of classes. The *Epistles to Several Persons* are rarely taught as a group, *To a Lady* and *Burlington* apparently being used as representative of the set. The surprise for me was how rarely *Eloisa to Abelard* is taught; only three of the respondents mentioned it.

Editions and Anthologies

By far the most widely used text is Aubrey Williams's edition, *Poetry and Prose of Alexander Pope*. For the poetry, Williams uses the Twickenham texts; for the prose, he uses the first editions (with a few later additions to *Peri Bathous*). This collection contains the more popular poems, including the *Pastorals*, "The Episode of Sarpedon," *An Essay on Criticism*, *Messiah*, *Windsor-Forest*, *The Rape of the Lock*, *Eloisa to Abelard*, "Elegy to the Memory of an Unfortunate Lady," and *An Epistle to Dr. Arbuthnot*, plus the full text of all the *Epistles to Several Persons*, *An Essay on Man*, and *The Dunciad, in Four Books* (with some abridgment of the critical apparatus). The good selection of Pope's prose includes "A Discourse on Pastoral Poetry," the *Guardian 40*, *Peri Bathous*, "Preface to the *Iliad*," and "Preface to the Works of Shakespeare." Williams's introduction is in two parts, one part focusing on Pope's life and one on Pope's poetry, but Williams's historical orientation rightly blurs his own distinction, using Pope's poetry to illuminate his life, and his life to illuminate his poetry.

Also useful, especially for graduate students, is John Butt's one-volume edition of the Twickenham Pope, *The Poems of Alexander Pope*. It contains the complete poetry, with the exception of Pope's translations of the *Iliad* and the *Odyssey*. In his preface, Butt lists the other omissions from the original edition:

> The text is the Twickenham text but without the variant readings, without the Latin original of the *Imitations of Horace*, without the mock indexes to each version of *The Dunciad*, without the poems of doubtful authenticity, the 1712 version of *The Rape of the Lock*, and a few small pieces in volume VI that were subsequently incorporated in longer poems.   (vii)

All of Pope's notes have been retained, "but without variant readings and without indication of the editions in which they are to be found" (vii). One respondent to the survey says that she uses both Butt and Williams because "the format of *The Dunciad* in four books in the Butt edition is absolutely frustrating"; she does not elaborate. This edition contains a good chronological table, Pope's preface to the 1717 *Works*, and some prose incidental to the poetry ("Discourse on Pastoral," the various letters, testimonies, appendixes to *The Dunciad*). It does not contain *Peri Bathous* or any other prose, nor does it include any of the Twickenham introductions.

A third volume being used is *Pope: Poems and Prose*, edited by Douglas Grant. One respondent said that she uses it because it is "comprehensive, inexpensive." Another respondent, however, reported having ordered it sight unseen and having been greatly disappointed. He said that it had the poems he wanted, but with few notes and no line numbers. The absence of line numbers would seem particularly unfortunate for classroom use.

One volume that was not mentioned by the respondents but that I found on the bookstore shelf is Robin Sowerby's *Alexander Pope: Selected Poetry and Prose*. It is one of the Routledge English Texts, under the general editorship of John Drakakis. This is a book with a mission. Sowerby is a classics and eighteenth-century scholar and translator (he provides the translation and additional notes in David Lindley's edition of *De puluerea coniuratione (The Gunpowder Plot)*, and his edition of Pope's work seeks to overturn the lack of attention given to Pope's translation of Homer (see the omissions from Butt's edition above). In the "Critical Commentary," which focuses primarily on Samuel Johnson and Joseph Warton, Sowerby writes, "The Homer translation is a major poetic achievement, unjustly neglected on the grounds that it is not 'original,' and any assessment of Pope's output and career that ignores it will be deficient" (229). Toward the goal of righting this wrong, Sowerby's critical discussion follows Johnson, focusing in large part on the originality of Pope's translation; of the 180 pages of Pope's writing here, almost a third are passages from the *Iliad* and *Odyssey* (poetry, preface, or postscript). Although the collection also contains a few letters, there is little other prose, and some standard works get surprisingly short shrift (for example, none of the epistles in the *Essay on Man* is presented in its entirety). In the introduction Sowerby presents a modest biographic account and then uses *An Essay on Criticism* as the basis for a broader "Introduction to the Poems." There is also a very brief "Select Bibliography."

Five general anthologies were also mentioned as being in regular use. Two of these are of marginal importance. Wylie Sypher's *Enlightenment England* is out of print now, but the interested teacher might learn from it something about the way attitudes change toward Pope. It contains *An Essay on Criticism*, the *Rape*, *Eloisa*, *Arbuthnot*, and an excerpt from *Windsor-Forest* but none of the *Epistles to Several Persons*, book 1 rather than book 4 of *The Dunciad*, and all of epistles 1 and 2 from the *Essay on Man*. Hazard Adams's *Critical Theory since Plato* provides a convenient way to include Pope in classes on critical theory. Of Pope's works only *An Essay on Criticism* is included, but also represented are works by Aristotle, Horace, Longinus, Dryden, Dennis, and Addison, to name the critics most relevant to Pope.

The three more important general anthologies are *Eighteenth-Century English Literature*, edited by Geoffrey Tillotson, Paul Fussell, and Marshall Waingrow; *The Restoration and the Eighteenth Century*, edited by Martin Price; and, of course, *The Norton Anthology of English Literature*, volume 1, fifth edition, edited by M. H. Abrams and others. Of these, with reference to Pope, there is little difference between the Norton and Price's anthology: Price includes all of book 4 of *The Dunciad* but no complete epistles from the *Essay on Man*; Norton includes epistles 1 and 2 from the *Essay* in their entirety but only excerpts from *Dunciad* 4. Price has *To a Lady* and *Burlington*, but only excerpts from *An Essay on Criticism* and no *Eloisa*; Norton has *Eloisa*, the full *Essay on Criticism*, and *To a Lady*, but no *Burlington*. Both include *Arbuthnot*, but Price also includes *The First Satire of the Second Book of Horace* and the *Epilogue to the Satires*.

The anthology by Tillotson, Fussell, and Waingrow contains as many selections from Pope as Norton and Price put together. Here are "Winter,"

An Essay on Criticism, Messiah, Rape, Windsor-Forest, Eloisa, An Essay on Man, Arbuthnot, Burlington, To a Lady, Dunciad 1 (1728), *The New Dunciad*, and several Horatian imitations, all complete, together with other poems and selected prose, including *Peri Bathous* and the preface to the 1717 *Works*. It also contains such relevant items as John Denham's *Cooper's Hill* and Swift's *On Poetry: A Rhapsody*, neither of which appears in any of the other general anthologies surveyed.

Aims and Issues

If these are the texts we are using in class, what do we think we are doing with them? In response to the survey question, "What do you expect the student to understand chiefly about Pope at the conclusion of the course?" the answers reflect current debates about Pope's career and about the canon. One sequence of three responses seemed particularly telling. The first of these suggests a concern with making Pope accessible to a new, young audience: the teacher wants his students to see that Pope "is not as difficult or abstruse as he appears at first. That he is very funny and clever. A great social satirist. That he can illuminate his era." This same concern about the distance between our students and Pope's work surfaces elsewhere in a different respondent's statement that he wants to instill an "awareness (if not also appreciation) of [Pope's] imaginativeness and creativity" and an "awareness (if not also enjoyment) of his wit, humor, energy, and liveliness." Apparently there is a fear that despite Plato's claims about the irresistible nature of truth, the truth about Pope may be revealed to our students without convincing them of its value.

Indeed, several respondents seem themselves unconvinced by the truth about Pope. The second respondent in my sequence recognizes the usual marks of Pope's greatness, but for her this "greatness" would seem to require quotation marks: she wants her students to see "that Pope is canonical because his poems combine genteel learning, structural and syntactic complexity, the subordination of overt social and political investments to a frequently psychologistic rhetoric, and a tendency to produce wit at women's expense: all characteristics valued by a traditional liberal arts education in Anglo-America." This teacher is more concerned than was the first with the basis and targets of Pope's humor and cleverness, with the issues informing current canon debates, including the questions of ideology and gender raised by critics like Laura Brown and Ellen Pollak. For her, Pope's canonicity makes it possible to study the canon and its standards of inclusion.

These issues are of considerably less concern to the respondent who came third in this sequence: he wants his students to see "Pope as supremely gifted wordsmith; Pope's ideas of civilizedness." Pope's "civilizedness" would probably include his "genteel learning," and perhaps even his "tendency to produce wit at women's expense"; his status as "supremely gifted wordsmith" almost certainly implies his "structural and syntactic complexity." The difference between the second and third respondents in this sequence is the sort of work they want to make Pope do. While the third respondent is not as reductionist as still another respondent, who said simply that she wanted her students to understand his poetry — she also requested that this collection include "nonideological analyses" — he clearly speaks from a New Critical, old formalist position. He intends to teach the greatness of Pope; the second respondent wants to use that claim of greatness to teach skepticism toward the institutions that endorse the claim.

Most often, however, we seem to teach some combination of an idealized Pope and a historicized Pope: idealized either as craftsman or moralizer or both, historicized either as marginalized satirist or representative central spokesman. Several respondents referred to Pope's "insight into human nature," "the moral issues he raises," "his great moral significance," and "his conviction that proper use of language and moral stature are closely allied." This moral quality is, not surprisingly, often coupled with Pope's role as satirist, although the historical implications of that satire occasionally seem to be subordinated to Pope's aesthetic; for example, one respondent teaches "the power [Pope] gives to satire by the marvel of his verse," while another refers to "his power as satirist; the beauty of the closed couplet as used in satire." A different approach focuses on Pope as a guide to, if not representative of, his period: as one respondent put it, his students should "appreciate Pope's works in the wider context of eighteenth-century critical thought and understand the intellectual and cultural assumptions of the age." Another says that his students should see Pope's "range and variety as a poet and as a critic of his age." Still another desires her students to see that Pope, "following Dryden, believed that the poet was a public figure."

Which Pope is it that we are teaching? Which Pope is it that we want to teach? Two respondents suggest the difficulty of deciding. One teaches different Popes to different class levels: "For sophomores — an appreciation of his enormous technical skill; some understanding of the notion of wit, decorum, satire, and Great Chain as metaphor for metaphysical and social reality. For Women in Literature — cultural stereotypes of 'the female.'" How does one separate Pope's complicity in perpetuating "cultural stereotypes of 'the female'" from a full appreciation of his "technical skill" in *The Rape of the Lock* or *To a Lady*? A second respondent does not even try; he wants his students to see Pope's "'greatness' but also his pettiness; his frustration with his outsider status and how that contributed to his choices about his work and his life; his place in a literary community, if only by letter; his place in a long literary tradition that seemed to him to have an uncertain future; how his work partakes of tradition and deviates from it."

This is the Alexander Pope we finally must address. Like all of us, a mass of contradictions. Unlike Chaucer or Shakespeare or Milton, Pope is not usually granted an entire semester for study. He usually must share the semester at least with Swift and Johnson, if not with everyone else in the *Norton Anthology*, volume 1. Given the limited time we have for Pope in the classroom, perhaps we can hope for no more than that our students come away with "some understanding of Pope's social and political concerns, with an appreciation of Pope's wit and artistry." Even that seems a tall order.

I think our intentions in teaching Pope can help explain why we teach the poems we do. The *Rape* is popular because it is reasonably accessible even to modern readers, and it requires relatively little of the historical annotations that are needed for most of Pope's other poems, such as *The Dunciad*. *The Dunciad* is popular, I think, because it provides an interesting contrast to the mock-epic of the *Rape*; it is also more broadly humorous than the *Rape*, even if it requires — and brings with it — a more extensive critical apparatus. Moreover, *The Dunciad* allows the teacher to counter the misconceptions of many students that the eighteenth century in general, and Alexander Pope in particular, are somehow stodgy, humorless, or over-refined. The choice may, of course, be more explicitly self-interested; one teacher of *The Dunciad* admits frankly to an "obsession" with it. We teach the *Essay on Man* because it balances the darkness of *The Dunciad* and allows discussion of Pope as philosopher and moralist. The *Epistle to Dr. Arbuthnot* grants a more homely, and Horatian, glimpse of Pope.

The shape of literary history depends in many ways on how literature is taught in the classroom — which poets and what poems, how much "context," whether the teacher "likes" the material. If you don't like Pope but you have to teach him, these essays may not change your mind, but they should make your job easier. If you do like Pope, then the job is half done already; these essays can show you what others are doing and perhaps give you some practical information and new ideas. It is still up to you, however, to decide which poems to teach, what shape you want to give to your Pope. The survey shows that the shape we collectively give to Pope in our classrooms is informed primarily by *The Rape of the Lock*, the *Epistle to Dr. Arbuthnot*, and parts of *The Dunciad* and *An Essay on Man*. Perhaps the essays here on the less frequently taught poems, like *Windsor-Forest*, *Eloisa to Abelard*, and the *Imitations of Horace*, book 2, satire 1, will begin to change that shape. Whatever shape you give to your Pope, we hope all these essays will prove helpful.

A Bibliographic Essay

Critical commentary on the writings of Alexander Pope seems to have begun at about the time that Alexander Pope began to write, and the commentary — both positive and negative — has continued virtually nonstop since then. When I began this study I consulted the MLA's online *Bibliography*, requesting titles on "Pope, Alexander" from 1980 to 1990; the search turned up 442 items for that decade alone, and the list was by no means exhaustive. From the perspective of the 1990s, a bibliographic essay on the state of Pope studies, especially one that will fit within the constraints of this volume, would seem as monumental — and silly — a task as moving Timon's villa to Twickenham.

But if we consult the "Genius of the Place," perhaps we may construct a useful edifice. The genius of this place is pedagogy, and so I offer some practical information that I hope teachers of Pope's work at all levels will find helpful. I have made no attempt to provide a complete bibliography of discussions of Pope's life and works, as several good annotated bibliographies exist that can help the teacher of Pope survey the critical history. Instead, I have divided my own discussion into two parts: (1) books that should be on a "reserve book" list for your students, including supplemental primary texts, biographies, introductions, and those bibliographies I have mentioned; (2) selected books and articles on important topics in Pope studies (Pope's politics, Pope and the other arts, etc.), including book-length studies of major poems.

Reserve Books

The most important work to have available to your students is the eleven-volume *Twickenham Edition of the Works of Alexander Pope*, John Butt, general editor. The standard edition of Pope's poetry, it serves as the basis for the texts of most of the classroom collections discussed above in "A Course Survey." It comes equipped with extensive annotations, authoritative introductions, and all the items omitted in Butt's one-volume edition. The Twickenham edition replaces *The Works of Alexander Pope*, edited by Elwin Whitwell and W. J. Courthope, in ten volumes, which may still be useful as a reference work. Two concordances will help your students trace particular words or ideas through Pope's work. Keyed to the Twickenham edition is *A Concordance to the Poems of Alexander Pope*, in two volumes, edited by Emmett G. Bedford and Robert T. Dilligan. This concordance supersedes Edwin Abbot's *A Concordance to the Works of Alexander Pope* (1875), which is useful in a different way since it refers to the Warburton 1751 edition of Pope's work.

There are also critical editions of several poems by Pope that your students may find useful. Earl Wasserman's *Pope's "Epistle to Bathurst": A Critical*

Reading with an Edition of the Manuscripts considers Pope's revisions of the poem between the first draft (1732) and the 1744 text used in the Twickenham edition. Robert M. Schmitz's *Pope's* Windsor-Forest, *1712: A Study of the Washington University Holograph* includes not only the manuscript but also historical background and some discussion of Pope's creative process. Maynard Mack's "Pope's *Pastorals*" (1980) provides a facsimile of Pope's manuscript with introduction and bibliographic remarks.

Pope's prose has at last been brought together in a modern edition, *The Prose Works of Alexander Pope*. To Norman Ault's volume 1, *The Earlier Works, 1711–1720* (1936), has been added Rosemary Cowler's volume 2, *The Major Works, 1725–1744* (1986). Also important is George Sherburn's edition of *The Correspondence of Alexander Pope* in five volumes. A useful compilation of Pope's own critical commentary, drawn from his prose, poetry, and correspondence, is provided by Bertrand A. Goldgar in *Literary Criticism of Alexander Pope*. Paul Hammond's edition of *Selected Prose of Alexander Pope* offers a handy selection of fourteen prose works, including the major pieces and some correspondence. For teachers who wish to address Pope's relationship with the other Scriblerians, the important editions are *Memoirs of the Extraordinary Life, Works, and Discoveries of Martinus Scriblerus*, edited by Charles Kerby-Miller, and *The Art of Sinking in Poetry* [*Peri Bathous*], edited by Edna Leake Steeves.

The lack of a modern biography has recently been remedied by Maynard Mack's excellent and monumental *Alexander Pope: A Life*. Still useful is George Sherburn's *Early Career of Alexander Pope*, which considers the poet's life up to 1726. A more personal account of Pope appears in Joseph Spence's *Observations, Anecdotes, and Characters of Books and Men*, edited by James Osborn, which includes anecdotes about Pope. Among the several other biographic studies, the most notable is *"This Long Disease, My Life": Alexander Pope and the Sciences* by Marjorie H. Nicolson and G. S. Rousseau, which provides a medical case history of Pope.

For introductory material, the introductions in the Twickenham edition may be recommended, as well as Pat Rogers's *An Introduction to Pope*, I. R. F. Gordon's *A Preface to Pope*, Brean S. Hammond's ideologically oriented *Pope*, and Felicity Rosslyn's *Alexander Pope: A Literary Life*. If you prefer a less predigested approach, the following three books can provide your students with a relatively quick overview of Pope's career and context: Reginald Berry's recent *A Pope Chronology* is just that, a chronology of Pope's career coordinated with contemporary public events; Reginald H. Griffith's *Alexander Pope: A Bibliography* is a list of Pope's publications from 1709 to 1751; Joseph V. Guerinot's *Pamphlet Attacks on Alexander Pope 1711–1744: A Descriptive Bibliography* can help outline Pope's adversarial entanglements. Together, these works should allow the interested student to grasp quickly the contours of Pope's career and the controversies of his contemporary reception.

One might also consider including, for critical background, the three most often cited pre-twentieth-century commentaries on Pope: Joseph Warton's *An Essay on the Genius and Writings of Pope*, Samuel Johnson's *Life of Pope* in *Lives of the English Poets*, edited by G. Birkbeck Hill, and Matthew Arnold's "The Study of Poetry." The first two of these set the tone for discussions of Pope in the nineteenth century, Warton pigeonholing Pope as the best of the second rank of writers, Johnson noting conversely that, if Pope's work is not poetry, then poetry is nowhere to be found. About a hundred years after Johnson, Arnold confers on Pope the dubious distinction (for a poet) of being one of the English language's best prose writers. Most twentieth-century commentary on Pope is an attempt to defend Pope against Warton and Arnold, and the defense more often than not begins with Johnson.

Finally, the bibliographies of secondary works, useful for student and teacher alike, include James Edward Tobin's *Alexander Pope: A List of Critical Studies Published from 1895 to 1944*; Cecilia L. Lopez's *Alexander Pope: An Annotated Bibliography, 1945–1967*; Geoffrey Tillotson's "Pope" in *English Poetry: Select Bibliographical Guides*, edited by A. E. Dyson; Wolfgang Kowalk's *Alexander Pope: An Annotated Bibliography of Twentieth-Century Criticism, 1900–1979*; "Alexander Pope" in Donald C. Mell's *English Poetry, 1660–1800: A Guide to Information Sources*; *The Eighteenth Century: A Current Bibliography (ECCB)* (Borck), published annually and now up to 1985; and the section on Pope in *An Annotated Critical Bibliography of Augustan Poetry* by David Nokes and Janet Barron.

Critical Studies

In this part of my discussion I divide critical study of Pope into the following, admittedly artificial but pedagogically useful, categories: (1) recent collections; (2) books on specific poems (*Rape*, *Essay on Man*, *Dunciad*); (3) Pope and Horace (including work on the Horatian poems); (4) Pope, Homer, and the classical tradition (excluding Horace); (5) Pope and the other arts; (6) Pope and gender; (7) Pope and Jacobitism; (8) studies of Pope's career, backgrounds, and versification. The first group includes (among others) the tercentenary collections as a ready guide for the uninitiated to the state of Pope scholarship as we approach the end of the twentieth century. The second and third groups describe the book-length studies (and a few single-focus collections) that can handily present to the teacher of Pope's most popular poems both an overview and a depth of study wholly different from what any single article can do. In groups 4 and 5 will be found respectively (but not only) work on Pope's translations and work on Pope and gardening. The items in groups 6 and 7 should be useful to the teacher who wishes to engage students with Pope in the light of the advances of women's studies and a sort of new (or at least revisionary) historicism. The last group includes the more important of the full-length studies of Pope's career, as well as works useful for discussions of Pope's context and craftsmanship. Given the number of articles on Pope's work, the constraints of the present volume, and the strengths and limitations of the annotated bibliographies mentioned above, I have chosen to mention only the more significant articles and to comment only in passing on most books published before 1980; I have briefly described, however, just under thirty of the books published since 1980. This strategy will, I hope, provide the teacher of Pope's work with both a ready guide to scholarship useful in class preparations and a description of recent books, many of which have not yet been annotated elsewhere.

Recent Collections

Teachers of Pope have profited from the Pope tercentenary in 1988, for it saw the publication of four collections of essays exclusively on Pope, plus a special number of the *Yearbook of English Studies* devoted to Pope and Swift. These five volumes, together with a more recent collection, edited by David Fairer, provide a handy means for scanning the current state of Pope studies. Not all the essays in these collections are easily categorized, so let me simply describe each volume separately. *The Enduring Legacy: Alexander Pope Tercentary Essays*, edited by G. S. Rousseau and Pat Rogers, brings together thirteen essays under six headings: *The Rape of the Lock*, Pope and women, *An Essay on Man*, landscape gardening and the villa at Twickenham, Pope and translation and criticism, and Pope and posterity. The contributors are Patricia Bruckmann, Howard D. Weinbrot, Felicity Rosslyn, Penelope Wilson, Howard Erskine-Hill, David B. Morris, John Dixon Hunt, Morris Brownell, A. D. Nuttall, Wallace Jackson, Pat Rogers, G. S. Rousseau, and Donald Greene. The level of thought and scholarship here is what one might expect from a group of critics of this caliber.

Alexander Pope: Essays for the Tercentenary, edited by Colin Nicolson, contains essays by H. T. Dickinson, Brean S. Hammond, Martin Malone, John Price, Ian Bell, Colin Nicolson, Roger Savage, Peter France, Geoffrey Carnall, Colin Manlove, Alastair Fowler, Michael Phillips, W. W. Robson, R. D. S. Jack, Don Nichol, and Wendy Jones. The essays are celebratory, and several present useful summaries of information on Pope. Price, for example, offers a brief guide to what Hugh Blair, James Beattie, Adam Smith, and George Campbell had to say about Pope. Nicolson discusses Pope's involvement in the South Sea Bubble and its relation to *The Dunciad*. Fowler makes good use of John Dennis's criticism of the *Rape* to discuss the possible implications of the poem's machinery. Jones places Pope's publication of his edited letters within the context of his ongoing battle with the dunces (see also her book-length work in "Backgrounds," below).

A special number of the *Eighteenth Century: Theory and Interpretation*, edited by David B. Morris, contains essays by Morris, James Grantham Turner, Susan Staves, Carole Fabricant, Leo Damrosch, and Carey McIntosh. Morris's introductory essay attempts to use subatomic "Bootstrap Theory" to suggest the range of new possibilities in Pope studies. The other five essays constitute a selection of these possibilities. Turner focuses on the contradictions in Pope's attitudes toward women, the tension between his avowed high moral position and his rakish affectations. Staves considers Pope's entrepreneurialism and the creation of a social class of readers capable of appreciating the "refinement" of his verse. Fabricant takes a skeptical view of Pope's representation of himself as holding the moral high ground and sees rather "a poet seeking both to translate complex ideological issues into clear-cut moral categories and to address posterity" (174). Damrosch examines the tension between narrative events in Pope's work and his detailed descriptions of the relatively static scenes in which those events occur. McIntosh discusses the orthodoxy of poetic styles and Pope's efforts in the 1730s "to expand the expressive range of English satire" (221).

A special number of the *New Orleans Review*, edited by Ronald Schleifer and titled *The Poststructural Pope*, attempts to bring Pope within the scope of modern critical theories. It contains eleven essays, all of which, except the introduction by Schleifer and the afterword by G. Douglas Atkins, are explicitly about *The Rape of the Lock*; the contributors include Elizabeth Hinds, Pamela Slate Liggett, David S. Gross, Kate Beaird Meyers, Grant I. Holly, Tom Bowden, Robert Markley, and Richard Cassetta. There is a good deal of poststructuralist fun in these essays, and Pope is found in the company of, among others, Marx, Bakhtin, Roman Jakobson, and—of all people—William S. Burroughs. Cassetta's piece is an annotated bibliography of works on the *Rape* in the 1980s, and Markley examines the polemics of review essays to suggest that current rifts among Popians of various ideologies may finally be irreconcilable.

The *Yearbook of English Studies* for 1988, edited by C. J. Rawson, is a special issue titled *Pope, Swift, and Their Circle*. Of the fifteen non–review essays here, seven are specifically about Pope, and in one essay, "Scriblerian Self-Fashioning," Brean S. Hammond discusses Swift and Pope together. The Pope essays are by Douglas Brooks-Davies (on *Windsor-Forest*), Robert Cummings (on *Windsor-Forest*), Frederick M. Keener (on Pope's *Homer*), Patricia Bruckmann (on *An Essay on Man*), Ian Donaldson (on *Epistle to Dr. Arbuthnot*), and Howard Erskine-Hill (on Pope's "Epitaph for Dr. Francis Atterbury"). Of the review essays in this volume, at least twelve consider books on Pope, including the studies by Laura Brown, Ellen Pollak, Brooks-Davies, Hammond, and Fairer.

The most recent collection, *Pope: New Contexts*, edited by David Fairer, provides an overview of what Pope studies became in the 1980s and where they may go in the 1990s. The collection brings together thirteen essays that in various ways seek to "tackle the issue of appropriation, the awkward question of '*whose* Pope?' which is audible now as ever" (7). The authors in this endeavor include Fairer himself, J. A. Downie, Christine Gerrard, Thomas Woodman, Carolyn D. Williams, Steve Clark, Susan Matthews, Stephen

Bygrave, Rebecca Ferguson, John Whale, Nicholas Roe, Stephen Copley, and Brean S. Hammond. Among the issues raised are Pope's alleged Tory sympathies (Downie), Pope and the depiction of women in the novel (Matthews), and Pope's relation to the Romantics (Whale, Fairer, Roe).

Useful collections of essays published before the tercentenary include *Essential Articles for the Study of Pope*, edited by Maynard Mack; *Alexander Pope: A Critical Anthology*, edited by F. W. Bateson and N. A. Joukovsky; *Alexander Pope: Writers and Their Backgrounds*, edited by Peter Dixon; *Pope: The Critical Heritage*, edited by John Barnard; *The Art of Alexander Pope*, edited by Howard Erskine-Hill and Anne Smith; *Pope: Recent Essays by Several Hands*, edited by Mack and James A. Winn; and Mack's *"Collected in Himself": Essays Critical, Biographical, and Bibliographical on Pope and Some of His Contemporaries*.

Books on Individual Poems

Only three of Pope's individual poems have attracted book-length consideration: *The Rape of the Lock, An Essay on Man,* and *The Dunciad.* About Pope's most popular poem, the *Rape,* there are six books, apart from the tercentenary *New Orleans Review,* that may be useful. Robert Halsband's The Rape of the Lock *and Its Illustrations, 1714–1896* considers the relationship between the *Rape* and the various illustrations that accompanied it, from the first edition of the five-canto poem to the 1896 edition illustrated by Aubrey Beardsley. Among the artists considered, in addition to Beardsley, are Thomas Stothard, Henry Fuseli, and C. R. Leslie. In this short but interesting book, Halsband obviously cannot explore Pope's poem in great detail, but the volume's six color and sixty-eight monochrome plates could easily provide a good starting point for class discussion of possible interpretations for the various scenes.

Joseph S. Cunningham's *Pope:* The Rape of the Lock provides an introduction to the mock-heroic, and William Kinsley's *Contexts 2:* The Rape of the Lock uses facsimile reproductions of contemporary sources to situate the poem in its time. The remaining three books are all collections of essays: The Rape of the Lock: *A Casebook,* edited by John Dixon Hunt; *Twentieth Century Interpretations of* The Rape of the Lock: *A Collection of Critical Essays,* edited by G. S. Rousseau; and *Alexander Pope's* The Rape of the Lock, edited, with an introduction, by Harold Bloom.

The most recent full-length study of the *Essay on Man* is A. D. Nuttall's *Pope's* Essay on Man. The poem, Nuttall says, "tells you more of the thought of the time than any other single literary work" (192), and he insists on Pope as "not just a source but a potent, *organizing* source" (1). His discussion of Pope's life is followed by a consideration of "Augustan" versification; his close reading of the poem touches on such issues as the decline of theodicy and Pope's engagement with Milton. Before Nuttall, the poem had been discussed at length by Martin I. Kallich, in *Heaven's First Law: Rhetoric and Order in Pope's* Essay on Man, and by Douglas H. White, in *Pope and the Context of Controversy: The Manipulation of Ideas in* An Essay on Man.

Perhaps because its chaos seems to require the most explication, *The Dunciad* has drawn more extended commentary than has any other single poem: Aubrey L. Williams's *Pope's* Dunciad: *A Study of Its Meaning*, John E. Sitter's *The Poetry of Pope's* Dunciad, Howard Erskine-Hill's *Pope:* The Dunciad, and Douglas Brooks-Davies's *Pope's* Dunciad *and the Queen of Night: A Study in Emotional Jacobitism*. In this last study, Brooks-Davies argues that, in *The Dunciad*, images of Isis, Elizabeth I, Queen Anne, and Pope's own mother conspire with a critique of monarchy based on Virgil and Milton to make possible, at least, a Jacobite reading of the poem. This is the longest sustained discussion on the topic of Pope's alleged Jacobitism (see "Pope and Jacobitism," below). Since Brooks-Davies's work, David L. Vander Meulen has produced two books useful for discussing the textual intricacies of *The Dunciad*: *Where Angels Fear to Tread: Descriptive Bibliography and Alexander Pope* and *Pope's* Dunciad *of 1728: A History and Facsimile*.

Pope and Horace

As a group, Pope's Horatian poems have attracted by far the most extensive critical attention recently. Reuben A. Brower's *Alexander Pope: The Poetry of Allusion* is probably the most influential study, positing a Pope whose life and work become progressively imitations of Horace; Maynard Mack's equally important *The Garden and the City: Retirement and Politics in the Later Poetry of Pope, 1731–1743* reaches much the same conclusion. (These two books were also mentioned most often by respondents to the MLA survey.) Between the publication of these two works, Thomas E. Maresca situated Pope's Horatian imitations in a Christian context in *Pope's Horatian Poems*. Other work on Pope and Horace includes Ronald Paulson's *The Fictions of Satire*, Peter Dixon's *The World of Pope's Satires: An Introduction to the* Epistles *and* Imitations of Horace, John M. Aden's *Something like Horace: Studies in the Art and Allusion of Pope's Horatian Satires*, and Malcolm Kelsall's "Augustus and Pope." Also, Caroline Goad's early *Horace in the English Literature of the Eighteenth Century* (1918) attempts to do for Horace what Raymond Dexter Havens did for Milton four years later.

The 1980s saw at least five new full-length studies of Pope's Horatian poems. Allen G. Wood's *Literary Satire and Theory: A Study of Horace, Boileau, and Pope* adds a more European strain to the mix, while Fredric V. Bogel's *Acts of Knowledge: Pope's Later Poems* is less a book on Horace or on Pope's moral judgments than an exploration of Pope's attempts to "know" the world, as opposed to "evaluating" it. Bogel has a bit to say about the *Essay on Man* and *The Dunciad*, but his primary focus is on the *Epistles to Several Persons*, *Imitations of Horace*, and *An Epistle to Dr. Arbuthnot* as he charts Pope's movement between the extremes of an isolating "schematic" knowledge and a more engaged or worldly "substantial" knowledge. Bogel does not mention Keats or negative capability, but his Pope does exhibit the ability to exist in uncertainties "in a sustained process of human discovery" (234).

Howard D. Weinbrot's *Alexander Pope and the Traditions of Formal Verse Satire* counters the arguments of Brower (*Poetry of Allusion*), Mack (*The Garden and the City*), and others that Pope's career becomes more Horatian as it develops. Instead, Weinbrot argues that Pope's work develops "from an essentially Horatian ethic epistle . . . to mingled satire with a variety of Horatian, Juvenalian and Persian emphases, to the overwhelming Juvenalian-Persian elevation and gloom of the *Epilogue to the Satires*" (331).

Frank Stack's *Pope and Horace: Studies in Imitation* is an examination of the "intertextual field" (xv) created by Pope's publication of his *Imitations of Horace* with parallel, facing-page Horatian originals. Stack uses this publication decision to explore how Horace was read in Pope's day and to suggest a dynamic, almost symbiotic relationship, in which Pope's imitations both inform and are informed by our reading of Horace's originals.

In *Reading Pope's* Imitations of Horace, Jacob Fuchs seeks a middle ground between the Horatian Pope of Brower and Mack and the Juvenalian and anti-Augustan Pope of Weinbrot, destabilizing the eighteenth-century view of Horace in order to liberate Pope: "My point is that eighteenth-century thinking on Augustus and his age could not have constrained Pope in any significant way" (30). Fuchs's discussions of the *Imitations*, including the *Epistle to Dr. Arbuthnot*, are intended to "reveal and in part account for Pope's growing conviction that his satire cannot even hurt his enemies, much less improve them, and that the darkness gathering over his country will envelop Twickenham too" (62).

Pope, Homer, and the Classical Tradition

Pope's relation to Homer has received somewhat less attention than his encounter with Horace has. Modern work on Pope and Homer begins with Douglas Knight's *Pope and the Heroic Tradition: A Critical Study of His* Iliad and includes Knight's "Pope as a Student of Homer," H. A. Mason's *To Homer through Pope: An Introduction to Homer's* Iliad *and Pope's Translation*, Norman Callan's "Pope and the Classics," and George Fraser's "Pope and Homer." More recently, in *Pope's Iliad: Homer in the Age of Passion*, Steven Shankman has set out to support Samuel Johnson's statement that Pope's translation of the *Iliad* "is certainly the noblest version of poetry which the world has ever seen." Shankman pits Pope against George Chapman, aligns him with Longinus, and argues that he is more faithful to the passions of Homer's original than his Renaissance predecessor is. Shankman finds that Chapman's translation is marred by the tendency to moralize Homer, a tendency that a later aesthetic context enabled Pope to resist.

G. F. C. Plowden's *Pope on Classic Ground* is an interesting study of Pope's borrowings from several of the more obscure classical sources and/or their English translations, particularly Manilius's *Astronomica*, translated by Thomas Creech, and George Sandys's notes to his translation of Ovid's *Metamorphosis*. Plowden focuses on Pope's use of astrological imagery to trace his enduring interest in cosmic and microcosmic creation in *The Rape of the Lock*, the *Essay on Man*, and the relatively little-discussed *Epistle to Cobham*.

Pope and the Other Arts

On the relation between Pope and the arts other than poetry, the standard work is Morris R. Brownell's *Alexander Pope and the Arts of Georgian England*, which considers painting, landscape gardening, architecture, and sculpture, with a briefer comment on music. Of the more specialized works, those on the visual arts include Robert J. Allen's "Pope and the Sister Arts," David Ridgely Clark's "Landscape Painting Effects in Pope's *Homer*," and James Sambrook's "Pope and the Visual Arts." In *The Character-Sketches in Pope's Poems*, Benjamin Boyce argues that Pope's poetic portraits owe less to eighteenth-century theories of painting than to literary antecedents. On Pope's work with playwrights and the theater, see Malcolm Goldstein's *Pope and the Augustan Stage*. John A. Jones has considered the musicality of Pope's verse in "The Analogy of Eighteenth-Century Music and Poetry: Bach and Pope."

Pope's interest in gardening has attracted considerable attention. Earlier works on Pope and gardening include Frederick Bracher's "Pope's Grotto: The Maze of Fancy," Reginald Harvey Griffith's "Pope on the Art of Gardening," A. L. Altenbernd's "On Pope's Horticultural Romanticism," Maynard Mack's "A Poet in His Landscape: Pope at Twickenham," John Dixon Hunt's "Emblem and Expressionism in the Eighteenth-Century Landscape Garden," and Irving N. Rothman's "The Quincunx in Pope's Moral Aesthetics."

More recently, Peter Martin's *Pursuing Innocent Pleasures: The Gardening World of Alexander Pope* presents a biographic rather than a literary-critical account of Pope's work, focusing on the reciprocal relation between his poetry and his interests in landscape gardening. Martin discusses the gardens visited or influenced by Pope and includes a consideration of, and speculation about, Pope's own garden at Twickenham.

Pope and Gender

As women's studies has assumed its place in academe, feminist and related studies of Pope have become more common. Most of the tercentenary collections listed above include at least one essay on Pope and feminist issues. Among the other, shorter discussions of Pope and gender, one might also consult Carol Virginia Pohli's "The Point Where Sense and Dulness Meet: What Pope Knows about Knowing and about Women," Penelope Wilson's "Feminism and the Augustans: Some Readings and Problems," Molly Smith's

"The Mythical Implications in Pope's 'Epistle to a Lady,'" Taylor Corse's "Heaven's 'Last Best Work': Pope's *Epistle to a Lady*," Wolfgang E. H. Rudat's "Sex-Role Reversal and Miltonic Theology in Pope's *Rape of the Lock*," and Laura Claridge's "Pope's Rape of Excess." For an extended discussion of the general background, see Felicity Nussbaum's *The Brink of All We Hate: English Satires on Women, 1660–1750*.

Ellen Pollak's *The Poetics of Sexual Myth: Gender and Ideology in the Verse of Swift and Pope* and Valerie Rumbold's *Women's Place in Pope's World* are the more important book-length considerations of Pope and women. Pollak presents a deconstructively influenced feminist reading of Pope's *Rape* and *To a Lady*, as well as of Swift's *Cadenus and Vanessa*; she also discusses *Eloisa to Abelard* in the epilogue. Pollak presents a good exploration of "the socioeconomic determinants of what, by the early eighteenth century, had become a culturally dominant sexual mythology" (159), showing how women's expected role became more passive as the developing middle-class family became the center of values. Rumbold examines Pope's poetry and the women in his life. Rejecting the temptation to read Pope simply as sexist, Rumbold focuses on the trope of the "unfortunate lady" to explore in detail Pope's relationships with the women important to him, including his mother, Teresa and Martha Blount, Lady Mary Wortley Montagu, Henrietta Howard, and Mary Caesar.

Pope and Jacobitism

One of the most hotly debated topics in Pope studies today is the question of whether Pope was a Jacobite. This question is closely related to the issue of Pope's attitude toward his Catholicism, and the debate is characterized by a surprisingly vehement tone. References in modern criticism to Pope as a Jacobite appear as early as George Sherburn's *Early Career of Alexander Pope* (1934), and the debate continues as recently as J. A. Downie's "1688: Pope and the Rhetoric of Jacobitism," which opens *Pope: New Contexts* (1990). Despite Sherburn, a modern critical consensus developed that Pope was not a Jacobite and that, while he was indeed Catholic, his religion mattered relatively little to him. During the mid-1970s, however, this opinion began to come under fire. Among the various examinations (pro and con) are the following: John M. Aden's "Pope and Politics: 'The Farce of State'" and Pat Rogers's "Pope and the Social Scene" (1972); Chester Chapin's "Alexander Pope: Erasmian Catholic" and Aden's *Pope's Once and Future Kings: Satire and Politics in the Early Career* (1978); Howard Erskine-Hill's "Literature and the Jacobite Cause: Was There a Rhetoric of Jacobitism?" (1982); Brean S. Hammond's *Pope and Bolingbroke: A Study of Friendship and Influence* (1984); Douglas Brooks-Davies's *Pope's Dunciad and the Queen of Night* (1985); Chapin's "Pope and the Jacobites" (1986); Hammond's *Pope* (1986); and Erskine-Hill's "Alexander Pope: the Political Poet in His Time" (1988).

Studies of Pope's Career, Backgrounds, and Versification

The items in this group include critical efforts to characterize Pope's body of work either by some sort of internal logic or by reference to a presiding interest or motif. Also included are works that provide information about Pope's intellectual and political context. I have grouped these works together because career studies usually rely heavily on the establishment of a particular vision of Pope's context and can therefore also be useful as "background" sources.

There have been seven discussions of Pope's career since 1980 alone. In *Vision and Re-vision in Alexander Pope*, Wallace Jackson "elaborat[es] a coherence of symbolism" in Pope's work from *Windsor-Forest* and *The Temple of Fame* to *The Dunciad*. Jackson sees this symbolism as the trace of a mythology that informs all Pope's work. He seeks to place Pope squarely in the company of Milton and Blake. Pope's work, Jackson argues, replays in various registers the Miltonic myth of the Fall, charting the destruction of a "special place," the internal resituating of that place, and the subversion of the "master passion" by the "monster passion" (191).

In *Pope's Imagination*, David Fairer seeks to enlarge our understanding of Pope's broad notion of imagination. Fairer undermines our assumptions about early eighteenth-century distinctions between imagination and fancy, for example, and situates Pope's views within the English tradition. He discusses *Eloisa* (in the light of Milton's *Comus*), the *Rape* (in the light of *Paradise Lost*), *Epistle to a Lady*, and *The Dunciad*.

In *Alexander Pope: The Genius of Sense*, David B. Morris surveys Pope's entire career through the lens of Dryden's influence, including an economic understanding of the poet's relation to the past (as reflected in the word *borrowing*, for example). Morris sees "refinement" and revision as characteristic Popian activities and focuses on Pope's concern with the "Man of Sense" rather than with the Man of Wit or the Man of Feeling.

Laura Brown's *Alexander Pope* has generated a great deal of controversy, and the responses to it are often quite telling (see, for example, G. S. Rousseau's essay in this collection). Brown offers a Marxian revisionist reading of Pope's career based on his major poems, from *Windsor-Forest* and *The Rape of the Lock* to *The Dunciad* (not, however, including *Arbuthnot*). Brown argues for a consistency in Pope's rhetoric and poetic forms based on the nascent commodity culture of empire and capitalism, and she provides a useful account of the historical forces at work behind Pope's work, diagnosing in him an ambivalence about the "new world" of capitalism.

In 1986, G. Douglas Atkins, *Quests of Difference: Reading Pope's Poems*, offered the first book-length reading of Pope "in light of deconstruction" (xi). Drawing predominantly from Derrida and de Man, Atkins attempts to read both "with" and "against the grain" to "open" *An Essay on Criticism, An Essay on Man, Moral Essays, Imitations of Horace*, and *Dunciad* 4. His close readings focus on the questions of definition and difference that inform Pope's work.

In *The Unbalanced Mind: Pope and the Rule of Passion*, Rebecca Ferguson studies Pope's notion of passion — evident in *Eloisa to Abelard* and "Elegy to the Memory of an Unfortunate Lady" — as it develops into his understanding of the "ruling passion" in the *Essay on Man* and the *Epistles to Several Persons*. Ferguson argues that Pope's focus on passion finally sponsors the explorations and depictions of the unbalanced mind in the later poetry.

Leopold Damrosch's *The Imaginative World of Alexander Pope* emphasizes Pope's marginality — sexual, financial, political, artistic — to depict him as the first modern poet, a writer who had to contend with skepticism and the loss of social values and generic authority. Damrosch argues that in response to this relative isolation, Pope worked to imagine himself as an "insider" with the ability and authority to speak for the group.

Before 1980, the more important career studies include Geoffrey Tillotson's *On the Poetry of Pope*, Norman Ault's *New Light on Pope*, Thomas R. Edwards's *This Dark Estate: A Reading of Pope*, Patricia Meyer Spacks's *An Argument of Images: The Poetry of Alexander Pope*, Miriam Leranbaum's *Alexander Pope's "Opus Magnum," 1729–44*, and Dustin H. Griffin's *Alexander Pope: The Poet in the Poems*.

For background on Pope's time, Howard Erskine-Hill's *The Social Milieu of Alexander Pope: Lives, Example, and the Poetic Response* is a storehouse of valuable information. Wendy L. Jones's *Talking on Paper: Alexander Pope's Letters* situates Pope's correspondence in its classical and contemporary contexts, including the eighteenth-century debates over the ownership of private letters. Other recent background studies include Anthony Easthope's *Poetry as Discourse*, Allan Ingram's *Intricate Laughter in the Satire of Swift and Pope*, Christopher Fox's *Locke and the Scriblerians: Identity and Consciousness in Early Eighteenth-Century Britain*, Maynard Mack's *The Last and Greatest Art: Some Unpublished Poetical Manuscripts of Alexander Pope* and *The World of Alexander Pope* (a descriptive catalog of the exhibitions in the Beinecke Rare Book and Manuscript Library and the Yale Center for British Art), and Gretchen M. Foster's *Pope versus Dryden: A Controversy in Letters to the* Gentleman's Magazine, *1789–1791* (the introductory essay provides a history of the Dryden-Pope critical rivalry).

The last topic is Pope's versification, which, as one might imagine, has received a good deal of attention. The first major modern work on Pope's literary craft is Rebecca Price Parkin's *The Poetic Workmanship of Alexander Pope* (1955), followed, nine years later, by Jacob H. Adler's *The Reach of Art: A Study in the Prosody of Pope* and, five years after that, by John A. Jones's *Pope's Couplet Art*. Among the more interesting articles on Pope's language are Maynard Mack's "On Reading Pope," George Sherburn's "Pope at Work," Peter Dixon's "'Talking upon Paper': Pope and Eighteenth Century Conversation," and Irvin Ehrenpreis's "The Style of Sound: The Literary Value of Pope's Versification."

Such is the state of Pope's studies as of this writing—healthier than the poet was during most of his life, but with a contentiousness similar to that which characterized so much of his career. In the classroom, both the health and the contentiousness can be useful, informing the teacher of new and different ideas and approaches, demonstrating to the student the possibility of discovery and differing interpretations, inspiring spirited interchange and thoughtful discussion.

Part Two

APPROACHES

BACKGROUNDS: FORMAL, THEORETICAL, LITERARY

Wit, Rhyme, and Couplet:
Style as Content in Pope's Art

David B. Morris

Although he may seem at times among the most artificial or old-fashioned of poets, Pope speaks our language. His vocabulary, syntax, and clear style make his verse much more accessible to modern readers than, say, the poetry of Chaucer, Spenser, and Milton. My approach in teaching Pope is to take advantage of his (deceptive) accessibility to reopen questions we normally do not consider. What happens when poems rhyme? What is wit and what is it good for? What meanings and feelings does a couplet (or "coupletness") convey? I prefer to address these questions here not as purely literary issues that call for explanations drawn from rhetoric or poetics. Rather, I want to think of wit, rhyme, and couplets as forms of social practice. Students who feel insecure about literature in general or about Pope in particular have spent hundreds of hours listening to rock lyrics (which almost always rhyme) and trading witty remarks. The art of teaching Pope, I think, lies in asking students to reflect on knowledge that unknowingly they already possess.

This brief essay makes a twofold claim: that we must know something about the heroic couplet to understand Pope's wit and that we must know something about wit to understand Pope's heroic couplets. For Pope, couplets and wit are overlapping, intersecting concepts. The sad fact is, however, that scholarly studies of the heroic couplet rarely manage to get a handle on its mysterious attractions. Discussion quickly bogs down in technical details about figures of speech, from anaphora to zeugma, that few students remember except under duress. Worse, style is treated as strictly divisible from content, a mere overlay, and Pope might even seem to encourage this division when in *An Essay on Criticism* he calls expression "the *Dress* of *Thought*" (line 318). Dressing, however, viewed as a social practice, is not a mere laying-on of clothes but a precise and highly coded art by which the person makes his or her appearance, in public or in private. Content and style, while not indistinguishable, prove finally inseparable. Ask students about dress: Does their clothing acknowledge various unspoken cultural codes while also making a significant personal statement? Here, in a slightly more extreme move, I argue that wit in effect *constitutes* the infinitely variable content of Pope's couplet.

Wit, of course, is central to Pope and his era. Dryden in his preface to *Annus Mirabilis* (1666) identified what we might consider the bedrock of a neoclassical poetics when he wrote, "The composition of all Poems is or ought to be of wit" (1: 53). Yet wit serves as a central value for Pope and his age precisely because it was a focus of conflict. Critics attacked earlier metaphysical and Restoration practices of wit as too convoluted or too bawdy. Addison in the *Spectator* and Pope in *An Essay on Criticism* contributed directly to the ongoing process of redefinition designed to identify and separate false wit from true wit. Reflecting this spirit of historical change, Johnson's *Dictionary* (1755) offers eight definitions of wit, at least two of which ("fancy" and "judgment") stand in direct contradiction. We will get nowhere with Pope if we start by trying to define wit through dictionaries or handbooks. Even Locke's famous philosophical definition of wit — as the quick-acting mental power that creates pleasing pictures in the mind by linking similar or congruent ideas (156; 2.11.2) — is far too narrow and abstract.[1]

An attempt to discuss wit and rhyme as forms of social practice helps students understand Pope's verse less as a self-contained artifact than as an action. It is worth pursuing slightly unorthodox questions, such as, Why does wit give us pleasure? Why is it that we tend to admire people who make witty remarks? Does wit serve as the sign of other qualities, say, intelligence? Can it be a source of power? Is there a point at which someone becomes too witty? Students won't have any trouble describing how we use wit to deflate or injure people. (Hobbes and Freud offer full theories of aggressive laughter; see Morreall.) Is an insult more cutting — or at lease more effectively insulting — if it rhymes? How does rhyme function in political slogans or in advertising jingles? What is the relation between rhyme and memory? When and why does wit become taboo? The sign beside the baggage-inspection table at my local airport reads, "Joking Forbidden." Isn't it strange that at the wrong spot in Kalamazoo a clever remark about Havana or Beirut can get you arrested? The irreverent wit of *A Tale of a Tub*, so the story goes, cost Swift a bishop's seat.

This line of thought soon makes it plain to students that wit and rhyme are literary devices that carry a powerful extraliterary charge. The extraliterary dangers implicit in wit were clear to Pope — who carried pistols on his walks from Twickenham to Richmond — but we often ignore less obvious ways in which wit functions within social contexts. Swift in *The Intelligencer* once wrote of clergymen that "[n]othing is so fatal as the Character of Wit . . . or that Kind of Behaviour which we contract by having too much conversed with Persons of high Station and Eminency" (*Prose* 12: 40).[2] Here wit is regarded not only as a social practice — a form of human behavior — but also as divided along rough lines of vocation and class. It is not just a mode of expression but a form of life (a way of being) that separates, say, a footman from a lord. Who hasn't experienced how a witty remark can transform one suddenly into an outsider — or insider? Wit, in J. L. Austin's phrase, is a very social way of "doing things" with words.

One thing that wit typically does with language — especially in conjunction with rhyme — is to compress it. This compression, in turn, tends to exert a subversive influence on meaning. We cannot assume that Pope's commitment to clarity as an aesthetic virtue means his verse is always clear. The compression intrinsic to wit requires that much is left out. The aphorism — that typical Augustan sign of wit — always sacrifices precision to achieve its illusion of generality. Further, couplets take their place in a chain or paragraph of linked couplets, so that the apparent completeness of couplet A is regularly disturbed by couplet B, which supplements or modifies it, and so on. The heroic couplet in its brevity seeks to imply more than can possibly be said: it suggests reserves of meaning left unexpressed or inexpressible. Couplets *look* clear and complete; that is their job. But wit and rhyme make sure that clarity is never transparent.

An example may help suggest how wit often serves to disturb or to destabilize sense. Consider this familiar couplet from *An Essay on Criticism*:

> For *Wit* and *Judgment* often are at strife,
> Tho' meant each other's Aid, like *Man* and *Wife*.
> (82–83)

In this couplet, marriage is not so much a poetic image (in the modernist sense) as a model of social practice somehow applicable to understanding wit.[3] Yet what does it mean or imply that Pope should represent wit as female, as a wife? How should we think about wit if its relation to judgment follows the stereotype of an ancient and unending struggle for sexual mastery?

A related couplet later in the poem continues to suggest, through its reference to culturally charged models of social practice, that wit seems to possess an inherently destabilizing function. Pope now abandons direct statement altogether in favor of a wistful and self-reflexive questioning:

What is this *Wit* which must our Cares employ?
The *Owner's Wife*, that *other Men* enjoy?
(500–01)

Pope sometimes makes wit nearly synonymous with poetry, but here he complicates the classical image of the female muse by describing wit in relation to specifically eighteenth-century ideas of marriage and masculine power. Further, this is no celebration of male dominance. The description implies that wit as female subverts the masculine power and reason that seek to dominate it and reduces the male poet to a cuckold unable to control his own muse, doomed to a life of self-betrayals.

Does wit — in its subversiveness and compression — necessarily embrace an element of the uncontainable? Is it among the social functions of wit to elude or to destabilize the very structures that poets and reason, like a jealous husband, would build to contain it? Certainly Pope at times exploits the slipperiness of wit, which allows us to say two things at once, as in irony. *An Essay on Man* contains numerous couplets that bear very different readings — even the notorious phrase "Whatever is, is RIGHT" (1.294) — precisely because Pope did not wish to commit himself, on controversial points, to a single meaning and because single meanings often proved inadequate (even impoverished) for a poet drawn to describe the many-layered nuances of social relationships and to orchestrate the dialogical clash of opposing idioms and ideas. Like innuendo and allusion, which for Pope as satirist sometimes provide the slim margin of uncertainty crucial to frustrate prosecution for libel, wit serves indispensable social purposes in a world where words still carry great power, for good or for ill.

These last examples reflect my belief that wit for Pope must be understood at last as something that the critic, like the poet, cannot hope to pin down in a final victory of reason and judicious explanation. It is one social function of wit, we might say, to remain always ungraspable, to employ its lightning speed and characteristic spontaneity in defeating our ineradicable fantasies of control. We might recall a couplet — which Maynard Mack quotes in the title of a famous essay — where Pope laments that he is so often unjustly abused:

Poor *Cornus* sees his frantic Wife elope,
And curses Wit, and Poetry, and *Pope*.
(*Arbuthnot* 25–26)

Once again wit brings us mysteriously round to the figure of the cuckold. Poor Cornus certainly finds himself in a position to confirm that poetry possesses a destabilizing power, even as Pope (wittily) suggests that he, a mere poet, is not to blame if wives can be seduced and lawful marriages destroyed by wit.

The cuckold — that Restoration dupe who moves in the shadows of Pope's verse — might serve as a summarizing image of wit's power to tap unlawful and unregulated pleasure. Cuckoldry, too, shows us the comic defeat of the desire to possess and to control the other. Wit for Pope seems to possess an irreducible otherness: it stands not only beyond the control of the poet but also in open or covert resistance to the entire range of social discourses and practices that might be summarized, metaphorically, in the institution of marriage. Marriage, after all, is perhaps our most enduring social invention for domesticating contradictions and for subjugating difference. It is the nature of wit as a social practice, Pope shows us, to stretch, twist, mock, elude, subvert, and reaffirm bonds that it cannot completely overcome. Like the marriage vows of a restless wife, such constraints not only create the occasions for wit to practice its repeated escapes but also no doubt increase the pleasure of successful transgressions.

Rhyme always involves bonds, and there is good reason for considering it a basic mode of Augustan wit. It draws together far more than merely similar sounds. The similarity in sound brings disparate words and ideas into close contact (as in Pope's famous rhymed pair from *The Rape of the Lock*, "chaste" and "embraced"). Like the rules governing the last two feet of the Latin hexameter, rhyme gives shape and closure to an individual line, and inevitably it influences the thought that the line expresses. If the first line of a couplet ends with the word *chaste*, the second line obviously cannot conclude with the word *promiscuous*. The poet has to find another way to say it; and, because no two words are ever exactly synonymous, saying it in a new way means saying something slightly or entirely different. The wit of rhyme lies in finding exactly the right word for the right place.

All writing, of course, in one sense involves finding the right word for the right place. (Swift's succinct definition of style was proper words in proper places.) Rhymed couplets, however, like sonnets or sestinas, make the game more difficult. The pleasure of reading well-composed couplets involves our knowledge that the writer works under rigorous self-imposed constraints: a Houdini in handcuffs. Further, a successful couplet has the rightness of words falling precisely into place like the tumblers of a combination lock. It is language at the point where it cannot be revised. The wit of rhymed couplets — even when the writer is not saying anything particularly witty — lies in the exercise of skill and talent required to bind idea, image, meter, sound, and language into a perfect fit. As Pope puts it in *An Essay on Criticism*:

> True Ease in Writing comes from Art, not Chance,
> As those move easiest who have learn'd to dance.
> (362–63)

One does not dance by chance. Wit creates within the couplet an ideal movement of words that cohere with the effortless grace of Rogers and Astaire. Rhyme is the symbol for this social dance of wit.

The couplet, indeed, possesses a symbolic power that owes much to the specific historical moment in which it became, for a brief time, the reigning poetic form. The aesthetic values of balance, control, politeness, refinement, correctness, and reconciled opposites so fundamental to Pope's couplet also embody political and social virtues that seemed indispensable in the period immediately following the wild disorder of civil war and constitutional crisis. The couplet stands as a model of social practice: it offers, as in much of Pope's verse, an image of conflict redirected into ideal form. Later in his career, when Pope begins to despair of political and social solutions to the turmoil of British life, he begins, quite deliberately, to disorder his couplet.

There is a danger, however, in overemphasizing the control, skill, and intelligence that Pope's couplet wit normally displays for our appreciation. One cannot find in Pope the devotion to rules so characteristic of French neoclassicism. Wit in fact may be for Pope a paradigm of the unintentional. Certainly it is painful to watch someone *trying* to be witty. Think how often we find ourselves punning as if by accident — forced to add the lame excuse "No pun intended." We didn't intend to pun but we punned nonetheless, as our listeners at once recognized. Puns, of course, were regularly condemned by Augustan critics as examples of false wit, but that did not stop writers from punning or from exploring similar ways in which ironies and ambiguous words set off an almost unstoppable play of suggestion. Rhymes, like puns, are the purest instance we know of what Heidegger considered an otherness or uncanniness inherent within language that continually breaks through despite our best efforts to control or exclude it (see Bruns 140–49, 170–73). The next time a rhyme slips into your speech, someone is likely to say that you're a poet but don't know it. Wit and rhyme, like poems, tap into a permanent unseen otherness with language: it is perhaps among their most important social purposes to make contact with this forgotten power.

Uncanniness is a concept that Freud (in "The 'Uncanny'" [1919]) linked directly with the return of the repressed, and it seems pertinent that rhyme echoes our earliest, forgotten encounters with language and the social world. The repeated monosyllables *ma-ma* or *da-da* are primitive rhymes, so primitive that the child has not yet discovered the slippery pleasure of joining not quite identical sounds. Researchers are currently studying how the brain processes rhyme in a complex relay between the left hemisphere, where linguistic processing normally occurs, and the almost mute but music-rich right hemisphere (see Temple et al.; Rayman and Zaidel). Certainly, in the development of children, repetitive baby talk soon passes into the singsong enjoyment of nursery rhymes. Pope might find such precedents repugnant. Any full discussion, however, needs to ask why rhyme so often accompanies music and why — from limericks and doggerel to contemporary rap lyrics — it so often accompanies the social practices of transgressive, and even childlike, pleasure.

Pope was clear about the uncanniness of language in poetry, which transgresses (or at least overleaps) the boundaries of art and rules. As he wrote in *An Essay on Criticism*:

> Some Beauties yet, no Precepts can declare,
> For there's a *Happiness* as well as *Care*.
> *Musick* resembles *Poetry*, in each
> Are *nameless Graces* which no Methods teach,
> And which a *Master-Hand* alone can reach.
>   (141–45)

Pope's triplet rhymes are almost always tacit homages to Dryden, for whom they constituted a kind of signature. Dryden, too, had asserted the need for genius in the poet and emphasized the bond between poetry and music, which rhyme so clearly invokes. Pope's key term *Happiness*, however, refers to something more than the mysterious pleasure great poets such as Dryden give. It means that the finest poetry contains moments of inexplicable ("nameless") beauty beyond language and method—a beauty that, somehow, just "happens."

Wit, at its most elevated, is another name for the creative and uncanny power that is never entirely under the poet's control. It flashes out inexplicably, it makes things happen, it gives no account of itself. For Pope, this mysterious power cannot be summoned. Skill and art create the precondition that permits it to appear, but it achieves in an instant, effortlessly, beauties that the highest skill cannot produce and cannot explain. Wit may seem a tame word for such an untamed power. Yet—to return to the most homely of social practices—think of the moment when we reach the punch line of a joke. Suddenly the body shakes with laughter. We didn't plan to laugh, we can't control it, it just happens. William Empson once wrote—in what I interpret as a fruitful exaggeration—that there is no appearance of the word *wit* in *An Essay on Criticism* that does not carry the clear, if submerged, implication of joking. Like an exquisite rhyme, the joke is a useful image for everything in language that somehow escapes us, that lies outside our power, that gives us a pleasure we never fully succeed in explaining. Wit and rhyme, if we do not reduce them to mere artifice, open a way for students to understand what Samuel Johnson meant when he wrote that, in addition to good sense, Pope had genius: a mind "always imagining something greater than it knows, always endeavouring more than it can do" (217).

The argument winding its way through these pages can be summarized in a few final sentences. The Augustan couplet disappears toward the end of the eighteenth century along with wit as a supreme value in poetry. We cannot separate style from content in talking about the Augustan couplet, because to a large degree style *is* content. Not the ostensible content, perhaps, which may describe shepherds or coquettes or dunces or critics. But Pope's couplets, through their sequences of unobtrusive or ingenious rhymes, through their patterns of compressed, ironic, paradoxical, playful, punning, uncanny language, whisper to the reader a continuous subliminal reminder to beware: we are now in the presence of wit. A magazine advertisement for a high fashion line once credited Jean Cocteau with the statement that style is a simple way of saying complicated things. A student who understands the complex social function of dress is not likely to dismiss wit and style as mere trivial external adornment. Like rhyme, they remain potent sources of pleasure and complication.

NOTES

[1]For a provocative rethinking of wit throughout the period, see Sitter, *Arguments of Augustan Wit.*

[2]On wit and social class, see Woodman, *Politeness and Poetry in the Age of Pope.*

[3]The classic starting point is Stone, *The Family, Sex, and Marriage in England, 1500–1800.*

Alexander Pope: Ideas of Order
and the Sense of Form

Martin C. Battestin

In my time — and I have been teaching Pope for thirty years — it has never been easy to open students' minds to the qualities of his thought and sensibility or to the miracle of his verse. But the effort is worth making. Samuel Johnson, the most celebrated critic of Pope's century, could ask simply, "If Pope be not a poet, where is poetry to be found? . . . Sir, a thousand years may elapse before there shall appear another man with a power of versification equal to that of Pope" (251, 251n). And T. S. Eliot, perhaps the greatest critic of our century, as well as the founder of "modern" verse, was no less convinced of Pope's virtues: "it might be said in our time," Eliot wrote six years after the appearance of *The Waste Land* (1922), "that the man who cannot enjoy Pope as poetry probably understands no poetry. . . ." In the original version of that poem, indeed, Eliot had included what he considered "an excellent set of couplets" in imitation of *The Rape of the Lock* — nearly a hundred lines that his friend Ezra Pound persuaded him to scrap, saying, "Pope has done this so well that you cannot do it better; and if you mean this as a burlesque, you had better suppress it, for you cannot parody Pope unless you can write better verse than Pope — and you can't" (Eliot, Introduction xxi).

Pope's craftsmanship, his mastery of the form of the heroic couplet, helps explain why so few poets have attempted to match him. Pound saved Eliot from making a fool of himself, but no one prevented A. D. Hope from printing in 1970 his *Dunciad Minor*, in which, for all the fun of it, one of the best poets of our time stumbles in a good cause by inviting comparison with the original. By the end of the eighteenth century, as W. H. Auden observed, the heroic couplet had become "a dead end" (Rev. of Quennell 136), chiefly because Pope had exhausted its potential. And, though poets might still be found in our own time whose sense of form in verse conveys the kindred pleasures of order and elegance — Auden and Hope themselves come to mind, as well as Anthony Hecht and Richard Wilbur — order and elegance are values not much understood or prized by readers today.

But what, specifically, do Johnson and Eliot mean when they hold up Pope, before any other English poet — before Shakespeare and Milton, before Wordsworth or Keats — as the standard of poetry? They do not mean, certainly, that he was greater or more profound. They mean, I think, first of all, that he had an infallible ear for the harmony of the language. Pope himself points us in this direction in his anatomy of bad contemporary verse, *Peri Bathous; or, The Art of Sinking in Poetry*; and it is apt that when Wyndham Lewis and Charles Lee followed his example by putting together

their hilariously egregious anthology *The Stuffed Owl* (1930) — widening
their net, however, to collect specimens from three centuries — they had little
trouble culling howlers from Dryden and Johnson, Byron and Keats, Poe and
Longfellow — even whole pages of them from Wordsworth and Tennyson —
but they could produce not a single line from Pope. One test of great poetry
is how much of it lingers in the memory: Pope's lines have continued echoing in the collective memory of the English-speaking world — so much so
that I have heard unsympathetic students complain that his verse is a cento
of clichés. The columns devoted to him in Bartlett's *Familiar Quotations*
make the point adequately, but they are the merest selection.

The harmony I speak of is partly a matter of precision and economy of
phrasing: this is what Swift has in mind when he grumbles that Pope "can
in one Couplet fix / More Sense than I can do in Six" ("Verses on the Death
of Dr. Swift" 49–50). It is certainly not a matter of sound only — not, that
is, the deafening sonority of a Blackmore or the cloying mellifluousness of
a Swinburne. Nor has it anything at all to do with the poet's affecting a
foppish, artificial language. This is Auden's point:

> [I]f Wordsworth had Pope in mind as the enemy when he advised poets
> to write "in the language really used by men" he was singularly in
> error. Should one compare Pope at his best with any of the Romantics,
> including Wordsworth, at their best, it is Pope who writes as men nor-
> mally speak to each other and the latter who go in for "poetic" lan-
> guage. When Wordsworth tries to write according to his theories, the
> result is nearly always flat; to write well, he has to forget them. In
> Pope, theory and practice are one.   (136)

Where, for example, can we find in Wordsworth language as natural and
dramatic as the opening of *An Epistle to Dr. Arbuthnot*?

> Shut, shut the door, good *John!* fatigu'd I said,
> Tye up the knocker, say I'm sick, I'm dead,
> The Dog-star rages! nay 'tis past a doubt,
> All *Bedlam*, or *Parnassus*, is let out:
> Fire in each eye, and Papers in each hand,
> They rave, recite, and madden round the land.
>   (1–6)

Nor is the harmony I mean chiefly a matter of Pope's rhymes, as beginning students seem to suppose when they make the lines jingle and chime.
What matters in Pope's verse is the electric life of language and meaning
that happens before the last word of the couplet at once closes and breaks
the circuit. This, surely, is what Pound had in mind when he admired in
Pope the "dance of the intelligence among words and ideas" (424). For this

reason, it is better not to try to teach Pope until one has learned to read him well aloud, so that students can hear the harmony and move mentally to the dance of wit that Pound speaks of. But reading Pope aloud is a skill not easily acquired. The key to it, I believe, is to treat the lines as if they were dramatic blank verse, avoiding an exaggerated emphasis on the rhyme words: the rhymes will be heard anyway above all other sounds; Pope's syntax, his regular end-stopping, makes this effect inevitable. (In this context, I sometimes like to recall Browning's form in "My Last Duchess": most students know the poem, but they are usually surprised to find that it, too, is composed of couplets, the constant enjambment having the effect of submerging all the rhymes.) To test one's sense of how Pope's lines should sound, it can be helpful to listen to the readings by a trio of excellent actors — Michael Redgrave, Claire Bloom, and Max Adrian — available on cassettes from Caedmon.

But the quality of Pope's poetry that attests to his skill at versification — and indeed to his profound understanding of its possibilities — is most obviously illustrated by Pope himself in the poem that it is useful to assign first to students for other reasons as well (it includes, for example, a clear, concise statement of neoclassical poetics). I refer of course to the famous "sound and sense" passage in *An Essay on Criticism*, lines 337–83 — a delightful and, for a poet who was about the age of our college seniors when he wrote it, quite prodigious tour de force, in which Pope, declaring that good verse is no mere matter of smooth "numbers" and a knack at rhyming but rather the art of what may be called expressive form, embodies that theory in his practice. It is true, as such able critics as Johnson and Irvin Ehrenpreis have maintained (*Life* 230–32; "Style" 63–75), that the substantific effects of meter and sound are difficult to demonstrate: while the range of possible prosodic and sonic variations is restricted, especially in Pope's closed form of twenty syllables, the range of ideas and images these linguistic elements must convey is limitless and comprehends all imaginable contradictions. Even so, Johnson's objection seems to me actually to affirm the effects that Pope was consciously striving for and that sensitive readers of his works have felt: in the resemblance of sound to sense, Johnson scoffed, "the mind often governs the ear, and the sounds are estimated by their meaning" (231). The experience of reading, however, as we have come to understand, is inevitably subjective in this way; the sense of a passage of poetry will to a considerable degree control the way the sound of it affects us. More, perhaps, than any other poet, Pope understood this principle and successfully enacted it in his work. In the *Epistle to Burlington*, for instance, the verse enables us to feel, quite physically, the discomfort of being a guest at Timon's villa:

But soft — by regular approach — not yet —
First thro' the length of yon hot Terrace sweat,

>   And when up ten steep slopes you've dragg'd your thighs,
>   Just at his Study-door he'll bless your eyes.   (129–32)

And in *The Dunciad* one almost hears Handel's martial music: "To stir, to rouze, to shake the Soul he comes, / And Jove's own Thunders follow Mars's Drums" (4.67–68).

By beginning with the poetics in *An Essay on Criticism*, one can proceed to explore the principle of expressive form as Pope practiced it through virtually the entire range of his work. It reveals itself not merely in such sonic devices as alliteration and assonance or in subtle variations of meter but in a variety of rhetorical techniques ideally suited to the closed form of the couplet. Among these the most characteristic are those techniques of antithesis, of balance and symmetry and parallelism, that admirably serve to embody Pope's philosophy of order in the macrocosm and his keen sense of the inversion of order, morally speaking, in the characters of men and women. Focusing on Pope's versification — on his poetry "as poetry," in Eliot's words — can thus lead a student deeper, beneath the surface of the verse, to the intellectual assumptions that inform the poet's peculiar music. For besides the enhancement of the student's ability to "understand" poetry in general (even, as Eliot seems to imply in the passage I quote at the start of this essay, the poetry of such flagrantly formless poets as, say, Whitman or Ginsberg), there is another compelling reason for studying Pope and his contemporaries — a reason unsuspected by most students of English literature, who, when they have the curiosity to read anything at all before 1800, skip eagerly from Milton to Wordsworth in the belief that nothing much of any importance occurred during the intervening period of 125 years or so. To borrow Leo Spitzer's apt metaphor, the middle of the eighteenth century marked "the great caesura" in a continuous tradition of Western thought stretching from Plato to Pope (76). More recently, Marvin Mudrick made the same point, if somewhat more enthusiastically, declaring his conviction that the eighteenth century was "the most important century in human [i.e., Western] history": "Everything," as he put it, "comes to an end there, and everything has a beginning" (18–19).

What came to an end there is nowhere better illustrated than by the powerful metaphors of order expressed in *Windsor-Forest* and *An Essay on Man*: the idea of world harmony (of a *concordia discors*, in which opposing elements have been reconciled in dynamic equilibrium) and the idea of the great chain of being. These, for Pope, were complementary principles of the Christian humanist tradition as well as principles informing the objective aesthetic of classicism. For pedagogical purposes I have found no better illustration of the way Pope contrives to make his verse *embody* the first of these concepts than Earl Wasserman's analysis of a couplet from the splendid opening of *Windsor-Forest*, in which Pope, after explicitly stating the principle of *concordia discors* (lines 1–16), implicitly expresses that concept by describing the general prospect of nature:

> Here in full Light the russet Plains extend;
> There wrapt in Clouds the blueish Hills ascend.
>   (23–24)

Every idea, every image in the second line of the couplet directly opposes every idea and image in the first line, but the antithesis, complete as it is, is reconciled by the syntactical parallelism and harmonized by the rhyme, which unifies ideas as diametrically opposed as horizontal and vertical (Wasserman 111–12).

The concept of the great chain of being, expounded by A. O. Lovejoy and by Maynard Mack in his excellent introduction to the Twickenham edition of the *Essay on Man*, is widely taught as the key to Pope's idea of order, but it is less useful to an understanding of how his verse works and how, typically, he saw human life and human character, in which, instead of the harmonious reconciliation of opposing elements, he found only contradictions and unwholesome paradoxes:

> Or stain her Honour, or her new Brocade,
> Forget her Pray'rs, or miss a Masquerade.
>   (*Rape* 2.107–08)

> Now deep in Taylor and the Book of Martyrs,
> Now drinking citron with his Grace and Chartres.
>   (*To a Lady* 63–64)

> Sole judge of Truth, in endless Error hurl'd:
> The glory, jest, and riddle of the world!
>   (*Essay on Man* 2.17–18)

> His Wit all see-saw between *that* and *this*,
> Now high, now low, now Master up, now Miss,
> And he himself one vile Antithesis.
>   (*Arbuthnot* 323–25)

> We nobly take the high Priori Road,
> And reason downward, till we doubt of God:
> Make Nature still incroach upon his plan;
> And shove him off as far as e'er we can:
> Thrust some Mechanic Cause into his place;
> Or bind in Matter, or diffuse in Space.

Or, at one bound o'er-leaping all his laws
Make God Man's Image, Man the final Cause.
(*Dunciad* 4.471–78)

Pope's couplets are infinitely adaptable to expressing the sense of a world characterized by such antitheses, contradictions, paradoxes: the principle of harmony in *Windsor-Forest*, the riddle of man at the opening of epistle 2 of *An Essay on Man* or of woman in *Epistle to a Lady*, or the representation of Eloisa's divided mind. Similar in effect are the stunning inversions of the order of things that serve to reify the bright yet trivial world of *The Rape of the Lock*, on the one hand, and the dark estate of *The Dunciad*, on the other: Belinda at her game of cards, pronouncing the fiat of Genesis ("*Let Spades be Trumps!* she said, and Trumps they were" [3.46]); Cibber as "Antichrist of wit," emulating the bad eminence of Milton's Satan in Pandemonium ("High on a gorgeous seat, that far out-shone / Henley's gilt tub, or Fleckno's Irish throne, / . . . Great Cibber sate" [2.1–2, 5]). Once the student is alert to Pope's mastery of the rhetorical devices and strategies of his craft, it is possible to see — as one of my students, Andrea Nagy, saw in a prizewinning essay on the subject — that such a poet can make even the philosophical inanities of *An Essay on Man* seem almost plausible: "The spider's touch, how exquisitely fine! / Feels at each thread, and lives along the line" (1.217–18). Indeed, it becomes possible to see how (much like Dante in *The Inferno*) Pope can indulge his spite against an enemy such as Lord Hervey, mocking every particular feature of the man's moral and physical character — his foppishness and bisexuality, his sycophancy, his diet of ass's milk, his painted face, his toothlessness — while managing to transform his victim into the very type of depravity (*Arbuthnot* 305–33).

In addition to developing a keener appreciation of the beauty, drama, and intellectual substance of Pope's verse, students, I believe, should be encouraged to grasp something of the significance that the idea of art itself held for Pope: for one distinctive characteristic of "Augustanism," from Gay in *Trivia* (1716) to Gray in his exquisite sonnet on the death of his friend Richard West (1742) — the poem that Wordsworth in the Preface to *Lyrical Ballads* found so little to his taste — is the sense these poets had of the redeeming efficacy of artifice in the face of squalor, grief, disorder. I have a way of interpreting Pope's *Pastorals*, for instance, that enables me to make this point (Battestin, ch. 2). And in connection with teaching the *Epistle to Burlington* I find that at least one class devoted to an illustrated lecture on Pope's interest in Palladian architecture and in the artificially contrived "natural" garden can be extremely effective, since it reveals a gentler, more human side to Pope than we find in the satires while it graphically demonstrates concepts of ideal nature and ideal form that he shared with many of his contemporaries (Battestin, ch. 1). The lecture on *Burlington* helps answer a question that many students have concerning Pope: namely, what can this peevish little man, this snarling satirist, mean when he declares at the close of epistle 1 of *An Essay on Man* that Nature is Art, Discord is Harmony? It helps them understand what it is that, as Mudrick hinted, came to an end and what it is that will have a beginning at about the middle of the century.

In this respect, the lecture on *Burlington* can also help students understand how it may be that, as Northrop Frye observes, a great satirist is often an apocalyptic visionary (*Fearful Symmetry* 200). And so it is natural to conclude the course I have been describing with Pope's masterpiece, the final book of *The Dunciad*, which prophesies the collapse into anarchy of the Christian humanist tradition. Yet the power of his own poetry in that poem works subliminally to negate this "message": for at the moment when Pope affects to succumb to the stupefying torpor of Dulness, he produces the most sublime verse he ever wrote, in which satire for once achieves an epic grandeur.

Finally, in trying to cope with what seems to many students the difficult question of Pope's "relevance" to issues that interest us who live in the world he envisaged at the close of *The Dunciad*, I often find it helpful to refer to Eliot. As *The Dunciad* ends with a universal yawn, the world of *The Hollow Men* (1925) ends with a whimper; and *The Waste Land* vividly depicts the condition of "modernism" Pope foresaw. Pope, moreover, has always seemed to me to resemble Eliot in another respect, one clearly stated in Eliot's famous essay "Tradition and the Individual Talent" and one important, I believe, for students today to grasp and relate to: both poets, that is, depend on allusions to the literature and religious thought of the past to deepen and complicate the surface level of their verse. Pope could count on his audience — the readers he was writing for, at any rate — to recognize his allusions to the classics and to Scripture; for the age he lived in had not yet come to ignore or forget those traditions that were the common heritage of every educated person. By contrast, Eliot, attempting in our own century to recover a measure at least of that lost order, can only shore fragments of quotations — from Augustine and the Upanishads, from Dante and Gérard de Nerval, from Thomas Kydd and Baudelaire — against the ruins.

Imitating Pope

Deborah Baker Wyrick

Recently I joined a group of graduate students playing a Derridean parlor game in the faculty-student lounge. Whom would you erase from literary history, they asked one another, and why wouldn't this erasure make any difference? Alexander Pope, answered one. Samuel Johnson, said another. Boring, unreadable, artificial, overly topical, poetic and intellectual dead ends . . . they poured out an Arnoldian rain of reasons why eighteenth-century writers form a dreary puddle of words to be avoided on the journey from the metaphysical to the Romantic poets. It was small consolation that none of these students had studied Pope or Johnson with me. Most of them had no graduate work whatsoever in the period, and most planned none. They shunned it, I suspect, because their undergraduate courses had failed to make eighteenth-century texts interesting or exciting.

After leaving the lounge (without having convinced them that Henry James was a better candidate for excision than were their nominees), I searched through files, reviewing my approaches to teaching Pope and other Augustan writers. The most successful approaches involved the virtually obsolete practice of imitation. Imitating Pope, I think, works for two reasons. First, it forces students to become actively engaged with a poem, observing its formal structure, reenvisioning its rhetorical situation, transposing its concerns, enjoying the play between a model text and their own. Second, students begin to see how imitation is central to Pope's poetic activity; by imitating Pope, however haltingly, they're imitating his process as well as his product. The body of this essay attempts to describe how students implement various imitation exercises and how their writing makes them more engaged readers of Pope.

Imitation remained crucial to rhetorical studies in late-seventeenth-century England. Pope did not champion every aspect of it; in book 1 of *The Dunciad*, for instance, he criticized the emphasis on rote memorization and grammatical analysis that keeps students — as well as the poets they study — "in the pale of Words till death" (line 160). Nonetheless, Pope had not abandoned all the pedagogical methods to which he was exposed during his peripatetic formal schooling, and some had provided him with the means to instruct himself in literature and writing. Pope's juvenilia attest to his frequent imitations and translations of ancient and modern authors, including Homer, Statius, Ovid, Chaucer, Thomas à Kempis, Waller, Cowley, and Rochester. Pope's habitual modes of expression, such as allusion and mock forms, are varieties of imitation (Brower, *Pope* 13). Indeed, throughout his career, Pope continually rewrote his predecessors; works as various as the great translations of Homer and the imitations of Horace and of Donne's satires transform and critique poetic origins to enable personal mythopoesis.

For Pope, imitation did not mean slavish mimicry. As he wrote in the advertisement to *Messiah*:

> One may judge that *Virgil* did not copy [the Sybilline prophecy] line by line, but selected such Ideas as best agreed with the nature of pastoral poetry, and disposed them in that manner which serv'd most to beautify his piece. I have endeavour'd the same in this imitation. . . .
>
> (Pope, *Poems* 189)

Pope's interest focused on the "looser" stages of classical imitation: paraphrase, or retelling a text in one's own words to understand structure and to develop a personal style; transliteration, which encompasses direct translating, recasting prose into verse and vice versa, condensing or amplifying, and altering style levels (Murphy, "Roman Writing" 49–51); and modeling, following a set format but choosing one's own subject (Sullivan 13). Pope admired and practiced what today we would call "creative imitation," the use of preexisting texts both as grounds for invention and participation in "archetypal forms and ideas" (D'Angelo 283) and as models of style. Moreover, through imitation Pope could enter the discourse community of great poets; understanding, re-creating, and eventually augmenting their textual conversation produced a sense of shared moral, aesthetic, and political values that was as much a goal of classical rhetoric as was stylistic effectiveness (Sullivan 14). Imitation allowed cultural positioning, stimulated cultural production, and led to the cultural empowerment that nourished Pope's distinctive genius. By describing the field of Pope's imagination, imitation permitted Pope to reinscribe tradition, and himself within it.

Today, imitation is often seen as the antithesis of creativity. Writing instruction has largely moved away from the models-and-modes approach; developments in literary theory have disassembled the covert program of imitating master interpretations that underlay most instruction in literature until the 1970s. I believe, however, that imitation can be an extremely useful pedagogical tool. In literature classes, it bridges reading and writing and it can involve students in texts more intimately than do standard analytical practices. In eighteenth-century literary studies and, particularly, in the study of Pope, imitation offers a route into what for many young people is especially difficult textual terrain, and it turns their creative responses into guides for understanding matters as diverse as prosody, functional allusions, and social criticism.

I've used the following exercises in English literature survey courses, which at my university are thirty-member classes composed mainly of nonmajors, and in eighteenth-century period surveys, smaller classes composed mainly of junior and senior English majors or of graduate students. Since the assignments are designed to inaugurate and to supplement study of Pope, I treat them as homework or journal entries, commenting on the responses but not giving a letter or number grade. It is essential to redistribute student re-sponses (or selections from them) because the assignment's purpose is in part to generate class discussion and a sense of collective inquiry, although not necessarily consensus (see Trimbur).

Panegyrics and Mock-Panegyrics

Students who believe poetry to be either exclusively self-expressive or totally irrelevant are confused by poetry that involves itself with social and political issues. Drawing an analogy between Augustan poems and contemporary music — particularly rap — helps focus the general project; nonetheless, the unfamiliar form, tone, and allusiveness of Restoration and early-eighteenth-century poems remain baffling. I therefore ask undergraduates to write their own panegyrics or mock-panegyrics, requiring six to ten lines in heroic coup-lets. I specify the form in hopes that prosodic imitation enhances appre-ciation of craft. I specify the panegyric mode because praising or criticizing famous (and not-so-famous) people is central to Augustan poetry. While following a model, students choose their own subjects and tone.

In English literature surveys, this exercise begins our study of Pope, after the class has read Dryden's *Mac Flecknoe* and "To Congreve." I hand out copies of Pope's early "To the Author of a Poem, intitled, Successio" for in-class analysis of style and theme; this mock-panegyric of Elkanah Settle exhibits fairly obvious figures of speech, classical allusions, antithetical parallelisms, and combinations of artistic and political concerns. Student poems are due the class period following this discussion; selections of student work are redistributed the class period after submission. Thus the entire exercise follows the shape of the seven-stage *imitatio* (reading aloud, detailed textual analysis of the model, memorization, paraphrase, transliteration, recitation, correction of student writing), adapting Quintilian's sequence to contemporary classroom exigencies without, I hope, entirely losing the power of interrelation that made classical rhetoric an integrated approach to learning (see Murphy, "Modern Value").

Some students try to imitate the model precisely. The first two lines of "To the Author" ("Begone ye Criticks, and restrain your Spite, / *Codrus* writes on, and will for ever write") become:

> Begone ye doubters, ye who think you're clever.
> Elvis lives, and will live forever.

Other students are more concerned with counting syllables and forcing end rhymes:

> Jim Bakker now is in an ugly jam,
> His love of wealth before the love of Tam.

Both rewrites focus on mass-culture heroes, as did Pope in *The Dunciad* and elsewhere, and the second selection gestures toward commentary on societal malaise as well as on a current scandal. Since the interplay between specific references and general social criticism informs much of Pope's work, class-generated examples prepare students to read *The Rape of the Lock* or *An Epistle to Dr. Arbuthnot* from a dual perspective. Just as the names of Jim Bakker and Tammy Bakker will disappear into history whereas their actions and characters may remain as examples of hypocritical greed, Lord Hervey is unknown to today's students but his portrait as Sporus remains a powerful depiction of corruption.

The Bakker couplet ignores the element of praise integral to the panegyric. In contrast, the couplet below shows the fine line between straight and satiric commendation:

> Praise to high-flying Michael Jordan.
> He wears Nikes because he can afford them.

The writer explained in class that he both admires and envies the basketball star, a mixed attitude not dissimilar to Pope's toward the wealthy Fermor-Petrie circle or toward Addison/Atticus (see *Arbuthnot* 192–214). The tone of the following lines, however, is more clearly panegyrical:

> Some roommates always gab on the phone.
> My roommate can leave it alone.
> She lends me money when I need a loan,
> And sometimes does my wash with her own.

Despite difficulties with the heroic couplet, the writer plainly intends to praise her friend. In class discussion, students concluded that the identity of the roommate was of minor importance compared with the definition of friendship as a compound of consideration and generosity. A personal friend serves a public function here, as does Martha Blount in *Epistle to a Lady* or Pope's father in *Arbuthnot*.

In an eighteenth-century period course, more time can be devoted to the panegyric project and the results are usually more sophisticated. These lines, for instance, demonstrate knowledge of Virgilian formulas and Augustan typographic conventions:

> I sing not of the arms and man, although
> A man with arms would surely want to throw
> Them round my saintly nymph, should she appear;
> I sing *Madonna's* shapely f—t and r—r.
> I sing her acting, videos, and gall.
> I sing, I say, 'cause she can't sing at all.

Following the examples of *Mac Flecknoe* and *The Dunciad*, in which Dryden and Pope implicitly depose the dunces by exercises of superior wit, this student tries to insert himself as a corrective to inarticulate tastelessness.

After period-course students write first drafts, they work in groups to refine meter and diction. Group work simulates Pope's habit of asking friends to comment on his poems; I start this phase of the exercise by showing an early version of the first four lines of "Spring" and Pope's request for Walsh's advice (Mack, *Life* 112–13), asking the class to take Walsh's role. Group work also can develop a community of knowledge and a mutually reinforcing spirit important to the success of the class (see Bruffee, "Peer Tutoring" 10–14). Here is a first draft of a mock-panegyric on Nancy Reagan:

> Brave Ronnie's queen for our new material age,
> What gilded schemes and projects in her rage.
> Designer gowns, mink coats, new china plate,
> White House fortune tellers, affairs of state.
> Around her, sycophants kowtow and fawn,
> While homeless huddle on the White House lawn.

Group members suggested that the first line diluted the poem's focus; they were bothered by the repetition of "White House" in lines 4 and 6 and by the clunky rhythm of line 4. They didn't like the inversion in line 2 but couldn't decide how to fix it, and they wisely left the final couplet intact. Revised, the first four lines read:

> The Empress of our nouveau golden age—
> What gilded schemes and projects in her rage:
> Designer gowns, mink coats, new china plate,
> Hair-dos and horoscopes, affairs of state.

The final stage of the exercise is writing learned notes to one another's poems, in imitation of Scriblerian bibliosatire. The note to line 4 shows the annotator adopting the manner of Swift's *A Tale of a Tub* as well as of Pope's *Dunciad Variorum* (and of modern anthologies):

> The reference is to Joan Quigley, a high-society astrologer whom Mrs. Reagan consulted during her husband's terms in office. White House insiders revealed that Ms. Quigley's "readings" helped determine the president's schedule. According to R. Bentley, the word *horoscope* in the original Latin was written *whore-o-scope* but was changed by the timorous author to avoid a law suit. —W. Wotten

The Pastoral Wars

An alternative creative project appropriate to a period course is writing pastorals. I use this exercise when the course emphasizes transformations of pastoralism in eighteenth-century literature. After setting the social, political, and literary stage with Dryden, Mandeville, and the usual cast of Restoration characters, I move to Pope. Studying his early pastorals establishes his sense of poetic vocation and his reliance on classical models. It also prepares students for Pope's less overtly pastoral poetry and indeed for much of the work to be covered during the semester — including Gay's pastoral parodies, Swift's pastoral utopias in *Gulliver's Travels*, Gray's introverted pastoral myth, Johnson's antipastoral pronouncements (among which, I believe, *Rasselas* can be numbered), Goldsmith's and Cowper's pastoral responses to the looming industrial revolution, and ultimately Blake's *Songs*.

The first set of reading assignments lists Pope's *Pastorals*, "A Discourse on Pastoral Poetry," *Windsor-Forest*, and the *Guardian* 40; Ambrose Philips's "The First Pastoral"; Addison's *Spectator* 30, praising Philips and ignoring Pope; and Gay's "Friday" from *The Shepherd's Week*. The pastoral wars in which Pope was embroiled amuse students yet demonstrate, I hope, the serious and often adversarial positioning of pastoralism in the eighteenth-century intellectual landscape. Concurrent with the readings I ask students to write a pastoral or an antipastoral, six to ten lines in heroic couplets. As in the panegyric exercise, the responses are distributed to class members for purposes of discussion.

Some student pastorals are close imitations of Pope:

> Thy greenways, Raleigh! And thy verdant parks
> Breed noble deeds and poets' feeble marks.

While rewriting the first two lines of *Windsor-Forest*, the student has recognized the convention of moving the muse from classical to contemporary times. The student who wrote the following verse, patterned on the beginning segment of "Spring," reaches a similar understanding and also adds "authority" to her lines by citing place names (the "city of oaks" is the Chamber of Commerce's epithet for Raleigh, NC):

> The tuneful nymphs from Thessaly have fled,
> Abandoned Arcadia's grassy bed,
> To take up their abode with pleasant folks
> Who live and work in the city of the oaks.

A different sort of topicality occurs in this pastoral, which borrows one of the organizing repetitions in "Autumn":

Resound ye fields! My heart is cleft in twain,
To see the trees embrowned by acid rain,
To see the stream where children used to romp,
Turn to a stinking, sewage-ridden swamp.

When the class discussed *Epistle to Burlington*, the ecological pessimism in this student's pastoral lament was reexamined to highlight Pope's apparent trust in natural rejuvenation (173–76).

Imitation also reveals other pastoral themes. These lines echo the paean to Britain in *Windsor-Forest*, lines 377–84, and transpose nationalistic sentiment to current conditions and issues:

Behold! America's glittering towers arise
As Liberty illuminates the skies.
The Stars and Stripes in majesty unfurled,
The sign of peace and plenty for the world.

Just as this student text points from Pope's Stuartophilia to Thompson's imperialistic raptures in *The Seasons*, another student text points from Pope's parody of rusticity in *Guardian* 40 to Gay's *Shepherd's Week*:

Louetta drove the pigs a-down the hill,
And stopped to visit Jim-Bob at the still.
"Lawd sakes," he said, "you're looking mighty fine —
"A woman looks her purtiest in moonshine."
She sniffed, as Jim-Bob took a hearty swig,
"Don't need me no additions to my pigs."

Imitating the Virgilian program, Pope moved from pastorals to other genres, yet pastoralism never disappeared completely from his poetry. As class discussion of the America verses above suggested, pastoralism could be a political stance — for Pope, a generic taproot into Tory ideology. To try to avoid pigeonholing, I stress Pope's dexterity in manipulating monied interests (for instance, his subscription deals with booksellers) while creating a persona for himself of a landed gentleman who savors Horatian retirement (see Mack, *Garden*). Thus when we studied the moral epistles, students were quick to see ideological contrasts between Sir Balaam and the Man of Ross (*Bathurst*) or in the excesses of parsimony and profligacy imposed by Old Cotta and his son on their landed estate, pastoralism providing the backdrop for a drama of the new economics. Similarly, they identified the "Genius of the Place" in *Burlington* (57) as an essentially pastoral spirit, which authorizes not only taste in general but also the "Imperial Works" that turn the commercial growth of "happy Britain" (204) into elements of landscape architecture. The academic, nostalgic pastoralism of Pope's early work has been transformed into an active force that orders and directs Britain's national development. In addition, pastorally oriented students found that the tasteless and tasteful gardens in *Burlington* helped them discern a philosophic and aesthetic unity in Pope's diverse works, whether manifested in the balance between boldness and regularity or that between the systemic perspectives counterpoised in *An Essay on Man*. Attention to gardens also spurred attempts to define Pope's satires as revisions of the Fall from a succession of cultural Edens.

Yet students didn't lose sight of the class biases inherent in pastoralism. Juxtaposing Gay's loutish shepherds and "Newgate pastoral" commonfolk with the wealthy exemplars in the moral epistles and extending the lesson to Goldsmith's *Deserted Village*, the class concluded that both nostalgic and prophetic pastoralism were intellectual properties of the rich and the leisured. The relation between economic status and pastoral taste surfaced on a Christmas card I received at the end of the term, inscribed with lines inspired by Timon's villa:

> A fruited wreath on every door, a light —
> Just one — in every window, gives the night
> A prim display Colonial, celebration
> Williamsburg, Yule decoration.
> One is benumbed. Is it against their laws
> To prop the porch with a plastic Santa Claus?
> No front-yard creche or carolers are seen;
> The snooty neighborhood remains serene.

Rewrites of the Rape

Not all students lisp in numbers, as many of the above examples show. Thus I've devised another type of creative imitation, designed particularly for nonmajors and modeled on Quintilian's transliteration exercises. Since *The Rape of the Lock* is the one poem that almost everybody teaches in a general survey course — and one that I always teach, no matter how I arrange my syllabus — the assignment focuses on the *Rape* and addresses what seems a fundamental barrier to student understanding and enjoyment of the text, that is, what exactly happens in the poem. Thus I give students a choice of writing a plot summary of the poem's narrative or of rewriting a scene or episode in prose, imitating if they wish the style of a contemporary author. Less adventurous students choose the summary; their homework (often assisted, I suspect, by Cliff's Notes) at least familiarizes them with the events in the *Rape*, so they have a groundwork for considering other issues. The rewrites are usually more interesting and can lead directly to matters of character, ideology, and authorial stance. I distribute examples of student writing to the class for discussion and reference.

As with the poetry imitations, some students "translate" the *Rape* directly into prose. The first stanza of canto 3, for instance, becomes:

> The towers of majestic Hampton stand next to the proud river Thames, near fields constantly filled with flowers. Here British statesmen talk of foreign tyrants and local women. Here Queen Anne sometimes meets with her advisers and sometimes drinks tea.

This student ignores details, such as the triple realm, he doesn't understand, but by mimicking Pope's parallelism he does begin to understand the alternating inflations and deflations characteristic of the mock-heroic mode. Further, by highlighting the political dimension of the *Rape*, this rewrite generates discussion of how the poem may allegorize the Hanoverian rape of the kingdom (see Erskine-Hill, "Political Poet"). A more elaborate prose rendition, this of Umbriel's visit to the Cave of Spleen, remains faithful to textual specifics while expanding on them in an adjective-laden, modern-Gothic exercise in *copia*:

> Umbriel groped about blindly, brushing the clammy, slimy walls of the cave with trembling hands. Restless scurryings, nauseating rustlings echoed faintly, as if living teapots prematurely entombed in the stone were hissing in agony. Eyes adjusting to the gloom, Umbriel made out the dim shape of a glassy decapitated woman in one corner crying in vain for her lost head and in another a groaning male figure holding his swollen belly. The sinister scene terrified Umbriel, yet underneath the terror another emotion, a melancholy, bad-tempered whim, made him clutch his stomach. Fighting the urge to quit, he moved toward the bag and vial, the objects of his quest.

Besides causing the student to define words such as *spleen*, the exercise here demonstrates how imitation can generate invention. Invention in turn generates discovery; reconceived as horror fiction, Umbriel's quest discloses sexual displacements and usurpations latent in Pope's *Rape* that were not immediately apparent to the class.

The next two selections evidence a different approach to the assignment. Their authors are concerned less with fidelity to details than with interpretation of character and theme. This rewrite, broadly based on canto 1, is modeled stylistically on a popular teen-romance series:

> Belinda was in bed, rereading the note Baron had passed her in ombre class earlier that week. She couldn't help herself. She really had a crush on him. He was absolutely the cutest guy at Hampton High. No wonder she dreamed of him every night.
>
> She got out of bed and went to her dressing table. I wonder what Baron's favorite color is, she thought, as she experimented with pink,

coral, and fuchsia lipsticks. She watched herself in the mirror, pursing her lips into a kiss. I'm going to knock his eyes out at the party tonight, she promised herself, but I'm not going to let him go all the way.

"Who's going to go all the way?" said Ariel. Belinda hadn't noticed that her little sister had entered the room.

"No one. I mean, I'm not. Baron's not," said Belinda.

"Don't be so sure," said Ariel, who often acted wise beyond her size. "You lead guys on, and . . ."

"Cut it out," said Belinda. "Date rape only happens on TV."

Belinda appears as a modern icon of *vanitas*, structured in part by commodity fetishism (Brown, *Pope* 9), in part by quasi-innocent female predatoriness. The double focus on Belinda's mixed motives and on sexual aggression produced spirited discussion, introducing issues of gender and power that shaped the class's later consideration of *Eloisa to Abelard* as well as of the *Rape*. Similar interests inspired the following piece by an extremely competent student-writer:

"Can you help me?" she asked.

These society dames are all alike. So much jewelry you'd think she played center field in the bigs. Clothes that left nothing to the imagination, if you get my drift. A yappy furball of a mutt, whose shocking expression made me want to use it as a hockey puck. Yet something about this dame was different.

She took my hand in hers. Lee Press-On nails, Whore-of-Babylon red. "Please," she said, batting her Revloned baby blues. "Someone stole my lock. I need it back."

Her lock to what? Her diary? Her safe-deposit box?

She ran her hands through her hair, and then I knew.

Of all the perverts loose in our town, the Baron was the worst. Stalking women with scissors, maiming their crowning glory. I didn't want to think what he did with his trophies when he was alone. Probably wore 'em like rings.

It wasn't Belinda's fault that she was a society dame. She didn't ask to be born to money, maids, card parties. Just like she didn't ask to be attacked by the Baron. Really, she was a sweet kid underneath the paint.

"You got it, honey," I said. "I'll make sure you and your lock are never parted again."

I pulled out my notepad and started to write, iambs flowing as fast as Belinda's tears. "I'll restore your public reputation," I added, "or my name isn't Al Pope, Esquire."

This version also targets Belinda's guilt and innocence, and it negotiates skillfully between physical and psychological violation. Further, it foregrounds the narrator's function as redeemer of honor and guarantor of fame. Turning Pope into Philip Marlowe allowed the class to examine Pope's involvement in his poems, whether through his use of dialogue and monologue, as in the *Epistles to Several Persons*, or through the more oblique, metapoetic self-references that end poems like the *Rape* and *Eloisa*. Intersections between the personal and the public can be hard for undergraduates to locate; the medium of peer imitations and "translations" can make them more visible.

Student imitations are useful adjuncts to undergraduate study of Alexander Pope. Because only a few class periods can be spent on any single author in general literature surveys, the panegyric exercise has not been as successful there as I would like. The project may be too loosely related to the handful of Pope poems assigned, and class size and pace prevent adequate attention to technique and structure in student work. The exercise does stimulate student interest, but it does not always reach its goals concerning the craft of the heroic couplet. For these reasons, I believe the translation-to-prose exercise to be more effective for large classes emphasizing broad coverage.

Period courses are a different matter. In a smaller, tightly focused class, students write panegyrics and pastorals enthusiastically; group revision and discussion create a type of collaborative learning that includes social construction of a parallel text, one produced to interpret and to interact with Popian materials (see Bruffee, "Social Construction" 774). Writing their own imitations helps students understand not only the importance of imitation to Pope but also its flexible, generative power. And as students become interested in the theory and practice of imitation, some decide to explore Pope's imitations in formal papers and research projects.

To the extent that imitation has been resurrected in contemporary pedagogy, it has been primarily used in writing instruction. This article has tried to suggest its applicability to literary studies as well. By making their own intertext, students become aware of the intertextuality of their models. They learn that imitation both respects tradition and prospects within it, finding and transforming materials, forging new connections to past and present history. Imitation can help students perceive the "quick springs of Sense" in what can too easily be a stultifying "pale of Words" (*Dunciad* 4.156, 160). And as they write through, across, and within Pope's poems, their transcriptions enable Pope to make a difference that, I hope, cannot be completely erased.[1]

NOTE

[1] I would like to thank my colleague Mike Carter for his generous advice in matters of composition and rhetoric.

Autobiographical Reflections on
Teaching Pope Critically

G. S. Rousseau

My sense of Pope and of contemporary criticism are so intertwined with
my development as a teacher and scholar-critic, and with my belief that
"culture" is usually what the present discovers of interest in the past, that
it is impossible not to write autobiographically on this occasion. I hope that
the college teachers who constitute the main readership of this volume will
forgive me if I write throughout in the first person. Only by disarming myself
in this way and evoking the voices attached to the act of teaching can I
suggest to what extent good teaching of Pope depends on having been taught
well oneself, the raison d'être, I suppose, of our collective revaluation here.
My further hope is that undergraduate teachers will recognize that my
approach to the teaching of Pope is personal. Indeed, I cannot imagine what
an impersonal approach could be — one claiming that Pope's life and works
have little or no relation to our own times at the end of the twentieth century.

At Amherst College I studied Greek and English literature with, among
others, Reuben Brower, the author of *Alexander Pope: The Poetry of Allusion*, still the best general book written about Pope's couplet verse. Brower's
approach was the quintessence of the auricular. In class he read Homer
and Pope aloud at about a quarter of the speed usually read by us students.
Homer he recited often in Greek; both poets he read very deliberately, in
calculated slow motion, always demonstrating how sound ("the sound must
seem an echo to the sense") was primary to Pope's substantive meaning.
There was little talk of genres, the evolution of poetic forms, or historical
backgrounds; few apologies for the lack of intricate plots in Pope's poetic
satires; no deference to the novel as a form. This was high, heroic literature
versifying epic themes — poetry in a class of its own. The approach appealed
to those students who were in search of the aesthetic in the poetry of Shakespeare, Milton, Pope, the Romantics and moderns. Brower knew almost
by heart the works of both Homer and Pope and encouraged us to read
aloud in small groups. We had to capture the line's pace as well as the
inflection of both Homer's hexameters and Pope's couplets. From Brower's
vantage, students who could not master this essentially auricular aspect of
the verse could never proceed to a higher level of understanding. Pope's
mighty line depended first and foremost — according to our teacher — on
these varied cadences based on sound, rhythm, pace, inflection, crescendo,
and diminuendo.

When we had a grasp of the auricular we graduated to rhetoric, rhyme,
and allusion. Although in the late 1950s most students had not studied
Homer in Greek, they were able to learn from those who could recite Homer

in the original. Consummate classicist that he was, Brower commanded the tropes of rhetoric, but rhetoric in and of itself was never his point, nor had it been W. K. Wimsatt's point in his illuminating book *The Verbal Icon*, published six years before I was at Amherst. I remember our devoting at least half the class time to these matters. Brower stressed the marriage of sound and sense, no less in Pope's poetry than in a Mozart opera; that the musicality of Pope's couplets enforced his rhetoric and — reciprocally — the rhetoric heightened the poetry's musicality, as in so many famous couplets in *The Rape of the Lock* and even in the more didactic poetry of the 1730s (space does not permit examples, but each professor has favorites). How could lines like these be understood without paying attention to sound and sense?

The New Criticism was still flourishing at Amherst College circa 1960, when I was a student, and it was not unusual to be taught Pope entirely from the page, so to speak. Brower's own essays in *The Fields of Light* and *In Defense of Reading* approximate this approach, and the teacher could scan the chapter on Pope to see what a class with Brower was like. Little was said about Pope's life, friends, social milieu, or the literary history informing the poetry. All emphasis was on the aesthetic: on the beauty of the words, lines, couplets, organized verses. Works such as *The Rape of the Lock*, the *Pastorals*, *The Dunciad*, and translations of Homer were preferred over *An Essay on Man*, *An Epistle to Dr. Arbuthnot*, or the *Imitations of Horace*. Little sense of Pope's maturation was provided, of the transformation of his imagination, his growth as a human being, his relation to his complex culture — that marvelous range of erudition and information provided by Maynard Mack in his books. We learned chiefly about Pope's couplet art, emphasizing the varied tones and voices he could create, the power of his pen and the force of his line.

At Princeton I did graduate work in classics and English and studied Pope with Louis Landa, the Swift scholar. Here my background in Greek and training in New Criticism became important paradoxically — by providing me with a technique for reading that would complement the approach I was about to learn — for Landa's approach was anything but New Critical. As can be gleaned in his articles on Pope and economics, Landa viewed him as a poet of meaning. Landa's sense of Pope derived from the century's great Pope scholars: George Sherburn, John Butt, Geoffrey Tillotson, James Sutherland, James Osborn, Maynard Mack, Marjorie Hope Nicolson, and — of course — Reuben Brower. This view permitted access to all the backgrounds at once, to the poet's life, letters, contemporaries, and social milieu. To satisfy Landa we graduate students had to become minischolars. Within two years I was converted to what I then referred to as the "historical method." This approach suited me because it was based on a balance of formalism (New Criticism) and cultural critique (the historical approach). By the time I sat for qualifying exams with Pope as my major author, I knew the history of Pope criticism from Pope's death in 1744 to the present and had learned most aspects of the historical approach. Osborn's magnificent edition of Spence's *Anecdotes*—a gold mine for the critic-scholar of Pope—had not yet appeared, nor had Mack's brilliant books, including the biography; as a budding scholar-critic I could not yet assimilate these valuable sources or conjoin these dimensions of Pope, but I vividly remember the sense I then harbored that the 1960s were becoming a golden age of Pope criticism. Almost everything that could be known about Pope either was known or would soon be learned. In a short time Mack's biography and his edition of the manuscripts would appear. Then more or less everything that could be known about Pope would be known. I remember thinking of Johnson's pronouncement at the end of his *Life of Pope* and relating it to criticism: "New sentiments and new images others may produce, but to attempt any further improvement of versification will be dangerous. Art and diligence have now done their best, and what shall be added will be the effort of tedious and needless curiosity" (251).

But just when I thought there was no more to say about Pope, I found something new in the Enlightenment science I was learning. In 1964 I was introduced to Marjorie Nicolson, then at Princeton's Institute for Advanced Study. Both of us remarked how strange it was that no one had interpreted the wide range of scientific and medical references in Pope's poetry. We were soon collaborating on *"This Long Disease, My Life": Alexander Pope and the Sciences*, a book conceived in the historical and biographic mode—in what I call the second approach—rather than in the aesthetic or rhetorical method. *"This Long Disease"* was not a book destined to change anyone's notion about the basic material of satire or the essential nature of Pope's poetic genres. Rather, it placed the man beside the poet, showing the genius of both and how each arose out of the same basic stuff.

After receiving my PhD from Princeton in 1966, I taught briefly at Harvard and then at UCLA. At both institutions, after being assigned the undergraduate courses dealing with the age of Swift and Pope, I agonized over the approaches I would adopt. As everyone knows, the late sixties in America were rocked by war controversy and ideological debate, and I was profoundly affected by them. I came away believing that every philosophy and methodology, every system of aesthetics and metaphysics, even the New Criticism, had an ideological agenda. New Criticism had not died out in the classroom, and I soon found myself teaching Pope not according to Landa and Nicolson but more or less in the auricular way I had been taught at Amherst. But as the war wound down I began to ask new questions. I was further compelled to examine my pedagogical principles when Peter Dixon invited me to write the opening chapter for the volume on Pope in the Writers and Their Background series ("On Reading Pope"). My assignment was to compile a detailed account of the reception of Pope's critical heritage that would also be pedagogically useful (the Routledge Critical Heritage volume compiled by James Barnard did not appear until 1973).

I found it a difficult task principally because my experience compelled me to recognize the discrepancy between classroom teaching and my research and writing: I was a vestigial New Critic in the one realm, a convinced historicist in the other. Why could the two approaches not be brought together, especially with the excellent students I was teaching at Harvard and UCLA? Because – I reasoned – it was impossible for the instructor to reconstruct the historical backgrounds and also teach the students to understand the technical aspects of the heroic couplet (i.e., to read Pope) in a single term. Besides, adoption of the historical method would probably brand me as a "pedant," a fate no young college teacher wants. I discussed this dilemma with various senior colleagues at different institutions, and we agreed that a choice of one or the other had to be made. Given the reality, the couplet was more important than the background. Nevertheless, it seemed an entirely inadequate solution – no solution at all.

Then, in the early seventies, I began to read French theory, especially Foucault, Deleuze, Lacan, Derrida, and some of the Marxists and hermeneuticists. At UCLA I was still assigned the undergraduate courses in the age of Swift and Pope, but I found myself teaching according to one set of beliefs while writing according to another. Yet as I moved intellectually further away from formalism and closer to an invigorated historicism or contextualism (I use the two words interchangeably here) whose interdisciplinarity was unavoidable, I also noticed my teaching was starting to alter. Now it was not a matter of either/or but of both concurrently: somehow I would just have to learn to integrate the two; otherwise the hypocrisy would be overwhelming. For Pope, this meant telling my students something about his life as a cripple and a Catholic, a landscape gardener and a devotee of the visual arts; providing them with information about the turbulent political dimensions of his world. Besides, of what use was it for my students to learn the tropes of rhetoric and the paraphrases of couplets if they hadn't the vaguest notion of the poet's imagination, heart, and head? Furthermore, each semester I discovered myself shocked at the wild prejudices about Pope (and his period) held by a large number of my students. All this had to be changed in the classroom itself – the space where ideas can be freely exchanged – even if I had no clue as yet whether the theory I was reading (structuralist, poststructuralist, neo-Marxist) would be useful. To persuade myself, I wrote articles advocating "interdisciplinarity" without specific application to Pope, while naively thinking the endeavor would rescue Pope from formalism and bridge the "two cultures" syndrome of my teaching – not the Snowian two cultures, of course, but those of formalism and historicism.

For a period in the mid-seventies I thought I had succeeded to a limited extent. My students were responding more enthusiastically, claiming that I was liberating them from the prejudices they harbored about Pope and his age and that they were beginning to understand that Pope actually met the standards of other great poets. I remember how vindicated I felt when reviewing

Howard Erskine-Hill's *The Social Milieu of Alexander Pope*, a book that stressed the historical relevance of Pope's world to every aspect of his mature poetry. But as the seventies evolved, it became strikingly evident that we were living in a different world from that of the sixties and that the now old New Criticism was becoming virtually irrelevant. For our best undergraduate students were asking new questions about their world, about education, and about the past, and it was not enough to teach as I had taught in the sixties. The "me generation," they wanted to know explicitly why they should read Pope, what value he was to their education, and what he had to say, anyway, that was so important. I was back to square one: it wasn't sufficient to proclaim him a great poet; he had to be shown to be one. All the more reason, I thought, to blend the two approaches. Here was a challenge and a risk well worth taking.

But by then, the late seventies, French criticism had reached its peak of influence in American universities. Theory had begun to permeate the whole fabric of the humanities, and it was only a matter of time until anyone not au courant with the most recent pronouncements of Derrida or Foucault would be considered barbaric. Yet the relevance of such thinkers to the Popian texts that I had now been teaching for a decade and that I practically knew by heart was less than obvious. Foucault barely read English, let alone Pope; Derrida had never written a word about Augustan satire (except a brief summary of the plot of *Gulliver's Travels*) — I doubted that he knew anything about Pope's poetry or life. Foucault's theories could, of course, be applied to Pope's social world, but this would mean re-creating and then commenting on that world in detail; in other words, seriously reconstructing the historical matrix. Pope's poetry could be deconstructed along the lines of Derrida's theories, his works could be "unraveled" in the ways Derrida demonstrated that every text unraveled; but to my way of thinking, the first problem was that Derrida had no means of coping seriously with referentiality, and what, then, was I doing if all I did was replace one type of formalism (the New Criticism) with a newer one (deconstruction)?

Foucault was another matter. By about 1980 I had become a converted Foucauldian, without having surrendered my firm grounding in English or British contextualism. Fortunately no contradiction existed between the two approaches. Foucault's studies of madness and sexuality, words and things, power and authority all converged at one point: the place where certain social figures and cultural structures are marginalized while others are empowered. The brilliance of his analyses lay less in his command of historical periods or national traditions than in his sense of the complex historical patterns in which marginalization occurred.

What could be more relevant to the interpretation of Pope's life and work? Pope himself had been a highly marginalized and problematic figure for the most pressing personal, religious, homosocial, and political reasons. If not exactly an outsider (a semantically treacherous concept no matter how interpreted), he was nevertheless no insider: his poetry rebels against established mores and authority more often than it endorses a traditional or empowered position. This was the poet whose religious allegiance was with the minority Jacobites (Catholics) more than with the Church of England; the poet who trembled when the Jacobite Bishop Atterbury was called to stand trial, lest his own brand of Catholicism be interrogated; a man whose deformed body — he eventually shrank to not much more than four and a half feet — probably precluded any type of intimate heterosexual life. Furthermore, he was a poet who defied the authority of classical rules, urging writers to reach "for a grace beyond the reach of art"; who, as a member of a Catholic minority, espoused the quasi-deist metaphysics of *An Essay on Man* and *The New Dunciad*; who dared to brand the Howards — the richest family of the realm and allies of the prime minister (Robert Walpole) and the New Whigs — "the sons of sons of whores." If Pope's personal health (his dwarfish, humped body, deformed by kyphoscoliosis, and his numerous chronic illnesses), bachelorhood, and homoerotic sexuality had also been taken into account — aspects of Pope that I remember Brower and the other New Critics at Amherst as rarely mentioning — he most surely would have engaged the attention of a Foucault — that is, if the French philosopher could have read anything by or about him.

So it was a matter not of deconstructing Pope — of further unraveling and decontextualizing him — but rather of somehow bringing him into the Foucauldian fold and hermeneuticizing him, conveying to his already richly allusive poems a historicism with a higher degree of literary pertinence. The task was more easily said than done, because my undergraduates found Foucault difficult to read and grasp, no matter how slowly I explained his theories. I was now teaching with a higher threshold of understanding — that is, expecting my students to know more than how to read and paraphrase Popian couplets — but I had to admit that few of them learned any historical background whatever.

G. Douglas Atkins's *Quests of Difference: Reading Pope's Poems* had a minimal effect on me. Pedagogically speaking, it had no effect at all. I could, of course, have assigned it as required reading (which I never did) and taught my students how to deconstruct Pope, but to what avail? Why deconstruct Pope when there were so many more pressing needs and when I myself had not been converted to Derrideanism? My search was for a method integrating the aesthetic-rhetorical and historical approaches, not for a newfangled theoretical gimmick that would work for a few years, only to fall out of fashion and leave me searching for another handle. Perhaps that is why Maynard Mack's biography seemed a much better solution for the classroom instructor than Atkins's valiant attempt. For my own reasons I had been awaiting the biography for years; but I also knew that it would be pedagogically useful, not as a reading assignment for the students but as help in presenting the figure of the great poet and the age in which he lived. I needed the biography to combat the profound prejudice of many undergraduates that the eighteenth century was irrelevant to our times and that Pope was a best-forgotten minor poet. I had read and commented critically on the opinions of foreign critics who contended that we Americans esteem Pope too highly. Most of all, I was excited about the Mack biography because I thought that through its anticipated new insights I would somehow improve my presentation of Pope the poet by sharpening and focusing his image for the undergraduates.

My long review praised the book (although it disturbed Mack); still, as persuaded as I was of the excellence of the new biography — and it is a superb biography — it was also the work of the biographer of another generation. I tried to explain why to my students. Mack could not, or would not, ask questions that we asked in the eighties — and still ask today — about the relation of a poet to his or her culture. I assured them that although no one in the world knew more than Mack did about Pope and his milieu, the historical approach was not, in itself, adequate for undergraduate English majors who wanted to know why Pope was a great poet and what he said that was so great. I quoted the opening of my essay in the Dixon collection:

> We live in an age of multidimensional disorder — disorder that is evident in every walk of life and by no means confined to governments, courts, or great affairs. Intellectuals and other men who live "by their minds" — to echo the late Bertrand Russell — experience this welter and have as much difficulty and anxiety in mustering an energy necessary to cope with it as soldiers and ministers of state had in previous ages. . . . What can an "ancient poet" who was a member of at least three minorities: a Catholic, a cripple, and — not least of all — a poet teach such a disordered age?   ("On Reading Pope" 1)

I continued to tell my students that Pope's greatness lay not primarily in his poetic technique (Mack had placed it first in the critical books and in the biography) but in the fusion of that technique to thought about his society and environment and thought about the universal lot of humankind. When my practical-minded undergraduates asked what Pope's poetry could do to solve current socioeconomic problems, I not only assured them it could but explained how his views of bureaucratic corruption, sycophancy, party politics, degenerate moral values, the old-boy system, and other sociopolitical issues had rendered him not some robotlike couplet versifier, turning out frivolous rhymes, but rather one of the most socially relevant poets of all times. Too often, undergraduates derived the notion in their early surveys of English literature that Pope was an armchair poet who sat by the hearth in Twickenham churning out meaningless ditties in rhyme. I always tried to eradicate this preposterous view as early as possible in the course.

For just these reasons Laura Brown's work about Pope the imperialist seemed outrageous to me. It undid all the benefit of Erskine-Hill's work of a decade earlier, undermined Mack's historicism, and—more consequentially for me—effectively made me a liar to my students. Brown claimed that Pope was the early-eighteenth-century poetic mouthpiece for a vicious and unrelenting imperialism—for a capitalism, moreover, that was appallingly male-centered and chauvinistic—and that he secretly despised women and did anything possible to keep them in check. This was just the opposite of what I had been telling my students for two decades. I had stressed Pope's compassion for the downtrodden and the overlooked, despite his fixation on the aristocracy and the ways it might live better. I had dwelt on his vision—expressed in the magnificent concluding lines of *Windsor-Forest*—of a fair social order existing within a unified globe, organically breathing as a single entity; emphasized his denunciation of political corruption and the odiousness of flattery; cultivated his images of the New World to show that he felt its lands and natives must not continue to be ravished by the reckless Europeans; spent class time to prove that Pope's attitude toward women was too complicated to be simplified by denunciation or stereotyping (a view that has now been confirmed by numerous feminist scholars—see Landry in this volume); explained that as Pope matured he grew critical of—indeed less and less the mouthpiece of—any form of humanistic tradition and political establishment and increasingly became its bad conscience; demonstrated that he was not the conventional king of wit but—as he himself subtly proclaims in *The Dunciad*—an "anti-Christ of wit." If the students' sense of Pope derives almost entirely from *The Rape of the Lock*, then, of course, students derive the impression that Pope was the self-appointed ambassador of an elite patrician culture into which he desired entry more than he did anything else; but those who read further—into the *Imitations of Horace*, the *Epilogue to the Satires*, and the last book of *The Dunciad*—glean what Pope's heartfelt mature beliefs really were.

I actually fantasized about undergraduates who might read Brown's book and then take me to the Committee on Academic Charges for misrepresentation and outright fraud because I had portrayed Pope as a liberal thinker. Here was Brown depicting a despicably tyrannical, imperialistic, colonial monster—anything but the temperate, fair-minded, honest, and ethical man I had presented, someone unafraid to "live among the great" and yet assault the aristocracy (implying that the Howards, the wealthiest family of the realm, had been "sots, slaves, and cowards," nothing but "the sons of sons of whores" [*Essay on Man* 4.205–16]).

Brown's argument struck me as not having been made in the name of an explicit feminism historically derived from the structures of Pope's world. Pope's attitude to women was equivocal, even by the most charitable standards of his own age. Pope relished the company of women—although he also felt women had starved his emotional life because those he fell in love with would not have him — and his representation of them in his couplet poetry and magnificently expressive letters is varied and complex. Nevertheless, his love for them is not sympathetic enough — does not sufficiently compensate for their lot (as viewed from our contemporary perspective) to permit the notion that he was a champion of, or spokesperson for, them. No one who consults a major poem (the *Epistle to a Lady*) beginning with the lines "Nothing so true as what you once let fall, / 'Most Women have no Characters at all'" can expect charity from Pope's female readers, despite the fierce irony of this couplet and the poet's ironic inversions staunchly defending women later in the poem. The Pope who in thousands of couplets nowhere mentions the Chinese, who stereotypes Africans as "sable Sons" and "Monsters" near "the Race of *Reptiles*," and who invokes

> . . . the poor Indian, whose untutor'd mind
> Sees God in clouds, or hears him in the wind;
> His soul proud Science never taught to stray
> Far as the solar walk, or milky way
> (*Essay on Man* 1.99–102)

should not expect progressive readers two centuries later to valorize his Anglocentric approach to these non-Western ethnic cultures. Nevertheless — and everything rests on this significant qualification — it is hard for me to perceive what value accrues from the application of these progressivist approaches when Pope himself lived in a socioethical milieu so different from ours. One might as well judge Plato or Russell by a set of standards altogether alien to their contemporary social vision and criticize Plato for not objecting more vehemently to the status of Greek women as slaves and Russell for not marching in the front lines to abolish apartheid. Pope's sense of social justice can, I believe, be usefully compared with that of our most progressive groups, and inculcating of social awareness in our students is surely one of the most important tasks of college professors, but the wisdom of doing it in the classroom, when there is so little time to teach students how to read Pope's lines, is debatable, even controversial.

Although in the eighties I was skeptical about the relevance of theory for Pope in the classroom (be it deconstructionist, feminist, minority discourse), I was encouraged by the advent of new historicism, even if this approach has now manifested serious limitations. New historicism, like earlier interdisciplinary methods approached through the writings of Marx, Bakhtin, Foucault, and Raymond Williams, juxtaposes often diverse texts and authors for the purpose of rehistoricizing them. As such, new historicism often teases out metaphors and tropes that had lain dormant — invisible, so to speak, to the best critic's eye. It is also true that today the new historicism has become a buzzword for a constellation of historicizing approaches, often without consistent method or recognizable content. All the same, despite its myriad shortcomings, its effect on students has been the invigoration of the historical approach to literary studies and the championing of methods of interpretation whose threshold of explanation insists on grounding literary tropes — especially recurrent metaphors — in historical structures and cultural patterns.

Some will maintain that Pope stands to gain less from the new historicism than other authors do because the best Popian criticism has always been historicized, so to speak, but this rebuttal is surely beside the point. The genuine matter relates to the *way* texts are historicized. I have no desire to defend new historicism here, though in fairness I must admit that its best ideas — for example, the notion of art as material production and of texts as interventions into historical realism rather than as pale reflections of it — have barely been employed in interpreting Pope. Pope's satiric attacks are often so rhetorically charged and auricularly precise ("*Sporus*, that mere white Curd of Ass's milk . . . he himself one vile Antithesis" [*Arbuthnot* 306, 325]) that they function as curse; indeed, he is a poet who despises the approximate in either sound or sense. Yet this curse element, rich in the poet's mind with associations of an English historical past, has not been tapped. Nor has anyone tapped the all-important concept of body — Pope's grotesque physical body, his genital disability and dysfunction, his metonymics of the quill as surrogate phallus, the relation of his deformed body to his gender and aesthetic identifications, the sizable body of his writings, the images of bodies found in his poetry and prose. As long ago as 1968, the British critic Emrys Jones commented in passing that "[t]he *Dunciad* is both a work of art and something else: it is, or was, an historical event, a part of literary and social history, an episode in the life of Pope as well as in those of his enemies" (232). For Jones, *The Dunciad* represented something more than "a poem," yet Jones's aperçu has gone virtually unnoticed even by the new historicism. Despite the variety of critical approaches that have been adopted to interpret *The Dunciad*, the giant lampoon's status as a material event, as a vigorous incursion into the mainstream of Georgian cultural history — especially the ways it shaped rather than reflected the tone and tenor of the Walpolian era and the king's administration — has never been studied. And *The Dunciad*'s status as a material object — its colossal size, its bulky weight, its typography, the homoerotic consequences of its versions of authorial collaboration, the economics of publishing and then imitating it for decades after Pope's death in 1744, its fiscal impact on the hacks it attacked, who were then writing for a consumer culture craving information delivered at breakneck speed — has been overlooked, even by the Popians. My point is surely not arcane. More critical work remains to be performed on Pope's metaphors in the large body of his poetry, even if much has already been completed, and it would be folly not to acknowledge the utility of the new historicism in this enterprise. This forward path, guided in part by new-historicist light, should not obscure the existence of previous bodies of criticism; and even in the classroom, students should be made aware, through Pope's metaphors, of the poet's ambivalent relation to power and authority, monarchy and democracy, reason and passion. Considered as a methodology in the abstract theoretical sense, the new historicism is far from perfect; but if sensitively used in the classroom, it has the resonance of a touchstone and may be more capable of altering the student's sense of Pope's poetry than deconstruction was in the late seventies.

Finally, something must be said, biographically and historically, about the diversity of class, race, gender, and sex—that is, the representation of the rich and the poor, white and black, male and female, straight, gay, bisexual, and so forth—in Pope's poetry. A reviewer of Pat Rogers and my recent book of Pope criticism complained that Pope's (mostly male) critics still conceptualize the poet and write about him as if they were the members of a small and (mostly male) elite club. The charge is serious and ultimately invalid, but one can see why it appeals to college students whose collective fantasy imagines a highbrow authoritarian Pope writing about elite circles that despise the hoi polloi. Yet the reality is that some of the best teachers of Pope today were trained by New Critics and, although unlikely to concede it publicly, remain New Critics themselves. Over the years they have been unwilling to surrender any of their dearly held pieties about the poet and his couplet art. But other caveats about, and desiderata for, Pope are equally pressing. By sometimes forgetting to place Pope the man in perspective, teachers distort the poet in the poems by seeing him only as he wished himself represented and reflected in the poetry. This version of "self-fashioning" (to borrow another concept from the new historicism) must not be exempt from the critical act in the classroom setting. Pope's poetry carefully differentiates between rich and poor, famous and unknown, permanent and ephemeral, but Pope himself was not the son of rich or famous parents and was no more an "aristocrat" than his manservant was. Our students often get from their teachers confused messages to the effect that, because Pope discusses the wealthy and the great, he himself was one of them. When Pope wrote, "*Envy* must own, I live among the Great" in the *Imitations of Horace, First Satire of the Second Book* (line 133), he was self-fashioning himself in ways that have far-ranging implications for his own notions of gender and sex, power, authority, and fame—even for the self-fashioned masculinity of his persona and the machismo of his grotesquely deformed body. But the reality of his life was that he himself was anything but an authority figure, and it is nonsense to maintain he was one. His heart was starved; he searched for love without finding it. He harbored a notion of poetic creativity based on his own desperately ineffectual sexuality. He wasn't even a "majority" figure in this capacity, let alone in other areas.

Careful distinction should also be made in the classroom so that our students understand a range of contexts for Pope, including the reasons why he remained a bachelor (our students want to know) and, alternatively, why Pope often savagely attacked the important personages he versified. The same clarification must be made for Pope's relation to elitism. We live at a time when, in some circles, opportunity is encouraged for those who have been bypassed, even unlucky. Our students' attitudes to elitism — elite persons, elite ideas, elite professions, elite arts — become ambivalent and suspicious. Our students are even more confused and uncertain whether to endorse the unlucky and downtrodden or the successful and elite. Their conflict disturbs them more than we teachers like to concede and often manifests itself as disgust for, and rebellion against, those empowered to legislate in any capacity for them. But "someone empowered to legislate" sounds like the kind of motto students regularly use to describe canonical writers like Milton, Pope, and Johnson. They wonder how this odd creature Alexander Pope — this lump of grotesque physical deformity, this unfortunate dwarf of Twickenham, this solitary bachelor who took it on himself to judge not merely other men (our students are now questioning the vicious attack on Sporus, the openly sodomitical Lord Hervey) but also women (Sappho), children, families (the poetry indicts numerous families), political parties (Tories, groups of Whigs), governments (the whole of Walpole's regime), monarchs (the illiterate George I and the cultural baboon George II), the whole lot — dared inspect and condemn virtually every element of his society. We arouse their curiosity more if we deflect the question from the moral to the psychological dimension of this daring, that is, not the de jure right of Pope to judge but the psychological reasons driving and compelling him. Then Pope becomes a major figure in the history of outrage whom they want to know something about.

I have been suggesting that we must recognize that we are in the presence of a poet very much in need of balanced presentation to our students if they are to begin to understand him. I am far from gloomy about the prospects, but I think there will be no future for Pope if he is presented merely as a technician or rhetorician perfecting rhymes, prosody, and couplet art. Pope was also a significant *social* poet, and this is what our students want and need to hear about. My blueprint for an undergraduate course entails the presentation of him both as an artist perfecting his craft and as a social critic piercing deeply beneath the superficial patina and deeper fabric of society. The former approach deals with his technique and place in the lineage of great English poetry (Shakespeare, Donne, Milton, Dryden, Pope, Blake, etc.), the latter with his role as an astute social observer. I present some of his positions to my students as if he were commenting on social class, rank, and sex as his most pressing task, and I do this without worrying that I am not "deconstructing" him, because I know that in historicizing him I am creating the possibility of his enduring as a voice our students want to hear. This approach also removes the edge of specialization my students always seem to associate with those teachers of literature attracted to a poet like Pope, that is, narrowly focused critic-scholars who may themselves be rich, autocratic, elite persons.

My method permits me to do partial justice to Pope without worrying about the balance between traditional and innovative approaches and without feeling that all I have done is apply some newfangled theory. By maintaining his place as a great poet, such a generalist approach does him fuller justice without selling out to the theorists who were never interested in him or his poetry in the first place.

The approach isn't perfect and doesn't always work. I don't have a name for it other than historical and critical, but it's not "new historical," "New Critical," "new deconstructionist," or "new" anything else. Although I cannot name it, the approach demonstrates how far I have strayed from the New Criticism in which I myself was educated.

Teaching Pope Today: Satire, Resistance, Theory

Fredric V. Bogel

Nothing has more dramatically marked literary studies in the last twenty years or so than the pervasive and multifaceted questioning of authority—the authority of text and author, of meaning and intention, of the idea of the literary, and of much else, including an author's ability to control his or her meaning, the ability of language to coincide with or to deliver adequately the reality it seeks to render, the interpreter's ability to produce a coherent and comprehensive (though not complete) account of a whole work, the ability of the literary work to claim for itself a status distinct from the status of other kinds of writing, and the ability of the realm of the aesthetic to sustain its identity as a sphere distinct from the spheres of nonliterary language, history, ideology, power, interestedness, and more.

This questioning of authority has, of course, taken many different forms. We have learned to be newly alert to the politics of gender, race, and class encoded in literary works; to inquire into the assumptions and alignments that make possible those systems of inclusion and exclusion known as canons; to explore the complicities with power disclosed by texts that claim to be free from the exercise of power; to notice the force and presence of ideology —the ways in which authors may prove blind to the values they support or to the compromising import of values consciously espoused; to dwell on the tensions between a text's different aspects or modes of signification and on the challenge these tensions deliver to the idea of a unified text—that is, a text whose modes of signification are not at odds with one another; and we have learned to register and explore the continuities between literary texts and other phenomena of the culture contemporary with them, and to do so, at times, without recourse to the powerfully hierarchical metaphors of foreground and background, center and periphery, high culture and low.

In consequence, relations between text and reader have altered significantly. To put it briefly and crudely, a certain amount of authority has migrated from the text to the critic. Many readers have become accustomed to demystify the texts they analyze, and while they have not ceased entirely to regard those texts as authorities, they have recognized that to take a text as an authority is to decide to use that text in a certain way, not merely to use it in the only way possible (a way dictated by the very nature of the text itself). A new sense of critical and readerly authority has arisen, not the power to tyrannize over a text (though that has appeared too, and inevitably) but the freedom to assess as well as explicate a text's meanings, to decline as well as to recognize its seductions, to criticize as well as articulate or interpret its structures of value.

It is possible, of course, to describe this migration of authority as something other than simply an alert critique of the tendency to fetishize literary texts: perhaps as an attenuation of the ability to submit to, or imaginatively reenact, or provisionally trust a text long enough to see whether it is itself critical or less than fully supportive of the mode of authority that arouses the resistance of the wary reader. Any form of attention, after all, is also a form of inattention. It is therefore understandable that an alert readerly opposition to textual authority might produce a certain inability to notice the ways in which a text criticizes or questions its own mode of authority, the ways in which it resists itself.

Nonetheless, it is clear that, to some extent, we have all learned to become "resisting readers." What is curious about satire, though, is that readers *always were* resisting. A number of eighteenth-century readers found Swift and Pope petty malcontents or writers too ambitious for fame and too willing to blacken others' reputations; nineteenth-century readers found them unpoetic or pathological, or both; in the twentieth century, critics — even those critics who did the most to recover satire as a literary mode — displaced the charges of personal unpleasantness and moralistic superiority into an account of rhetorical convention but neglected to tell us why a smug or vindictive persona should arouse less resistance than a smug or vindictive poet does. And, of course, our own students tell us in numerous ways, if we let them, that they, too, are resistant, that they are made uneasy by the spectacle of the satirist sitting in judgment on a wide range of real and imagined political or poetic or moral failures. More than the difficulties of line and couplet rhetoric, or of literary and political allusion, it is this act of judgment that chills the sympathetic current of the undergraduate soul.

In consequence, the present moment in criticism gives us something analogous to a reinforcement of wave motion in physics. Traditional resistance to satire is seconded, and given interpretive and theoretical legitimacy, by the skeptical or resistant modes of critical reading that are now in the ascendancy. I suspect that this congruence of skepticisms has made things too simple for us. Finding ourselves uneasy with the satirist's claims to authority, *and* empowered by a generalized critique of literary authority as such, we may move too readily beyond the intricacies of satiric authority in this text or that text to a "larger" account of the satirist's ideological investments or of the structures of political power and social organization that satiric hierarchies and exclusions seem to reproduce.

For what these different modes of skepticism share is the assumption that satire asks us to endorse the satirist's authority, to align our reading selves with the satirist, and therefore to set ourselves against the object of satire. Each sort of reader — the Augustan contemporary or the tenderhearted undergraduate or the contemporary negative hermeneuticist — has a different reason for resisting such claims for endorsement and alignment, but all agree implicitly that these claims are indeed being made on them: that the "reader position" projected by the satiric mode is one that entails a fairly simple assent to the satirist's ethos and values. This assent, moreover, is not an isolated phenomenon, since the rhetoric of satirist-reader relations is bound up with the rhetoric of the relations between satirist and satiric object. The clarity of our alignment with the satirist and of our opposition to the satiric object reproduces, and is compact with, the clarity of the opposition between satirist and satiric object.

We are dealing here with a dynamic triangle whose points (satirist, satiric object, reader) are interactive; consequently, disturbances along any one side of the triangle generate disturbances along the others as well. To discover such disturbances may thus mean revising our sense of satire as a mode, and of Pope as a satirist. I want to suggest what sorts of difference such a revision may make, a revision that asks of us not a clear alignment with the satirist and a clear opposition to the satiric object but something more complicated and more likely to issue in that "unease" that Patricia Spacks finds the characteristic emotion generated by the reading of satire ("Reflections"): an unease that students should be encouraged to acknowledge and explore rather than sidestep.

First, though, I would like simply to list a few other revisions of the received view of satire that are required by the actual complexities of satiric texts as they appear to us today. These are, by and large, revisions of the view that the mid-century pioneers of satire criticism made available to us, and it is with no abatement of gratitude to them — to Maynard Mack, Northrop Frye, Alvin Kernan, and Robert C. Elliott, principally — that I propose these modifications. First, the idea that satire is a response to a perceived threat in the world external to the text and that it is a response to a preexisting difference between satirist and satiric object seems to me not quite true. It is certainly what the satirists themselves, in their apologias, claim, but the apologia is best understood, I think, not as a text commenting on satiric texts ab extra but as a principal convention of the rhetoric of satire itself. It makes at least as much sense to treat references to figures "out there" as part of a rhetorical convention of referentiality establishing the satirist as a person in touch with the external world rather than someone for whom generating fantasy-figure attacks serves a variety of psychic needs. Of course, a satirist certainly *may* begin by perceiving a repellent figure whom he or she wishes to attack. But the asumption that such is always, or almost always, the case seems to me evidence of a remarkable willingness to read satire "with the grain," as the satirist would have us read it. (The formalists attempted to solve this problem by arguing that Sporus was Sporus, a figure of symbolic and universal force, and not simply a textual encoding of Lord Hervey, but that attempt sidesteps the question of how we know whether the impulse to attack — Hervey *or* Sporus — precedes, or arises from, a perception of the object.) Moreover, the choice need not be a clear one; there is no special oddity in imagining a satirist who begins with the desire to conduct a satiric attack and *then* fastens on an actual historic figure capable of satisfying that desire, among others. We may kick the family dog because we have lost money that afternoon, but, then, we may never have really liked the dog anyway.

In addition, it is at least as likely that we attack a figure, distance ourselves from him or her, because we sense a threatening proximity to us, as that we attack the figure because he or she is already so different from us. I suspect that satire is often not a response to a prior difference but an effort to make a difference, to create distance, between figures whom the satirist — who is one of those figures — perceives to be insufficiently distinguished. In this connection, as Michael Seidel has already made clear in his study of "satiric inheritance," the work of René Girard on doubling, mimetic rivalry, and the violence these engender is extraordinarily useful, as is Mary Douglas's account, in *Purity and Danger*, of the extent to which "pollution behavior," the effort to cast out or classify or terminologically corral threatening forces and agents, is rooted in the threat those forces and agents offer to cultural differences and distinctions. What Girard and Douglas tell us, in their different ways, and what Roland Barthes also tells us in *S/Z*, is that it is not difference but the erosion or annihilation of difference that requires acts of ritual boundary policing and boundary establishment, acts among which I would include a sizable number of satiric texts. The satiric attack produces the difference that the satirist treats as already there, waiting to be registered.

In Girard's account, moreover, the selection of a scapegoat who may be sacrificed in order to end the murderous and potentially endless rivalry between doubles inevitably has something arbitrary about it; indeed, it is only this element of arbitrariness that makes the scapegoat sufficiently different from the rivals for his or her sacrifice to terminate the crisis of doubling rather than simply continue it. Douglas, too, alerts us to the element of arbitrariness, and thus the element of fictionality or half-knowing self-deception, that permits many social rituals to work. In one society she investigates, monstrous human births are dealt with by precisely such a fiction, for they are classified not as human infants but as baby hippopotamuses and are gently placed, therefore, in their proper environment, the waters of the river. Modern and "nonprimitive" analogues are not far to seek. One thinks of the crisp legal division of human beings into the guilty and the innocent and the criminal and the noncriminal and of the implicit social distinction between "bad" violence, such as criminals perform, and "good" violence, such as the criminal-justice system metes out to convicted criminals. The functioning of the cultural and social machinery demands that we not notice too clearly or too frequently how human those "hippos" look, how powerful and unregulated that criminal-justice system can seem. If something of the same arbitrariness — the same designation of what is threateningly ambiguous as distinctly other — is part of the construction of the satiric object, then satire doesn't operate simply by affirming social norms and casting out deviants from those norms; instead, it affirms them, but it also creates profound uneasiness about both the act of affirmation and the norms themselves.

Why, though, should readers have persisted for so long — and in the face of their own considerable uneasiness — in assuming that satire does affirm clear norms, does establish clean distinctions between satirist and object, does invite our unambiguous alignment with the satirist and against the object? In part, because there is a significant payoff for readers in that assumption. It allows us to mask our ambiguities of identity, our own troubled connectedness with satirist and satiric object alike, and thus to affirm an internally consistent subjectivity. By casting out the satirist's intricate and complex involvement with the objects of the satire, we cast out our involvement as well. We may pay a high price for doing so, but we purchase an intensely comforting product.

Another area in which I think actual complexity has been sacrificed to manageable clarity is that of the mock-form. In the usual account, the "mock-" in compounds like "mock-heroic" or "mock-epic" signifies mockery, and mockery of a relatively secure sort. Most often, mock-heroic is taken to be that form in which the relatively trivial is ridiculed in the light of the grandeur of the authentically heroic — or, less often, in which the limitations of the heroic are brought out by contrast with the uninflated solidity of the everyday. Occasionally, a critic will venture beyond this choice, as when Martin Price remarks that there is a sense in which *The Rape of the Lock* "is mocking neither its own world nor the imaginative world of the epic but simply putting them side by side, small and great, with a quizzical sense of their parallelism as well as their conflict" (headnote to *Rape*). But while this subtle formulation resists the assumption of hierarchy implicit in most accounts of the mock-heroic, it nevertheless preserves their faith in clear distinctions: between mock-epic and epic, small and great, and so on.

What the mock-epics, mock-pastorals, and mock-georgics of writers like Swift, Gay, and Pope suggest, however, is that such distinctions are far from clear and secure. These works seem to have sprung not simply from veneration for the ancient and elevated or from scorn for the modern and low but from a wild fascination with the possibility of writing as though such distinctions were inoperative or unreal. If these works are imitations, they are imitations — by writers for whom hierarchy and distinction are matters of second nature — of works in which hierarchy and distinction are themselves eroded, works that are elsewhere satirized in less ambiguous terms. They are, in a sense, imitations of failed imitations, and their own status is therefore powerfully compromised. Such works suggest that we take the "mock-" in formulas like "mock-heroic" to signify not mockery, but surrogacy, substitute or counterfeit status — like the "mock-" in "mock-turtle." To move into the realm of the counterfeit, of course, as Hugh Kenner has brilliantly shown, is precisely to enter a sphere of unclear distinctions and uncertain identifications, since the whole point of a counterfeit is to be at once not the real thing and virtually impossible to distinguish from the real thing. A counterfeit banknote, we might say, exists somewhere between a genuine banknote (which no one considers a fake) and play money (which no one considers genuine). I think the Augustan mock-form exists in an analogous space between the high and the low: a space where distinctions are rendered problematic rather than reinforced, where unsuspected continuities throw bridges across chasms of customary distinction, and where our meditations on genre—like meditations on counterfeiting generally—leave us not with a secure conclusion but with a set of troubling questions.

The topics I have been exploring here—of compromised authority, of the interrelations between difference and identity, of imitation, and of the rhetorical structures of satire—can be briefly illustrated from Pope's portrait of Atticus in *An Epistle to Dr. Arbuthnot.* I want to try to show this portrait in a slightly new light but also to illuminate some of the readerly investments that make it hard to see it with any freshness.

> How did they fume, and stamp, and roar, and chafe?
> And swear, not *Addison* himself was safe.
>   Peace to all such! but were there One whose fires
> True Genius kindles, and fair Fame inspires,
> Blest with each Talent and each Art to please,
> And born to write, converse, and live with ease:
> Shou'd such a man, too fond to rule alone,
> Bear, like the *Turk*, no brother near the throne,
> View him with scornful, yet with jealous eyes,
> And hate for Arts that caus'd himself to rise;
> Damn with faint praise, assent with civil leer,
> And without sneering, teach the rest to sneer;
> Willing to wound, and yet afraid to strike,
> Just hint a fault, and hesitate dislike;
> Alike reserv'd to blame, or to commend,
> A tim'rous foe, and a suspicious friend,
> Dreading ev'n fools, by Flatterers besieg'd,
> And so obliging that he ne'er oblig'd;
> Like *Cato*, give his little Senate laws,
> And sit attentive to his own applause;
> While Wits and Templars ev'ry sentence raise,
> And wonder with a foolish face of praise.
> Who but must laugh, if such a man there be?
> Who would not weep, if *Atticus* were he?   (191–214)

Atticus, it is clear, is being satirized for a certain combination of power mania and sleazy indirectness and for a form of jealousy that has strong links to self-hatred and might be described as a fear of being mirrored or doubled: "Too fond a rule alone," "Bear . . . no brother," and so on. Pope's principal strategy, as generations of commentators have noted, is to mimic

Atticus's own cautious undermining of others by treating him not as a real person or indicative actuality but as a mere subjunctive possibility: "*Were* there one," "*Shou'd* such a man," "*if* such a man there be." This little grammatical joke consigns Atticus to ontological limbo, the unreal realm of the hypothetical, and gets at the degree to which he has undone himself in seeking to preserve himself, or has fatally divided himself in refusing to allow himself to be doubled.

But this is to see the portrait as enacting satiric difference alone, when, in the context of the entire *Epistle*, it also does just the reverse, forging connections between attacker and object of attack. Like the satirist, Atticus is a figure of extraordinary natural talents; like the satirist, he is besieged by flatterers and talentless hangers-on; and like the satirist, he has a strong taste for regal solitude, the solitude of "the Turk" or of "Asian monarchs" (220). There is, moreover, a deeper connection between satirist and satiric object than these thematic parallels suggest — deeper because it is structural and virtually unavoidable and derives from the character of mimicry itself. Pope, we say, mimics Atticus so as to satirize him. That is, he imitates him in order to stress the difference between them. But as that more general formulation suggests, this is a very curious thing to do, and it forces us to ask ourselves how we can distinguish mimicry as distancing from mimicry as reenactment or as identification. Can the satirist possibly mime Atticus hinting a fault and hesitating dislike without thereby painting a portrait of himself as well as of his satiric object? Imitation may not always be the sincerest form of flattery, but one thing it always is is an act of identification, even when that identification is enlisted in an effort of repudiation. If we take that repudiative mimicry — the oxymoron is inescapable — as not entailing identification, we do so, I think, because we want to preserve a less complicated, a less compromised or contaminated, conception of readerly identity. The satirist's alleged distinctness from those he satirizes models our own safe distance from them. In fact, I think this portrait redefines identity as neither solitary nor undivided but implicated in otherness and internally divided.

For one thing, it is not quite accurate to call Atticus "unreal," as I earlier did, since the presence of the name "Addison" in the line preceding the portrait exerts a powerful gravitational pull, which keeps the object poised somewhere between the real and the hypothetical; and this ontological straddling is reinforced by the portrait's grammatical mood, which is a mixture of the indicative and the subjunctive (a mixture emphasized by Pope's revisions, which richly repay study, in this as in many passages). The famous last line — "Who would not weep, if *Atticus* were he?" — also holds within itself a powerful doubleness. It asks, first, "Who would not weep to discover that the pathetic figure I've just described is actually the revered Atticus?" But it also asks, "Who would not weep to discover that he himself was Atticus?" The line, that is, projects an Atticus who is *at once another and oneself* and, in so doing, mirrors that doubleness of identity that I have been ascribing to the satirist. It would be only a slight exaggeration to say that Addison is being satirized, in this portrait, for denying the kinship with others that Pope displays even in the act of satirizing him.

There are several ways of generalizing from this example, several "morals" that can be drawn for the reading of Pope and Augustan satire at the present moment. The first is that it is a mistake to read most satire as though it simply asked readers to identify themselves with the satirist and set themselves against the satiric object. That would only be possible if the satirists themselves enacted such unambiguous rituals of identification and rejection, and I do not think they do. They ask us, instead, to meditate on the problematic intricacies of identification and difference by which we define our own identities and our relations to others of whom we cannot fully approve or disapprove. I think our students should be told this. It will not make their reading any easier; quite the reverse. But it may save them from the difficulty of having to conceal their discomfort with systems of value and acts of judgment that make them uneasy but that they think all right-thinking readers are supposed to affirm. When they express their discomfort, I think we should tell them that they're doing fine, that they're doing what they're supposed to do. Reading satire is not so much about finding a position we can plug ourselves into as about exploring the complexity of what it means to take a position.

Second, we can think of satire's curious tendency to affirm strong positions and resist those affirmations as the expression of a kind of cultural wisdom. Having shown that pollution rituals clarify cultural rules by mastering the anomalies and ambiguities that threaten those rules, Mary Douglas goes on to affirm the need for such threats. They are necessary because cultural norms and unambiguous categories, taken alone, forestall the possibility of transformation, of change, of self-criticism. Threateningly ambiguous figures are dangerous, but they are also locations of power, and if a cultural system is to be vital as well as perspicuous it must incorporate some of that power. This is why the Lele do not simply shun the scaly anteater called the pangolin, an animal that is in many ways a cultural nightmare since it threatens so many of the classificatory systems on which that society is founded. Instead, the Lele hunt, cook, and eat the creature, incorporating rather than evading its threatening condition.

This incorporation, however, takes place in a ritual space that is designed to frame and limit the effects of the encounter with the pangolin's anomalous status, a space analogous to those we are accustomed to call the space of "parody," or "mock-forms," or "irony." If the ritual frame does not hold, that encounter will prove simply destructive. In much the same way, the identification of satirist with satiric object must in some way be controlled if the two are not to collapse into each other, undoing difference, identity, and satire at one stroke. A badly managed imitation of a bad poem simply *is* a bad poem. But the power cannot be had without the risk of danger; things must always *be able* to go wrong if they are to have a chance at going right. Similarly, the remarkable power of at least certain satiric and mock-forms depends on our inability to say with certainty where we are, to know with certainty that failure is being pointed to rather than exemplified, quoted rather than uttered — that it is a matter of "mention" rather than also of "use."

Third, this account of satire may help us formulate more usefully the relation of Augustan satire, especially Pope's, to the figure of Milton. *Paradise Lost* is structured, in part, according to the principle of demonic parody. Every time Satan attempts a subversive or rebellious act, it is fatally compromised by the fact that it imitates an act of God, yet in an altogether different mode. Such acts of imitation, in Milton's poem, do not bring Satan closer to God; they provide continuing evidence of the unbridgeable disjunction between them. It is as though God and Satan were the recto and verso of a single strip of paper, forever parallel yet forever disjunct. And this, it might be said, is also the way the relation between satirist and satiric object has often been figured. The Augustans, I think, twist this strip of paper once and join the ends, making a Möbius strip. The result is not that difference is annihilated, as an overly hasty reading of both Pope and deconstructive criticism might suggest it is, but that it must now *be produced*, and within a single ontological plane. Satiric difference no longer rests on a prior, metaphysical disjunction. It is, instead, what the satirist must create *within the sphere that he or she shares with the satiric object*. The difficulty and complexity of such acts of satiric creation have their counterpart in the exacting role that readers of Pope must perform now and in the future.

Don't Touch Me! Pope as *Pharmakeus*

J. Douglas Canfield

Perhaps the most serious problem in teaching Pope in the late twentieth century is not so much the particularity of his satires but that particularity's attendant nastiness. There appear, in effect, to be two Popes: one the detached observer of culture who points to the highest standards, both moral and aesthetic, and the other the spiteful avenger who gets even with his enemies. Critics of the latter half of the twentieth century, with Maynard Mack, quite properly, in the forefront, have been able to achieve a feat of legerdemain by subsuming the second Pope in the first, turning Pope into the defender of the faith — cultural, moral, religious, and political. And most of us have been complicit in the promulgation of this image in our classrooms. But even in a poem as seemingly free from the second Pope as *The Rape of the Lock*, students want to know the reason for such a gratuitous bawdy insult as having Belinda lament that the Baron had not snatched "Hairs less in sight, or any Hairs but these" (4.176). Why did Pope perversely insist on this particular vision of female hell: "Maids turn'd Bottels, call aloud for Corks" (4.54)? The insult is to Belinda/Arabella in particular and women in general. And if students are puzzled by this gratuitous nastiness in as innocuous a poem as *The Rape of the Lock*, they are exponentially more so by the nastiness in some of the so-called *Moral Essays* and in *The Dunciad*, *Imitations of Horace*, and Pope's several self-defenses.

In other words, even in a large survey course, where one usually only has time enough to teach the *Rape*, students encounter a typical problem of satire: the besmattering of the satirist himself as he attacks vices and follies, a problem Alvin Kernan addressed years ago as that of "the cankered muse." Even if the Pope that students are exposed to includes the ostensibly moral and philosophic *Essay on Man*, they realize, if only implicitly, that the best parts of the poem, the ones Pope endows with the greatest energy and power, are the satiric sketches of vain, foolish men and women. But if students reencounter Pope in an upper-division eighteenth-century course, they meet the beleaguered defender, armed for truth and on the counterattack. And if we teachers pursue the Christian-humanist line of our own teachers, we generally have to suppress our students' resistance.

Carole Fabricant's brilliant essay "Pope's Moral, Political, and Cultural Combat" addresses the absence of an objective correlative for Pope's rage and righteousness, especially in his so-called *Epilogue to the Satires* and the forgotten follow-up, *One Thousand Seven Hundred and Forty*. Fabricant transforms Pope as defender of a Tory vision into Pope as exploiter of a bourgeois cultural vision, one that has, through Matthew Arnold, become our own: we teach only the best that has been thought and said, and who taught us better how to discriminate than Pope Alexander, as his victims in *The*

Dunciad called him? In that sense, according to Fabricant, the apparently beleaguered Pope triumphed over Walpole and the other witwouds.

But Fabricant does not really deal with Pope's savage attacks on his enemies. I should like to propose a reading complementary to hers based on the notion of satire as *pharmakon* and of the satirist as *pharmakeus*, as these terms have recently been employed by Jacques Derrida in his essay "Plato's Pharmacy." The *pharmakeus* is a magician, a sorcerer who administers the *pharmakon*, a drug that is both remedy and poison at one and the same time. Just as Socrates in Plato's *Phaedrus*, according to Derrida, wants to obliterate the ambiguity of the threatening *pharmakon* by interpreting it solely as remedy — an interpretation that preserves the possibility of univocal truth — critics and teachers of Pope have tended overwhelmingly to obliterate or sublimate Pope's venomous nastiness. Even when some of the better recent critics — Dustin Griffin and David Morris especially — have insisted on his selfish motivations, they see those motivations as being transformed by Pope's higher purpose into what Griffin calls Pope's "best self" (18–25). Griffin sees the offenses to Pope as being subsumed into offenses against the values for which Pope stands. And when Morris acknowledges that Pope's muse is the "Muse of Pain" (*Genius of Sense* 214–40), he sees pain as Pope's weapon not, finally, to get even but to punish transgressors of Pope's cultural laws — moral and aesthetic.

Thus Griffin and Morris allow us a glimpse of Pope as venomous toad or snake, but they transform his poison into remedy, into cure for society. It is as if we are to take Pope at his word, that satire "heals with Morals what it hurts with Wit" (*Horace, Epistle* 2.1.262), that he only attacks pretenders, posers, hypocrites, and truly vicious transgressors. Pope himself is posing as a healer, but his satires are often motivated by vengeful spite. I propose that teachers and scholars of Pope pay equal attention to this poisonous side of the *pharmakeus* by contrasting his pose of healer with that of hurter, the implications of which are rooted in historical, biographical criticism.

In *An Epistle to Dr. Arbuthnot*, Pope insists that he endured the arrows of his enemies for years before responding. He boasts that "Three thousand Suns went down on *Welsted's* Lye" (375) — that is, as Pope explains in his own note, Leonard Welsted's supposed traducing of Pope's reputation by accusing Pope of being responsible for a young woman's death and of insulting the Duke of Chandos in his portrait of the vain, tasteless aristocrat Timon in the *Epistle to Burlington*. The Twickenham editor points out that the chronology is wrong and that Pope may have been referring to Welsted's attack in 1717 on *Three Hours after Marriage*, a failed play on which Pope collaborated with Gay and Arbuthnot himself. A more astute critic might hypothesize that Welsted's real crime was to be a party writer for Walpole, who had recently been attacking Pope, probably for political reasons (Mack, *Garden* 123–26). But the point is that even if Welsted had falsely accused him of something Pope didn't do, Pope didn't forget it, did he? Nor did he forget the insults and attacks of Dennis, Addison, Theobald, Lord Hervey, and Lady Mary Wortley Montagu — to name those Pope has made most prominent by the brilliance of their portraits.

What were their crimes? The senior playwright and critic Dennis took umbrage at an insulting portrait of him as the title character in one of his own tragedies:

> . . . *Appius* reddens at each Word you speak,
> And *stares*, *Tremendous*! with a *threatning Eye*,
> Like some *fierce Tyrant* in *Old Tapestry*!
> (*Essay on Criticism* 585–87)

However much subsequent critics have tried to justify Pope's caricature, was it not gratuitous? Did Dennis not have warrant to respond? The situation is analogous to an assistant professor's caricaturing a Harold Bloom in a review! Perhaps Dennis's response was inordinate and intemperate, concluding as it did with an attack on Pope's *Essay on Criticism* that caricatured Pope as a "venomous . . . hunch-back'd Toad" (qtd. in Mack, *Life* 183). But where are the morals that heal the hurt in Pope's subsequent caricature of Dennis among the divers in the mock-Olympian games of the first *Dunciad*?

> In naked majesty great Dennis stands,
> And, Milo-like, surveys his arms and hands,
> Then sighing, thus, "And I am now threescore?
> Ah why, ye Gods! should two and two make four?"
> He said, and climb'd a stranded Lighter's height,
> Shot to the black abyss, and plung'd down-right.
> The Senior's judgment all the crown admire,
> Who but to sink the deeper, rose the higher.
> (2.271–78)

Pope's note in *The Dunciad Variorum* mercilessly rubs salt in Dennis's wound by commenting on Dennis's advanced age.

The two squabbled with each other for the rest of Dennis's life. Pope may have removed Dennis from the diving contest in book 2 of the revised *Greater Dunciad*; he may have surreptitiously ameliorated Dennis's poverty as Dennis lay dying (Mack, *Life* 588); and he may have written a prologue for a benefit performance for Dennis at the time of his death. But even in the prologue Pope lampoons Dennis for his infamous "Thunders" (*Twickenham* 6: 355–56), an allusion to the standing joke that Dennis's tragedies may have failed but his sound effects were successful. Finally, Pope could not forbear jabbing at Dennis posthumously, for he refused to delete references in *An Epistle to Dr. Arbuthnot*, "To Augustus," and *The Dunciad*.

Addison appears not only to have criticized Pope's initial attacks on Dennis but also to have put one Thomas Tickell up to a rival translation of Homer (Mack, *Life* 172–89). Pope never forgave Addison, nursing the infamous portrait of Atticus through several versions, which circulated in manuscript and print until Pope included it as a posthumous attack in *Arbuthnot*. Supposedly, Pope withheld the portrait from publication and even published a friendly epistle "To Mr. Addison." Why then publish the portrait posthumously? How could it heal wounds in a dead man?

What was Theobald's crime? The apparent offense was his pointing out the flaws in Pope's edition of Shakespeare (and later doing a better job himself). There may have been earlier skirmishes between the men, including a thwart to his career that Theobald may have bitterly blamed on Pope (Mack, *Life* 430). Whatever the history of mutual provocation, Pope punished him for his public attacks by making him the antihero of the first *Dunciad*, caricaturing him as a contemporary creative writer (or literary theorist, for that matter) might pillory textual scholars who "explain a thing till all men doubt it, / And write about it, Goddess, and about it" (1.169–70).

At least one pattern in Pope's motivations begins to emerge in these few send-ups. Pope called the aging Dennis a "*Tyrant*," obviously meaning a tyrant over upstarts in poetry and criticism, like Pope himself. He accused Addison as Atticus of being "too fond to rule alone"; "like the *Turk*," he could "[b]ear . . . no brother near the throne" (*Arbuthnot* 197–98). In short, Pope could not tolerate being criticized. He took it personally as being *touched*. In his first satire of self-defense, *The First Satire of the Second Book of Horace*, comparing himself with the great French cardinal who indefatigably sought peace on the Continent, Pope declares threateningly:

> Peace is my dear Delight — not *Fleury*'s more:
> But touch me, and no Minister so sore.
> Who-e'er offends, at some unlucky Time
> Slides into Verse, and hitches in a Rhyme,
> Sacred to Ridicule! his whole Life long,
> And the sad Burthen of some merry Song.
> (75–80)

"Don't touch me!" It seems disingenuous to interpret Pope's threat here as merely a warning to the vicious not to mess with his Christian-humanist values or his heroic, patriotic friends. I should like to stress that darker side of satire explored in Robert Elliott's *The Power of Satire*. Pope seems to me like Phormio, in Terence's play of that name, who does not have to reveal the one brother's adultery but reveals it nevertheless merely because both brothers have roughed him up. Once they have touched him, like a venomous toad he spits poison — and then, remarkably, turns to the audience to ask if there are any other challenges (Terence, *Comedies* 279).

A second inference from Pope's attacks seems probable, especially when we consider that Pope replaced Theobald with Cibber in the revised *Greater Dunciad*. What did Pope have against Cibber? Again, there is a previous history of enmity — or better, of rivalry. But is it not obvious that Pope was simply furious that Cibber was poet laureate and that the rightful heir to that laurel was languishing in exile like the Stuart king across the water? That rightful heir was, of course, Alexander Pope. Dennis, Addison, Theobald, Cibber — all were rivals who ignited Pope's envy.

Did Pope have ambitions? His whole career demonstrates inescapably that he did. In his early *Temple of Fame*, Pope acknowledges a "Lust of Praise," which he attempts to exorcise in a prayer that he not rise on "the fall'n Ruins of Another's Fame" (see lines 513–24). The lines are disingenuous. Did not Pope, the same year he wrote them, publish a poem gratuitously attacking Dennis, an older critic whom he, a Young Turk, hoped to supplant? Long before Cibber published his *Apology* or his *Letter to Mr. Pope* (see Mack, *Life* 774–81), Pope had asked — in a section of *Arbuthnot* that begins incredibly, "Whom have I hurt?" — "And has not *Colly* still his Lord, and Whore?" (95, 97). Pope spent a lifetime climbing up on reputational ruins he himself had created.

A larger point is at stake here. As a Catholic, a hunchback, a son of a tradesman, and a supporter of the opposition, Pope was marginalized. He spent his lifetime also ingratiating himself with people of higher station. He obviously desired to be near the scene of power. When Bolingbroke fell, when Anne died, not only Swift's but Pope's aspirations seem to have been inevitably dashed. By 1728 Pope, like Swift, was in a form of exile, growing increasingly estranged from Walpole's circle, where he had his own *Lord* and *Whore* who turned against him.[1]

Why Pope's relations with Lady Mary Wortley Montagu turned sour remains a matter for biographical speculation (see Halsband, *Lady Mary*; and Mack, *Life*). Perhaps as she grew more aristocratically disdainful of him (Halsband 130–32), his political ambitions became obnoxious to her. But Lady Mary appears to have exacerbated his sense of marginality and emphasized its sexual component. Apparently, he made repeated overtures to her (as he had to the Blount sisters), and she spurned him, according to her granddaughter, with laughter (*Twickenham* 4: xv). So, typical of the threatened male, Pope turned his lady into a whore, associating her in *The Dunciad* with French whores who give the pox (2.115–16). And when Lady Mary appears to have threatened him with a typical aristocratic beating through the spurious narrative of a fictive beating, *A Popp upon Pope* (Anon.), Pope responded even more savagely. Right after Pope's lines about touching him in "To Mr. Fortescue," he maliciously expands the misogynistic insult:

> Slander or Poyson, dread from *Delia*'s Rage,
> Hard Words or Hanging, if your Judge be *Page*.

> From furious *Sappho* scarce a milder Fate,
> P—x'd by her Love, or libell'd by her Hate:
> Its proper Pow'r to hurt, each Creature feels,
> Bulls aim their horns, and Asses lift their heels,
> 'Tis a Bear's Talent not to Kick, but hug,
> And no man wonders he's not stung by Pug.
> (*Horace, Satire* 2.1.81–88)

Pope's point is that each creature hurts according to his or her nature, so
Fortescue should be no more surprised at Pope's hurting through satire than
at a bull's hurting with its horns or a lapdog hurting not with a sting but
with its teeth. The sheer vindictiveness of his lines about Lady Mary are
apparent from the pun on the pox: Lady Mary had been disfigured by smallpox and had returned from Turkey an advocate of inoculation. Pope equates
her supposed libeling of him out of mere hatred to her infecting a lover
with not the small but the great pox, syphilis. Is Pope healing with morals
here or in his subsequent lampoons of Lady Mary as Sappho, Avidien's wife,
Fufidia, and in propria persona (*Twickenham* 4: xix)?

Griffin has pointed out Pope's preoccupation with his littleness, including
his fears of sexual inadequacy (43–46). Did Pope sublimate his sexual energies
into his pen? Did he attack women as stridently, as misogynistically as he
did (*To a Lady, Sober Advice from Horace*) because of his fears, because
of his desire to dominate through his pen? Whatever the case, my point
is that Popian satire is not just *pharmakon* as remedy but *pharmakon* as
poison—intended to hurt, to get even, to destroy enemies and rivals. Lady
Mary's brilliant counterattack, abetted by John Lord Hervey, attacks Pope
where he seems to have hurt most—his sexual inadequacy: "No more for
loving made, than to be lov'd?" (*Verses Address'd to the Imitator of Horace*,
line 49, in *Essays* 265–70).

Griffin has also handsomely argued that, in attacking Lord Hervey, Pope
was attacking an "antiself" (182–89). Griffin goes too far, however, when
he implies that Pope transcends meanness because he exorcises such anti-
selves. I think not. Whatever the reason for the falling out of these two
erstwhile friends, when Pope attacks Hervey as Sporus at the queen's ear
(*Arbuthnot* 319), is he not jealous that he himself does not have the queen's
ear? Does Pope attack Hervey for being effete, effeminate, androgynous
because *he* wishes to appear manly, because *he* therefore has the right to
the queen's ear (bawdy pun intended)? Of course not; because she was
corrupt, the whole court corrupt—so Pope tells us, so his critics and our
teachers tell us, so we tell our students.

We return to the problem: as long as we deny the poison Pope administers,
we delude ourselves in the glib acceptance of the "Truth" as Pope portrays
it, the "Truth" Pope claims as his object, his province (*Arbuthnot* 341). Consequently, we are in danger of accepting Pope's self-portrait as *pharmakos*,
as martyr, sacrificial lamb, scapegoat, who, after his *Epilogue to the Satires*,

announced his self-imposed silence in a world too corrupt to amend (*Twickenham* 4: 327). As Fabricant points out, in *One Thousand Seven Hundred and Forty* Pope complained bitterly — and self-pityingly — "The plague is on thee, Britain, and who tries / To save thee in th' infectious office *dies*" (75–76). These poses of martyrdom are gestures designed to erase the ambiguity of his pharmaceutical satire.

Of course, Pope did not remain silent but instead published the revised version of *The Dunciad* — his attack on cultural abuses, yes, but also on his enemies, his mimetic rivals. *The Greater Dunciad* is a great poem. So also, I would argue, is the *Epilogue to the Satires*. But they draw their power, they appeal to us at a visceral level as much because they hurt as because they purport to heal. The power of satire, Elliott argues, is its primitive power to hurt, to inflict injury, through words — a verbal voodoo. And that fact has a great deal to do with why we like it. But we do not experience the hurt as simply punitive deterrence to further transgression, as Morris argues we do. We experience it vicariously as the sweetness of revenge, as the beautiful pen stroke of dominance.

Such a reading means we cannot give our students an univocal interpretation of Pope: they know we are lying. Nor can our approach to ambiguity be the New Critical version, focused on the paradoxes of a Christian-humanist vision. Pope's satires display radical ambivalence as well as ambiguity, an ambivalence that summons divergent responses, that requires perpetually supplementary readings of Pope.[2] For Derrida, that is the ultimate potency/danger of the *pharmakon*: it is the dangerous supplement; it suggests that no one vision, no one word will ever suffice, not Pope's, not ours. We will always find radical *différance* at the heart of Pope's greatest poems. In that sense, we will never really touch him. But perhaps by combining both historical *and* theoretical strategies — as in my attempt to supply both biographic information and the Derridean deployment of the trope of *pharmakon* — we can better teach our students how to account for Pope's dual self-image.

NOTES

[1]Walpole and Pope had had friends in common, Pope had visited Walpole in court, and Walpole is said even to have visited Pope in his grotto (Mack, *Garden* 196).

[2]To give Mack his due, perhaps because he was influenced by Griffin, his student, he has tried to acknowledge Pope's ambivalence, especially in his section "The Man Reborn in the Poems" (*Life* 719–26). His great integrity and intellectual honesty will not permit Mack to completely whitewash a poet whom he obviously deeply identifies with and loves. Nevertheless, Mack insists that, while Pope's great satiric portraits may "take their beginnings from personal antagonism, they are transfigured by his imagination into warnings of universal application" (*Life* 647). It is that sublimation which this article hopes to counter, especially as it relates to the Pope we re-present as teachers.

Pope and Imagination

David Fairer

I find that to use "imagination" as the starting point for a class on Pope can encourage students to make the immediate experience of reading him the element from which other intellectual challenges grow. Normally this would not need saying, but for a teacher of Pope's poetry it locates a basic pedagogical problem — how to deal with the wealth of context. A major challenge in teaching Pope is helping students negotiate between the words on the page and the contextual knowledge required for reading them, and it is here that "imagination" can help, by being an area of contact between the student's own vision and the disciplined intelligence of Pope's work. Such an approach would try to move outward from the personal and immediate to take in the wider elements ("the centre mov'd, a circle strait succeeds . . .") rather than to establish a framework in which Pope is then placed.

Perhaps no poet is so traditionally packaged for consumption as Pope. On one side, a survey course may find it convenient to present him as the representative poetic voice of the eighteenth century, at the center of a society whose Augustan "structure" of ideas disintegrated with the approach of the Romantic "movement." This is convenience packaging. On the other side is the complex "added value" packaging that offers the student a whole range of background material and terminology: the classical writers (Homer, Virgil, Horace), genres (mock-heroic, georgic), technical terms (caesura, zeugma), and wider concepts (deism, *concordia discors*, Augustanism), not to mention those notorious words *decorum, wit, sense, nature*. No wonder some students, if confronted too soon by this material, find they are not so much reading Pope as merely being inducted into an intellectual discipline with Pope as the means of delivery. At worst the poet becomes a tyrant mediated by an academic priesthood. A survey course will often exploit this approach by using the succeeding figure of Blake to unmanacle the student and, in the process, make a telling point about Romanticism and 1789/98 in terms of imaginative liberation.

Our view of Pope has suffered from a persistent notion that he is a less imaginative poet than, say, Wordsworth or Coleridge and that imagination was somehow less important to him. This idea has been encouraged by scholars such as Walter Jackson Bate and James Engell, who have presented a scenario in which an embryonic eighteenth-century imagination develops from mid-century and grows to maturity in the Romantic period. Such readings back from Coleridge are a weakness in much writing about the eighteenth century, and they assume a Coleridgean view of the "imagination" (as organic, unifying, and creative) divorced from the supposedly more trivial and wayward qualities of the "fancy." But such a distinction of terms would make no sense to writers like Hobbes, Milton, Addison, Johnson, and of course Pope, for whom a prime characteristic of imagination was its ambivalence and contradictoriness. For Pope, to hive off the shaping and unifying aspects of the mind into a separate category labeled "the creative imagination" would have been a nonsense. We should not allow Coleridge's theorizing about the "organic" imagination to displace other conceptions of it.

Pope draws on a much older tradition of imagination, one that centered on faculty psychology and that saw the power of "imagination," or "fancy" (Lat. *imaginatio*, Gk. *phantasia* — the two terms were generally not distinguished until late in the eighteenth century), as being placed in ambivalent relation to the rational procedures of the mind. Many scientific theories located these faculties in separate ventricles of the brain, and they were understood as being able to cooperate with each other, so that imagination receives and projects images within the mind for reason (acting as "judgment") to sort out, categorize, and evaluate (see, for example, *Paradise Lost* 5.100–13 or the opening of Dryden's preface to *The Rival Ladies*). These faculties are, however, opposed in their principles, in that imagination expresses the combinative or synthesizing powers of the mind, and judgment the distinguishing or analytic powers (Hobbes and many others make this distinction). Where imagination saw similarities between ideas, the rational faculty understood distinctions. It would make no sense, therefore, to speak of "imaginative truth," since truth was not the imaginative faculty's province.

Pope's imagination is consciously not an organic and unifying one; rather, it is the seat of human contradiction, and just as much as Coleridge's it is the source of his power as a poet and thinker. A poet who wants to explore the tragicomedy of human pride and self-deception will not be well served by a synthesizing imagination that splits off other aspects under a separate term and enshrines "the creative" as a purely positive idea. Pope needs to be able to exploit the contrasting elements in a faculty that is alternately penetrative and superficial, revelatory and deceptive, creative and chaotic, inspired and mad. Where Coleridge's quest turned contradiction into a creative interplay of part and whole in which a unifying self is enshrined, Pope's principles were radically different: his esemplastic Dulness is the nightmare of an organic "one life" that privileges the poetic sensibility at the expense of all the paradoxes of the social world.

All this sounds like a theoretical preemptive strike on the students, and I think it is important not to compartmentalize Pope in advance of discussion. So where to begin? In my own teaching I tend not to have a prearranged structure but to work from the responses of the class, ready to pick up a point and allow the impetus of discussion to move things in a fresh direction. I like the class to start theorizing only at a later stage. Rather than begin by establishing "Pope's attitude toward" or "eighteenth-century theories of" the imagination, I would expect my students, first, to think about how our imaginations might be at work as we read a Pope text and, from there, to discuss the satirical and other possibilities a visual image can create — how images, for example, may combine with or jar against one another. After that stage it would be useful to introduce wider and more theoretical questions into the discussion: is imagination a faculty of the mind, or a way of perceiving? Is it to be set against concepts of reality, truth, and judgment? How does it relate to creation and deception, illusion, or delusion? To what degree are moral issues raised or evaded by an image? Is it morally loaded in some way, and, if so, what makes us think that? Is it possible to speak of a single authorial "attitude" to an image? Is imagination by nature an accomplice in the vision it expresses? Are we aware of a wider frame of reference encouraging us to "read" the image more objectively? Ideally discussion should alternate between general and particular, returning regularly to the words on the page and setting local effects against wider implications, verbal detail against structural patterns. From a single grouping of words it is usually possible to work outward to one of the themes of that poem and, beyond that, to other Pope texts and more theoretical issues.

Someone in class may begin by choosing an "imaginative" passage:

> For lo! the Board with Cups and Spoons is crown'd,
> The Berries crackle, and the Mill turns round.
> On shining Altars of *Japan* they raise
> The silver Lamp; the fiery Spirits blaze.
> From silver Spouts the grateful Liquors glide,
> While *China*'s Earth receives the smoking Tyde.
>   (*Rape* 3.105–10)

When asked what they see, students are likely at this point to literalize. Guided by footnotes which explain that the "shining Altars of *Japan*" are lacquered tables, the turning mill is the coffee grinder, "*China*'s Earth" the cup, they may short-circuit their responses with an explanation (easily mistaken for a critical act): the cardplayers are breaking for coffee — the result seems ingenious enough. Yes, but what do you *see*? Reading the passage through several times so that individual words create pictures in the mind, we all begin to notice things. We start registering alternative possibilities of scale and location: the altars and silver lamp suggest a rich church interior; for someone else the last line shows a volcano erupting across the plains of China. How do these pictures relate to that elegant coffee break? How do we take our bearings between the salon, the shrine, and the landscape of elemental destruction? To what extent is Pope creating a drama of fire, water, and earth? And how does this scenario relate to the poem's machinery of spirits? The discussion here would probably lead to a consideration of the many shifts of scale in this poem full of the heroically trivial (is it a storm in a teacup? — almost literally, yes) and to an assessment of the "mock-heroic" in terms of an imaginative procedure that entangles values along with visions and raises pertinent questions about the presence of moral issues in the text. Does the satire merely help us locate the "trivial" in Belinda's society, or does it (more dangerously) bring into question our easy assumptions about priority itself? "We don't need Pope to tell us that drinking coffee is trivial," says one student. "Perhaps it isn't trivial," says another. "Surely mock-heroic works equally in the other direction, to enhance the apparently commonplace? I'll never pour coffee in the same way again."

At this point it would be useful to look at two places where the imagination is at work inside Belinda herself — whether the "moving Toyshop" of her heart, presided over by the coquettish sylphs, or the nightmare of her spleen, where the prudish gnome works his mischief. In what ways is the "pow'rful Fancy" (4.53) active in both? The sylphs may be a token of Belinda's fancy-free state early in the poem (their amoral profusion transforming Bibles and a cross into fashion accessories), but the darker incongruities and more insidious fusings in her spleen also show the fancy at work (where "Maids turn'd Bottels, call aloud for Corks" [4.54]). Perhaps, in expressing her superficial flirtation *and* her neurotic denial, these airy and earthy spirits show how, throughout, imagination insulates her from direct human experience? Is Belinda the prude just as misled as Belinda the coquette?

From here it is a natural transition to questions of imaginative "empathy," a term that is usually offered to students when they encounter Keats. The idea, however, under the concept of the "sympathetic" imagination (in the original sense of "like-feeling"), was an integral part of eighteenth-century imaginative theory. An early example is James Arbuckle's talking in 1722 about "this imagining *Faculty*, . . . A Facility of placing our selves in Circumstances different from those we are really in." In class there is no need, therefore, to shy away from discussing the sympathetic projection of the imagination and how it is used by Pope. I find this approach particularly useful in tackling *Eloisa to Abelard* and *Epistle to a Lady*, poems that in my experience readily engage students' emotions in a direct way. Twentieth-century criticism of *Eloisa* tends to be embarrassed by such engagement and construes it as a weakness of the poem. The established view is that Pope does not manage to distance himself from his heroine, that he somehow sanctions her "fantasizing" and fails to maintain the detachment from her that would allow him to stand free and "place" Eloisa by controlling the situation and tone. In this context of failure, sympathetic class responses tend to be outlawed and the focus shifted onto a discussion of the epistle's "rhetoric" — the only way to rescue the poem's art and thereby allow the teacher of an "Augustan" Pope to get a purchase on the poem. There is a degree of critical uneasiness at the extent to which Pope writes from inside Eloisa's imagination. But student responses can, I think, be usefully harnessed through discussion of how the poem exploits traditional contemplative procedures and the religious mysticism (the *Song of Songs*, St. John of the Cross, Bernini's *Ecstasy of St. Teresa*) that expresses itself through the language of desire and consummation. Viewed in this context Eloisa's dilemma lies in her being forced to polarize the spiritual and physical levels of the meditative experience and to set one against the other, to separate out the images of her former lover and her heavenly Savior rather than to fuse them into the complex experience of being the bride of Christ. A nun of the Paraclete, Eloisa confronts through her imagination an intense and unified emotional experience, which she relentlessly tries to split apart into the sacred and profane. Class discussion, therefore, can confront in detail the poem's formal patternings and structural procedures, but in the fuller context of her (and the reader's) imaginative experience.

The issue of imaginative "sympathy" is raised in a different way in *Epistle to a Lady*, where it has to contend with the demands we place on a simplified notion of satire. I find that my students judge Pope harshly in this poem for the way in which he seems alternately to attack and patronize these women. But rather than let the discussion disintegrate into disputes about the "fairness" of Pope's satire, I find it useful to see his procedure in terms of a complex interplay of satire and sympathy, with imagination once again the linking term. I encourage the class to consider Pope's satire as creative, not destructive. How easily we forget that satirists seldom attack or deface something that is already there (drawing a moustache on the Mona Lisa, for example) but more often bring into being, into artistic life, whatever disgusts, unsettles, or terrifies them. *Epistle to a Lady* can be approached as a pageant of imaginative failure, ranging from Flavia's self-destructive world of romantic fiction ("Lucretia's dagger, Rosamonda's bowl" [92]), through Papillia's inability to see the park for the trees, to Atossa's emotional and mental pyrotechnics ("No Thought advances, but her Eddy Brain / Whisks it about, and down it goes again" [121–22]). These case histories of the rapid and unfixed nature of imaginative activity are linked to a repeated misdirection of energies ("With too much Spirit to be e'er at ease" [96]), out of which come moments of tragic irony ("Who purchase Pain with all that Joy can give, / And die of nothing but a Rage to live" [99–100]). An idea Keats's palate might savor becomes for Pope a token of self-defeat. A slightly different irony is at play in Pope's sketch of the heartless Cloe:

> She, while her Lover pants upon her breast,
> Can mark the figures on an Indian chest.
> (167–68)

At a moment of emotional fervor, her eyes (and ours) shift to play over an intricate artificial surface. Cloe may be one of those who "don't want to get involved" (and her portrait is one of many where gender is fundamentally irrelevant), but notice the strange way in which Pope uses a hackneyed phrase ("pants upon her breast"). Pope is taking an artistic risk, but in doing so he hints at the routineness of a sentimental situation that leaves Cloe bored. As our own imaginations respond to the phrase, just for a moment we get a sense of how a predictable romantic posture might well make Cloe focus her eyes elsewhere. A sense of the subtle imaginative sympathy at such moments can enrich Pope's satire and help students test their feelings against its verbal details. It is interesting, too, that when Martha Blount steps forward near the end of the poem, she also is offered as a contradiction, but one for whom this is a positive enrichment. Rather than split her apart, her contrasting elements work with each other, and her ever-new "Fancy" engages positively with her "Fix'd Principles."

It is important to note that theories of the imagination up to Pope's day conceived of it not as a faculty malign or virtuous in itself but as an activity that included everything in which the human mind took part. For Pope and others, the one faculty was present in the widest range of experience, from divine ecstasy to society gossip, from female beauty to coprophiliac madness. The key was not how it functioned (for good or ill, it was profuse, combinative, rapid, and untethered) but how far it indulged the passions, obsessions, and delusions of humankind. Ideally, and when rightly related to the capacity to judge and act, it could be a vehicle for sympathetic projection or creative discrimination. One way of establishing this idea in class might be to examine two spider's webs. The first satirizes:

> Who shames a Scribler? break one cobweb thro',
> He spins the slight, self-pleasing thread anew;
> Destroy his Fib, or Sophistry; in vain,
> The Creature's at his dirty work again;
> Thron'd in the Centre of his thin designs;
> Proud of a vast Extent of flimzy lines.
>   (*Arbuthnot* 89–94)

The second celebrates:

> The spider's touch, how exquisitely fine!
> Feels at each thread, and lives along the line.
>   (*Essay on Man* 1.217–18)

From one point of view the "thread" is the mental thread of imagination, a finespun sensorium with the fancy's capacity for making connections (as opposed to the judgmental faculty's concern with separating out and discriminating). But the two passages could hardly be more different in what they make out of it. In the first, the scribbler is proud and self-pleasing, locating the self at the center of all he does; someone else may see the spider's web as "Fib, or Sophistry," but there is no way of engaging with him — each time it is brushed away, he spins out from the center a new thread, endlessly recycling his internal matter. In the second passage, however, the same thread is now a means of extended life; it is a mode of communication, of living "along the line," combining living and feeling, and suggesting variety and scope in the possibilities that offers. The emphasis is no longer on the "dirty work" of the spider's entrails, but the focus moves from process to product. For Pope, process by itself is predictable, whereas product has endless possibilities.

The goddess of imaginative process is Dulness, that presider over self-pleasing anarchy of mind who plays all kinds of imaginative tricks in *The Dunciad*, a text that immediately sets up barriers for the modern reader. I spoke at the beginning of a pedagogical problem regarding the contexts for Pope's poetry, and we need look no further than the thickly printed footnotes identifying insignificant dunces, who now only have life in the poem's pages, to realize that a seminar discussion must try to avoid slipping into a pedantic morass. I find again that the best tactic is to release its imaginative elements and confront at once its profusion and confusion. Dulness, says Pope in his note to book 1, line 15, is "a ruling principle not inert, but turning topsy-turvy the Understanding, and inducing an Anarchy or confused State of Mind." He expresses the difficulty all readers have in finding a stable or clear vantage point amid the poem's restless movements and wild visual effects. Aubrey Williams and others have found such a point in the template of classical epic underlying the poem. But a more immediate approach, and one that demands less knowledge of the footnotes added by modern scholarship, can be through the undisciplined *copia* of the poem's visions and by an attempt to characterize its controlling principle, the mistress of ceremonies for all its activities.

The energies of Dulness are directionless, undisciplined, and shortsighted (we should remember that to be "dull-sighted" meant, in the eighteenth century, to be myopic or have some defect of vision). She therefore presides over a confused spectacle:

> All these, and more, the cloud-compelling Queen
> Beholds thro' fogs, that magnify the scene.
> She, tinsel'd o'er in robes of varying hues,
> With self-applause her wild creation views. . . .
>   (1.79–82)

In presenting a picture of the imagination detached from any wider responsibility, Dulness combines the fanciful indulgence of the sylphs with the murky unconscious stirrings of the gnomes. Her world begins in chaos, out of which emerges a pageant of frantic human creatures, each pursuing a private vision or obsession, until Dulness draws their energies into her vortex and they implode into the dark primal soup that bred them.

Writers before Pope's time had expressed the imagination-as-process in similar terms, but none with the shattering effect of *The Dunciad*. There are two quotations I find useful in helping students appreciate, in turn, the artistic and spiritual connotations of this idea. The first is from Dryden's preface to his play *The Rival Ladies*, where he speaks of the early stage in its creation "when it was only a confused mass of thoughts, tumbling over one another in the dark; when the fancy was yet in its first work"; the second is from Lady Mary Chudleigh's essay "Of Pride," where she characterizes her own figure of Dulness as being "fill'd with sensible Images, crowded with imaginary Appearances, like the first Matter, dark and full of Confusion, and hardly receptive of pure Idea's, of simple intellectual Truths." These quotations strongly suggest how Pope's Dulness represents that primary, atavistic world of the "pre-," of the infinite possibility of desire. The infantile minds she nurtures never emerge from her power but remain in the grip of self-projected belief:

> Joy fills his soul, joy innocent of thought;
> "What pow'r, he cries, what pow'r these wonders wrought?"
> "Son; what thou seek'st is in thee! Look, and find
> Each Monster meets his likeness in thy mind."   (3.249–52)

Dulness is a driving force within human beings that takes the form of their desires, ambitions, and obsessions and manipulates them for global ends. As such she is the individual imagination titillated and exploited by a greater power. She is the private fantasy processed into the corporate vision. She creates the need, advertises the product, closes the sale. As she assures her hero in the above quotation, she is not an external power but an inner motivating force: everything you want to be, every way you've ever wanted it.

There need be no desperate bid to assert Pope's contemporary relevance: the class will take over at this point and offer a wealth of contemporary parallels for the imaginative world over which Dulness presides: perhaps the fluid techniques of video, the colored lasers and dry ice of rock concerts (with Dulness herself as Madonna, the profane goddess), the manipulation of our desires through advertising, or the hype surrounding movie stars, politicians, and other packages. Certainly we are eager to buy the dream, as all devotees of Dulness do, whether we are the couch potato purchasing direct from the screen or the infant mind worshiping whatever emerges momentarily from the media. Smedley's fecal "Land of Dreams" (2.316) is the place where base matter recycles itself as fantasy; British television's *Spitting Image* offered the graphic adventures of "Teenage Mutant Ninja Turds," nameless somethings living in subterranean sewers, feeding on the scraps of our throwaway civilization.

Pope's Dulness still provides the sharpest indictment of present-day Western culture. She embodies the worship of life-style over life itself and the triumph of the commercial over the program, and to keep her system going she demands the surgical removal of skepticism, doubt, and conscience. As we buy the dream, we are drawn into a power structure that packages experience for us, and the empire of media and process expands endlessly, so that little can break free of it financially or intellectually. Even *PMLA* finds itself presenting an incongruous mix of intellectual product and processed matter, as it grows ever larger to incorporate lists, schedules, programs, advertising. Perhaps like the bees conglobed around their dusky queen we are all struggling less and less. Increasingly, however, we are coming to understand how the mad visions of the few, combined with the passive mindlessness of the many, could conceivably bring the end of the world. The prophecies of *The Dunciad* are impinging on us, and it is becoming easier to discern a relation between a pacifying mass culture (more and more international in its spread), the growth of mass movements (political, racial, and religious), and the concentration of power in the hands of a few charismatic figures (rock stars, religious figureheads, or national leaders).

I find that classes respond to Pope's imagination because it tackles some of the issues that arise from living in a frantic and desperate world. Instead of being involved in a theory about a semimystical process that privileges the genius of the poet, Pope's imagination homes in on human behavior and its many contradictions — its pretenses and failures. What is more, the principles with which it engages remain potent ones. When students discover the Pope who "feels at each thread, and lives along the line" they do so with enormous enthusiasm, and I believe that by encouraging them to use their imaginative responses as part of an intellectual argument, combining a wider vision with the discipline of verbal detail, we open up many other areas.

Pope and the Scriblerians

Oliver W. Ferguson

The inclusion of an essay on Pope and the Scriblerians in this volume may appear surprising. In all likelihood, when Pope is presented to college students, his relationship with the group that called itself the Scriblerus Club is given only slight attention at best. This is understandable, because the satire conceived by Pope, Arbuthnot, Gay, Swift, and Parnell and published under the pseudonym of Martinus Scriblerus is especially demanding for twentieth-century readers. Highly topical and intended to ridicule false or pedantic scholarship in fields ranging from contemporary medical theory to astrology, from antiquarian study to literary criticism, it requires some general knowledge of a variety of abstruse subjects as well as some understanding of the authors being satirized.

Such neglect, however, is unfortunate because the treatises, notes, and critical commentary that appeared under the name of Scriblerus are ironic counterparts to many of the articles of Pope's intellectual and artistic faith that inform the works of his mature period.

Because the focus will be on Pope rather than on the Scriblerians, it is not necessary for the instructor to provide students with exhaustive background material. One class lecture should be adequate for a brief account of the founding of the club, something on the careers of its members, and a survey of its activities and its dissolution. As for the writings of Scriblerus in which Pope played the sole or a major part, *Peri Bathous* is the most accessible, in terms of both availability and student appeal. In conjunction with this piece, Pope's *Guardian* 40 (also readily available) should be assigned. Though not one of Scriblerus's compositions, this attack on Ambrose Philips's pastorals is an interesting anticipation of the Scriblerian technique of quoting a satiric victim to his or her disadvantage. The study of *The Dunciad* can be enormously enhanced by having students read in *The Dunciad Variorum*. Charles Kerby-Miller's definitive edition of the *Memoirs of Martinus Scriblerus* is now available in paperback.

The Scriblerus Club has a particular appropriateness in a study of Pope because he was crucially involved with its founding and with the realization of its most ambitious aim. The idea for the club originated in an essay he contributed to the *Spectator* in 1712. In number 457 he proposed issuing a publication, *An Account of the Works of the Unlearned*, that each month would review the productions of those numerous writers who "make a very Eminent Figure in the Illiterate World." In 1713 he interested his friends Gay, Arbuthnot, Swift, and Parnell in the scheme, and by early 1714 the five were meeting regularly. (The occasional presence of Robert Harley, leader of the Tory ministry, inevitably gave the group a political identification that had not been Pope's intent and that would have serious consequences for the Scriblerians when the ministry fell from power.) In the preface to his edition of the *Memoirs*, Kerby-Miller recounts the story in detail. For present purposes it is enough to note that once the club got under way, Pope's original plan of publishing a monthly journal was significantly revised: the group determined instead to create a figure who through his own writings would extend the satire to many areas of intellectual endeavor. This character, Martinus Scriblerus, who "was dipped in every art and science but very injudiciously in each" (Pope, *Memoirs* 30), would serve as both object and agent of the satire. To this end the group planned to publish a biography of their persona, to bring out various of his writings, and from time to time to claim as Scriblerus's own the authentic works of some of their victims.

This design was largely frustrated by the collapse of the Tory ministry in 1714. The club dissolved, and its members scattered. However, as Kerby-Miller observes, "though the Scriblerus Club as such was never formally revived, the forces it set in motion continued to operate for nearly two more decades" (41). Both *Gulliver's Travels* (1726) and *The Beggar's Opera* (1728) have Scriblerian roots; and a letter from Swift to Pope shortly before the publication of the 1728 *Dunciad* attests to the de facto, if not programmatic, relation of the three satires: "The *Beggar's Opera* hath knocked down *Gulliver*. I hope to see Pope's Dulness [the title originally devised] knock down the *Beggar's Opera*" (Swift, *Correspondence* 3: 278). It was Pope himself, at this time and later, who most conscientiously tried to bring the Scriblerian plan to fruition. His *Peri Bathous* (1728) was issued under Scriblerus's name, and to Scriblerus was attributed a significant part of the elaborate editorial apparatus for *The Dunciad Variorum* (1729). When the long overdue biography of the pedant finally appeared in 1741, Arbuthnot, Gay, and Parnell were dead, and Swift was mentally incompetent. It was left to the active survivor of the club to fulfill its original design: *Memoirs of the Extraordinary Life, Works, and Discoveries of Martinus Scriblerus* — its authorship credited to Arbuthnot and Pope — was published in volume 2 of *The Works of Mr. Alexander Pope, in Prose*.

Before turning to *Peri Bathous*, students should read the *Guardian* 40. The piece is not from Scriblerus's pen. Its obvious irony is uncharacteristic of that pedant's laboriously earnest style. This satire on the pastorals of Ambrose Philips is appropriate in a study of Pope's Scriblerian activities, however, both because it shares the Scriblerians' concern over false taste in poetry and criticism and because it employs the device, used to such devastating effect in *Peri Bathous*, of offering especially banal or awkward passages of contemporary verse as models of excellence.

Peri Bathous; or, Martinus Scriblerus His Treatise of the Art of Sinking in Poetry is a revealing introduction to the manner, personality, and values of the pedant who will later emerge as the learned scholar-critic of *The Dunciad* and the subject of the *Memoirs*. With his reiterated assertion that bathos is an art, Scriblerus justifies his intention to supply "a regular *System of Laws*" for achieving the bathetic (*Poetry and Prose*, ch. 1). Such a system is necessary because although "the Taste of the *Bathos* is implanted by Nature itself in the Soul of Man" (ch. 2), "the Genius of no Mortal whatever, following the meer Ideas of Nature," can master the art of sinking in poetry (ch. 6). To illustrate the principles by which the aspiring poet can progress "many fathoms beyond mediocrity" (ch. 7), Scriblerus quotes passages from contemporary sources, including Richard Blackmore, the father and Homer of bathos; Ambrose Philips, Pope's victim in the *Guardian* hoax; and Lewis Theobald, the hero of the 1728 *Dunciad*. Some of the exempla are Pope's own facetious contributions: for "Shut the door" the would-be poet is advised to write: "The wooden Guardian of our Privacy / Quick on its Axle turn" (ch. 12). But the most risible of Scriblerus's illustrations are the authentic selections he quotes. Philips's pastorals once again are a convenient storehouse of the bathetic: "Teach me to grieve with bleating Moan, my Sheep" (ch. 11).

In teaching *Peri Bathous* one should emphasize the fact that, like the entire Scriblerian canon, it is a rich offering to the comic spirit but it does not employ its comedy gratuitously. Just as the title is an ironic inversion of Longinus's *Peri Hupsous* ("On the Sublime"), so Scriblerus's obtuse comments on taste and judgment are Pope's ironic treatment of a central issue in eighteenth-century critical theory. Pope had examined the relation between taste and judgment in *An Essay on Criticism*; and Scriblerus's insistence that a taste for the bathetic, though innate, must be nurtured is the grotesque version of a key point in Addison's landmark essay on taste in *Spectator* 409: "notwithstanding this faculty must in some measure be born with us, there are several methods for cultivating and improving it." Pope's remark to Spence that *Peri Bathous; or, . . . the Art of Sinking in Poetry*, "though written in so ludicrous a way, may be very well worth reading seriously, as an art of rhetoric" (*Memoirs* 55) validates the subtitle's implicit claim of ironic kinship with such works as Horace's *Ars poetica* and Boileau's *Art poétique*. Scriblerus's unwitting demonstration in *his* "Art of Poetry" that a perverted judgment will lead to a corrupt taste is, for all its comedy, a truth that will find a darker expression in *The Dunciad*.

Before students encounter *The Dunciad. With Notes Variorum, and the Prolegomena of Scriblerus*, they should be warned that the work at once clarifies and complicates Pope's poem. In providing identifying notes for many of his topical references, Pope was responding to a widely perceived need best expressed in a letter from Swift: "Twenty miles from London nobody understands hints, initial letters, or town facts and passages; and in a few years not even those who live in London" (qtd. in *Twickenham* 5: xxiii–xxiv). But by assigning this task to Scriblerus, Pope exposed his text and its readers to that scholar-critic's obfuscation. "Of the part of *Scriblerus*," he mischievously remarked in the advertisement to *The Dunciad Variorum*, "I need say nothing: his Manner is well enough known" (*Twickenham* 5: 9).

In addition to his annotations of the text of *The Dunciad*, Scriblerus's chief contribution to the variorum edition is his essay "Of the Poem." This piece is in the style of Scriblerus, but its content is uncharacteristically perceptive. In effect, Pope employs Scriblerus as his apologist, allowing the pedant to retain his own encumbered expression and manner of proceeding but endowing him with reliable insights into the poem's genesis, intent, and method. Thus Scriblerus locates *The Dunciad* in the mock-epic tradition of Homer's *Margites* and Dryden's *Mac Flecknoe*, justifies the moral aim of Pope's satire, describes the "action" of the epic, identifies its hero and vindicates Pope's satire of him and the lesser dunces, and comments approvingly on the poem's diction, descriptions, and narration. The Scriblerus of this essay is inconsistent with the variorum annotator and the author of *Peri Bathous*; nevertheless "Martinus Scriblerus of the Poem" is a useful introduction for readers of Pope's masterpiece.

If Scriblerus is out of character in his essay on *The Dunciad*, in his notes to the poem he is eminently successful in resuming the role originally designed for him in 1714. He makes his mark at the first possible opportunity, in a laborious disquisition on whether or not *Dunciad* should be spelled *Dunceiad*. His note occupies virtually the entire page in the Twickenham edition. If it is at all possible, students should be shown one of the contemporary editions of *The Dunciad Variorum*, wherein the disproportionate relation of commentary to text is visually even more striking. Each of the first three pages of the poem in the 1729 edition consists of a couplet, with the remainder of the page given over to Scriblerus's notes. Nor is this instance atypical. Consider the following passage from book 1:

> She saw old Pryn in restless Daniel shine,
> And Eusden eke out Blackmore's endless line;
> She saw slow Philips creep like Tate's poor page,
> And all the Mighty Mad in Dennis rage.
> In each she marks her image full exprest,
> But chief in Tibbald's monster-breeding breast.
> (101–06)

Even in the Twickenham edition the apparatus here gets out of hand, with text and notes running to five pages. In the smaller, 1729 octavo edition, these six lines and their annotations require nine pages.

Pope achieves a variety of aims with Scriblerus's commentary. Often one note serves more than one purpose. For example, the commentary on "Tibbald" in the passage quoted above pedantically discusses the proper spelling and pronunciation of "Tibbald/Theobald," quotes a disparaging remark on him by John Dennis, and defends Pope's edition of Shakespeare against Theobald's *Shakespeare Restored*. At times a note is deliberately wrong: H***, in 1.244, is not, the reader is assured, the Swiss impresario John James

Heidegger but "a strange Bird from *Switzerland.*" At times Pope uses Scriblerus's uncertainty about an identification to extend the applicability of the satire: is the "Ward in Pillory" (3.26) John the forger or Edward the poet? The note to the line will support either reading—or both. Finally there is the note of learned explanation. In 4.17–18, Dulness is described ascending her throne:

> She mounts the Throne: her head a Cloud conceal'd,
> In broad Effulgence all below reveal'd.

For the phrase "all below reveal'd," Scriblerus supplies this comment in boldface Gothic type: "The higher you climb, the more you shew your A—."

The remaining parts of the scholarly apparatus of *The Dunciad Variorum* that are explicitly assigned to Scriblerus are the errata of the 1729 edition and a compilation, "Testimonies of Authors concerning Our Poet and His Works." The former, a brief continuation of the parody of pedantic editors, need not be assigned; Scriblerus's editorial practices are shown to better advantage in his notes to *The Dunciad.* The "Testimonies," however, offers students an instructive insight into the literary controversy in which Pope was involved for so much of his career. To provide his readers with "the various judgments of the Learned concerning our Poet," Scriblerus sets against the abusive criticism of Theobald, Dennis, Welsted, and others of the dunces the favorable opinions of writers of the stature of Addison, Prior, and Thomson.

Although the index to *The Dunciad Variorum* is not specifically credited to Scriblerus, students should not neglect this delightful addendum. Everything about it is in Scriblerus's manner. Even its heading in the 1729 edition displays his characteristic verbal insensitivity: "INDEX of THINGS (including AUTHORS) to be found in the NOTES, &c." Scriblerus makes his dogged progress through the alphabetically ordered items, unaware of the absurdity of an entry such as "Flies, not the ultimate Object of human study, iv. 454," or the implicit contempt of "Owls, desir'd to answer Mr. Ralph, iii. 166," or the damning juxtaposition of

> Personal abuses not to be endur'd, in the opinion of
> Mr. Dennis, Theobald, Curl, &c. ii, 142.
> Personal abuses on our Author, by Mr. Dennis . . . *ibid.* —
> By Mr. Theobald . . . *Test[imonies]* . . . and their
> Brethren, *passim.*

These few examples are sufficient to illustrate the comedy in the index. When students read further in it, they will see how every part of *The Dunciad,* even so normally intractable an element of a book as its index, has been put to the service of Pope's satiric aim.

There are obvious difficulties in presenting the complex variety of *The Dunciad Variorum* to students. I have found that the most practical procedure is to supplement the class text with library assignments in volume 5 of the Twickenham edition. Readers of my essay will have noticed that I cite passages from the 1729 and 1743 editions without distinguishing between the two. I recommend that other instructors do likewise, without involving their students in the complicated textual history of *The Dunciad Variorum*. It should be enough to tell them that the work was — indeed, is — an evolving phenomenon; that after Pope's death his literary executor William Warburton added notes to the *Variorum*; that in 1943 James Sutherland added *his* notes in the Twickenham edition (followed by a second edition in 1953, "with Some Additional Notes"!); and that there is no reason to suppose that the "exercitations on this most delectable Poem" (*Twickenham* 5: 23) begun by Scriblerus in 1729 have been completed. However instructors use the *Variorum* in teaching *The Dunciad*, students should read at least some of Pope's poem with its full apparatus, for only by so doing can they see how the very form of *The Dunciad Variorum* expresses Pope's aim. In dissolving the distinction between elements that in a rationally ordered work would be clearly recognized as substantive and ancillary, *The Dunciad Variorum* forces the reader to assume Scriblerus's pedantic stance and values.

The *Dunciad Variorum* is the most successful of the Scriblerian undertakings. Some attention, however, should be given to the *Memoirs*, both because the work fulfills the club's original aim and because its satire on pedantry has resonances with other poems of Pope. Instructors may prefer to emphasize only selections from this brief but dense work. The "Double Mistress" episode is an exuberantly comic illustration of Scriblerian parody, and chapter 16, with its confident attribution of *Gulliver's Travels* to Scriblerus, plays a witty variation on the Scriblerians' practice of crediting to their persona various works of the dunces. The concluding chapter, "Of the Discoveries and Works of the Great Scriblerus, Made and to Be Made, Written and to Be Written, Known and Unknown," is a kind of catalogue raisonné of the fruits of Scriblerus's career. As Pope's disparate targets in *Dunciad* 4 are given thematic coherence by the inclusive meanings of the term *dunce*, so the various intellectual perversions celebrated in this chapter are subsumed in the character of Martinus Scriblerus.

Although Martinus and his father, Cornelius, anticipate the virtuosi of *Dunciad* 4, the *Memoirs* is, naturally, more a work of echoes. Cornelius's extravagant veneration for all things ancient illustrates an attitude satirized in "To Augustus" (35–68). His pleasure that Martinus was born with the same physical defects of such worthies as Cicero and Alexander recalls the sardonic passage on Pope's flatterers in the *Epistle to Dr. Arbuthnot* (115–24). And his rhetorical question, "Why should . . . [my son] not have the perfection of a Drill, or of any other animal?" (100), had previously been answered when Pope addressed the issue of metaphysical evil in *An Essay on Man* (1.193–204).

Parallels such as these clearly demonstrate the place of Pope's Scriblerian writings in his oeuvre. In none of his other works, with the possible exception of *The Rape of the Lock*, is the satire so consistently good-natured, but the difference is in Pope's angle of vision, not his indictment of the state of affairs he is observing. Pope treats the pedantry of Scriblerus and his father with amused contempt; but in the *Dunciad* he displays this intellectual failing in all its deadly potential.

Peri Bathous and the scholarly apparatus in *The Dunciad Variorum* are the dunces' response to *An Essay on Criticism*; *The Dunciad* is the negation of the values that inform *An Essay on Man*. Scriblerus seeks in *Peri Bathous* "to lead . . . [the geniuses of his age] the gentle down-hill way to the *Bathos*" (389), whereas in *An Essay on Criticism* Pope urges the would-be critic to "trace the Muses *upward* to their *Spring*" (127). This same antithetical movement is seen in *An Essay on Man* and the fourth book of *The Dunciad*, but now the concern is not aesthetic but spiritual. In the earlier poem, Pope describes the virtuous man as one who "looks thro' Nature, up to Nature's God" (4.332). In *Dunciad* 4, as the virtuosi parade before triumphant Dulness on her throne, the Goddess exclaims:

> O! would the Sons of Men once think their Eyes
> And Reason giv'n them but to study *Flies*!
> See Nature in some partial narrow shape,
> And let the Author of the Whole escape.   (453–56)

This quintessential description of pedantry inspires "a gloomy clerk," a free-thinker, to reply,

> Be that my task . . .
> . . . .
> Let others creep by timid steps, and slow,
> On plain Experience lay foundations low,
> By common sense to common knowledge bred,
> And last, to Nature's Cause thro' Nature led.
> . . . .
> We nobly take the high Priori Road,
> And reason downward, till we doubt of God.
>   (459, 465–68, 471–72)

Maynard Mack observes that the "*Essay on Man* represents the day side of Pope's visionary imagination, as the *Dunciad* represents the night side" (*Life* 540). Despite the good humor with which Martinus Scriblerus is presented, he inhabits with his fellow dunces the universal darkness of *The Dunciad*.

The Horatian View of the Poet

M. Elaine Dolan Brown

In his essay "Tradition and the Individual Talent" T. S. Eliot writes:

> We dwell with satisfaction upon the poet's difference from his predecessors . . . . Whereas if we approach a poet without this prejudice we shall often find that not only the best, but the most individual parts of his work may be those in which the dead poets, his ancestors, assert their immortality most vigorously.   (*Prose* 38)

Eliot here speaks of the relation of poet to predecessor and the habit of many readers who appreciate what is perceived as "new" in poetry at the expense of the traditional. Certainly in his remarks Eliot points to an obstacle that many of us who teach poetry from earlier eras have faced: our students' devaluation of the past. The problem becomes even more complicated, however, when students lack even a general historical perspective and sense of literary tradition through which to view poetry, thus blurring distinctions between old and new altogether.

This pedagogical problem is particularly acute for teachers of neoclassical works since students often look with suspicion on those works that consciously proclaim themselves as imitative. Indeed, the classical works that provide the foundations for so many neoclassical works appear as either inaccessible or elusive to our students; imitation itself is often seen negatively as an echo of an obsolete and impenetrable work and is thus derided as unoriginal and inconsequential.

Teaching the poetry of Alexander Pope would therefore seem to present a special challenge since all his major poems are linked in some way or another to classical prototypes; his literary forebears include Ovid, Homer, Virgil, and Horace. However, his relation to Horace is by far the most important because it affects almost all his mature poetry.

In response to these challenges of the classroom, I have developed an approach to *The First Satire of the Second Book of Horace* through which my students can discover Pope's Horatian qualities as well as examine the ways in which Pope molded and shaped the works of his Roman predecessor to create "original" works in the imitation. My goal is to show students how poetry can be invigorated by its relation to the past, to develop their knowledge of the past so that they may see its impact on the present, and to illustrate the creative and liberating qualities of the formal eighteenth-century imitation.

To achieve these ends, I first focus the attention of the class on Horace. To help sketch in some background about Horace's life and times for my students, I often assign for reading the entry in a literary encyclopedia. I point out that his influence in the eighteenth century was little short of canonical: his *Ars poetica* reigned supreme as a handbook for fine writing and good taste; in fact, it was the most frequently quoted literary authority throughout the century.

To get a sense of some of the attitudes about Horace's style, utility, and social and political characteristics, I preface our discussion of Horace in the eighteenth century with an assignment from Dryden's "Discourse concerning the Original and Progress of Satire." The "Discourse" crystalized for the age some of the views that were held about Horace, and Pope knew the essay well. Although contested in parts, in its general contours Dryden's essay contains the outline of Horace's portrait for the age. In my lower-level courses at New York Institute of Technology I have my students read selected passages from the essay, and in more advanced courses I assign the work in its entirety. In my advanced classes at Tulane I also included readings from Addison's *Spectator* 23 and Steele's *Spectator* 422, which address Horatian satire. (Additionally, in a senior seminar for English majors the instructor could put on reserve some remarks about Horace and his works from Shaftesbury's *The Life, Unpublished Letters, and Philosophical Regimen of Anthony, Earl of Shaftesbury* to flesh out the portrait further.)

In the ensuing classroom discussion, I ask my students to try to pinpoint the most important perceptions of Horace and Horatian satire that Dryden describes and that many others shared in the eighteenth century. As the discussion progresses, I try to emphasize three of the most important points that emerge from Dryden's portrait, and I list these on the board: Horace as (1) moral teacher; (2) the epitome of gentlemanly refinement; and (3) political poet. This list will be of assistance in the later stages of the analysis.

The most significant cultural assumption of the early eighteenth century was Horace's role as doctor, or moral teacher, particularly in the satires and epistles. That Horace saw himself in this way is clear from the *Ars poetica*, where he writes that poetry should both "instruct and delight." It is important for the instructor to stress that this attitude was the foundation for Dryden's essay, which tells us that "Horace is teaching us in every line and is perpetually moral" (62).

The second assumption that Dryden articulates in his "Discourse" for the neoclassical era and that students must appreciate is the view of Horace as the quintessential eighteenth-century gentleman. Closely tied to the assumption about Horace as the archetype of gentlemanly behavior is the view of the type and style of satire he wrote. He tells the truth with a smile; the smile in turn makes his criticism more palatable. According to Horace, laughter is a far more effective satiric tool than vituperation (*Satire* 1.10, 14–15). Indeed, Dryden writes, "But how hard to make a man appear a Fool, a Block-head, or a Knave, without using any of those opprobrious terms!" (70–71).

Third and perhaps the most hotly debated feature of the portrait of Horace in the eighteenth century is his role as a political poet. Dryden unfairly casts him in the part of "well-mannered court slave" (65). To the extent that critics followed Dryden's opinion, Horace became increasingly suspected of moral equivocation in political matters. Students will want to keep this in mind as they examine the politics of the imitation.

Having read Dryden, students are in a better position to see for themselves the degree to which Pope saw himself located in these various Horatian traditions. Once the students have looked at Horace through the same lens as Alexander Pope did, they are able to analyze and appreciate Pope's *First Satire of the Second Book.*

It is appropriate at this point for the class to read Horace's satire in translation since it is the model for Pope's eighteenth-century rendering. (The Loeb Classical Library translation works very well.) I stress to my students the importance of the original as an integral part of reading an imitation; I inform them that in the eighteenth century the need for a conscious parallel between ancient and modern work in the imitation often meant that poets printed the lines imitated along with the adaptations. All major imitators of the day, including Pope, did so.

Horace's *Satire* 2.1 was the opening poem in the collection of hexameter verses ridiculing the follies of Horace's fellow Romans. In form, the poem is a fictional consultation in dialogue between Horace and the lawyer Trebatius, the most famous jurist of his day. The poet approaches him for advice about what kind of satire he ought to be writing, and the poem consists of witty, informal, and sometimes even playful conversation on this topic between the two men, but it is built on a serious foundation: an impassioned defense of satire.

Once the students have examined and summarized the original poem in translation, I ask them to compare both the substance and the style of the two versions of the satire. Pope's imitation is also a discussion between the poet and a jurist, Fortescue, concerning the type and style of satire the poet should be composing. Students enjoy pointing out the differences though, however slight, and they are not disappointed here. Fortescue, the counselor, has an expanded role in Pope's imitation, and his role is not so much adversarial as it is coconspiratorial. Like the poet-satirist, Fortescue appears lively, witty, and satiric; Pope has captured Horace's ease and facility in rendering dialogue poetically. In an enlarged defense of satire, however, Pope's imitation also becomes a vehicle for a much sharper satiric attack than does the parent poem.

After comparing and contrasting the substance and style of the imitation with the original, we return to Dryden's essay and our list of eighteenth-century conceptions of Horace to see if these attitudes find their way into the imitation. First we look at Horace as moral teacher. Students are quick to point out that the theme of the imitation, like that of the ancient poem, is fundamentally moral. Indeed, the basis of Horace's poem that Pope explores in his imitation was how much of the motivation of satiric writing is moral. Pope writes, "What? arm'd for *Virtue* when I point the Pen, / Brand the bold Front of shameless, guilty Men" (105–06). The poet suggests that the inspiration for his satiric poetry was a great love of virtue.

Next, the class looks at the Horatian tradition of tact and gentility and analyzes Pope's application of that tradition in his imitation. As the students read the ensuing "debate" between the poet and Fortescue as to the efficacy of satire, they see how Pope has expanded the lawyer's role and exploited its dramatic possibilities. They also notice the playfulness of the debate and its great wit. But as the poem progresses, students should detect the shifts in tone. At points Pope may well seem to play the part of the gentleman full of Horatian wit and raillery, but he also complicates his satire at times with harsh and pointed invective. Indeed, this imitation contains perhaps the most vicious couplet Pope ever wrote, "P — x'd by her Love, or libell'd by her Hate" (83–84). Pope sometimes replaces the Horatian piety and decorum of the parent poem with invective — a fact not lost on the readers of the day, or on students analyzing the imitation.

This brings us to the third area of inquiry, determining Pope's view of Horace as a political poet in the imitation. In the satires Horace could imply praise for the world of Augustus and for the relation between Rome and her poets. Indeed, Pope notes Horace's association with his emperor and his patron, Maecenas, when, in the advertisement to Fortescue, he writes that Horace was acceptable to both the prince and the minister under whom he lived.

Pope, however, often aimed his satirical barbs at the politically powerful, and this imitation is no exception. Students are quick to point out that Pope's ending depends for its effect largely on the disjunction between Pope's world and Horace's. For example, in the concluding speech, Pope defines and defends his art when he distinguishes his work from the libels and satires that break "Man's law":

> *Libels* and *Satires*! lawless Things indeed!
> But grave *Epistles*, bringing Vice to light,
> Such as a *King* might read, a *Bishop* write. . . .
> (150–52)

The speaker here explicitly rejects Horatian values when he asserts that his satire is "Such as a *King* might read." Horace could use his emperor as part of his defense since Augustus was a patron of the arts and even tried his hand at writing verses. By contrast, Pope's monarch, George II, had little regard for poetry and indeed was ill at ease with English.

After completing their analysis of Pope's imitation, students see that, although Pope used Horace's satire as his model, he created a new and original work. An interesting exercise to reinforce this idea of the imitation's liberating possibilities is to assign a paper comparing this imitation of Pope's to Jonathan Swift's of the same model ("A Dialogue between an Eminent Lawyer and Dr. Swift Dean of St. Patrick's, Being an Allusion to the First Satire of the Second Book of Horace"); if time allows, Swift's much shorter and less substantive imitation can be placed on the syllabus as well.

Another assignment that is an outgrowth of this pedagogical approach is to ask students to debate the efficacy of satire after they have analyzed Horace's and Pope's defenses of satire. Finally, for a concluding project, and one that focuses students' energies with great success, I require students to write their own imitations of Horace's defense of satire, placing it in the modern context.

Dryden's "Discourse concerning the Original and Progress of Satire" has much to say about the eighteenth century and its classical inheritance — much more than is covered in an abbreviated pedagogical approach such as this. However, for the purposes of teaching Pope's *First Satire of the Second Book of Horace*, even a selected reading of Dryden provides students with a basic grasp of the stature and import Horace held for his audience — an appropriate lens through which to analyze Pope's Horatian mode. With an enriched understanding of the classical model, students are able to do much more than simply note the structural similarities and differences; they are able to recognize the ironies in subtle shifts in tone and voice, and they become conscious of the complex social and political agendas articulated by what at first appeared to be nothing more than a simple imitation. Pope has indeed created a new and original work in the imitation; as Eliot reminds us, "No poet, no artist of any art, has his complete meaning alone" (*Prose* 38).

APPROACHING THE POETRY: A SYNOPTIC ESSAY

Teaching Pope with a View to the Whole

Wallace Jackson

An early reader of my prospectus for this volume suggested that I not assume Pope to be a "major author" but rather ask if it is still worthwhile to discuss a major author as such. I propose that it is so, not because the category presupposes any sort of achieved imaginative coherence but because "major" is to be measured in accord with the ambitions implicit in a writer's work, the difficulties such a writer encounters and accepts as the condition of his or her writing life, the cultural density and historical rootedness to be found in that work, and finally, the institutional history of the poet. Many undergraduates will read no more than a few of Pope's poems, most likely *Eloisa to Abelard*, *The Rape of the Lock*, and, with the hope that they will find therein some formalized access to his poetry, *An Essay on Criticism*. In this hope they will be disappointed, but, more important, they will have read only the work of a very young poet; they will not have read his most ambitious (or longer) poems or the works that most complexly set forth his political and religious views. In sum, Pope is read today in a way that would be an academic scandal were Spenser or Shakespeare or Milton read similarly. It would mean that emphasis in the classroom was on Spenser's *Epithalamion* and *The Shepheardes Calender* (not *The Faerie Queene*), Shakespeare's *Venus and Adonis*, *The Rape of Lucrece*, and *The Comedy of Errors* (not the tragedies), Milton's "On the Morning of Christ's Nativity" and *Comus* (not *Paradise Lost*). Our undergraduates would be thus largely directed to those works that offer only a limited idea of why these writers survive for us as they do.

The purpose of this essay is not to give instruction in teaching Pope's poems but to offer, within relatively brief compass, an overview of Pope's work and a sense of what historical and literary touchstones are involved in reading that work. To the interested student I would suggest only that Pope takes seriously the challenge to teach and to delight, and thus my discussion here is informed by one leading question: how did Pope envision his role as an educator of the literate and enlightened in the early and middle years of the eighteenth century? To answer this question, and thus to read Pope with some understanding of his historical context, it is necessary to know a little about what Pope expected his audience to believe and of what he expected to convince them. And it is of particular importance that the present-day reader of Pope's poetry be mindful of what I might call the imaginative configuration that Pope's oeuvre assumes, not of course in the spirit of torturing poems into conformity with a critic's thesis but in the spirit of understanding the boundaries and contours of a poet's vision. This activity will always test a reader's engagement, for it is, I think, the last fidelity a reader can pay to the writer he or she reads both scrupulously and lovingly. The remarks that follow are based on a longer study I published a decade ago. My sense of the necessity to engage Pope in this way has not changed.

To some significant extent Pope's ambition to write an opus magnum (in effect, a great long poem) is the major impulse governing his career. His *Essay on Man*, the *Epistles to Several Persons*, and *The Dunciad* were to be parts of one large work comprehending the most important aspects of human life and providing a "science of Human Nature" so extensive as to describe humankind's place in the universe, the nature of "Civil and Religious Society," and "private Ethics or Practical Morality" (Brower, *Pope* 241). There are several ways to understand this project. One way is to see it in contrast to the epic poem, the magisterial accomplishment of which Milton's *Paradise Lost* is the greatest English example and Homer's *Iliad* and *Odyssey* and Virgil's *Aeneid* are the major classical models. Pope planned an epic poem, *Brutus*, on the early history of Britain, which was to be another part of his opus magnum, though he never advanced very far with it. A second way to conceive his ambition is that of spokesman to his age, the recreated role of public poet speaking on issues of public polity and providing religious and civic instruction. His poems were often designed to teach the age how to think of itself, how to know itself in relation to the pertinent subjects of historical discourse, and how to identify its interests as those best serving individual and national goals. Pope's opus magnum was to be therefore a philosophical poem presenting, under its discrete topics, systematic disquisition and a coherent conception of human life.

His central subject of disorder and order (the breaking away from and returning to divine design) over and again introduces metaphors of division, possession, obsession, and usurpation, which are in turn opposed by images of unity, freedom, dedication, and authority. Even the philosophical poem, the *Essay on Man*, includes a behavioristic thesis that purports to explain the relations among self-love, reason, pride, and the passions and depends on relocating the paradisal garden from an objective to a subjective status. The *Essay*, a more ambitious and later poem than *The Rape of the Lock*, nevertheless revisits the early poem by exploring further the action of subversion and by showing that reason, possessed by pride, issues in the closure of the divine and an alienation from nature, itself now seen by the one so victimized as empty of religious meaning. The *Essay on Man* is a philosophic poem, *The Rape of the Lock* a mock-epic, but no proper understanding of Pope's career or the progress of his imagination can disjoin the one from the other. In reading Pope one is always rereading him and searching the hidden paths leading from poem to poem. Pursued with sufficient rigor this enterprise would give us some sense of the range and scope of his imagination and of the exigencies of his own time to which he responded. We would see that political discourse is inevitably (and designedly) religious discourse and that a human being in the context of society is equally a human being in the context of eternity. The vision at which we would arrive might well undermine our sense of the "discreteness" of topics in the opus magnum, but the vision would be neither Miltonic nor Wordsworthian: it would be Pope's own and bounded by the moral philosophical concerns that are distinctively his and evident in one poem after another.

His formidable ambition as spokesman for an age required inevitably that he assume the role of prophet, a characterization not normally associated with Pope. It was necessary to assimilate the great and small texts of Western literature, its history, myth, and scripture, and then to deploy them imaginatively so as to reveal their bearing on the progress of civilization and on Pope's own historical moment and context. We will better understand this observation by recognizing the use he makes of Chaucer's medieval dream-vision poem, *The House of Fame*. Pope's *Temple of Fame* (1715) is modeled on Chaucer's allegory, in which Chaucer sees in his dream, among other notable figures of the past, the Jewish historian Josephus, as well as Statius, Homer, Lollius, Dares and Dictys, Guido de Columnis, and Geoffrey of Monmouth. Also present in Chaucer's dream are Virgil, Ovid, Lucan, and Claudian. Only very learned people can today identify most of Chaucer's eminent men. Few remember that Phrygius Dares was the supposed author of a history of the Trojan War; during the Middle Ages he was a highly important writer, and the work with which his name was associated (*De excidio Troiae*) became one of the most popular sources for medieval stories of the Trojan War. Much the same can be said for Geoffrey of Monmouth, whose chronicle of the kings of Britain was one of the chief sources for the Arthurian legend. Most of Chaucer's figures are gone from Pope's imitation, though Homer and Virgil remain; Pindar, Horace, Aristotle, and Cicero take the places of Josephus, Geoffrey, and others of whom Pope makes no mention. Implicit in these differences is a minihistory of European civilization from the Middle Ages through the Renaissance; Cicero is to some extent a discovery of Renaissance scholars, and the eighteenth century continued to ratify their judgment, though it is less the philosopher than the orator and public figure that Pope has in mind. The point, of course, is the obvious one of historical revision constantly carried on as an incessant human activity. Pope's figures are those who matter most to his age, and his modernizing of Chaucer's poem is perforce a modernizing of Chaucer's conception of historical relevance. Pope "imitates" Chaucer as a way of paying his respect to the father of English verse (Dryden before him did the same), but to invoke Chaucer in this way is to sustain Chaucer's enterprise and make it his own. To write *The Temple of Fame* is to write history; to compare *The Temple* with *The House* is to write a decidedly English history of cultural change between the 1380s and 1715. The continued presence of Homer and Virgil in Pope's "hallow'd Quire" validates Chaucer's judgment and affirms the importance of the epic poem as the first of literary kinds for the eighteenth century (though no poet was able to produce a memorable epic poem). Behind Pope's *Temple of Fame* we witness Chaucer's similar yet different testimony glowing through the four centuries separating the two works.

In the 1734 "Design" prefixed to the *Essay on Man*, Pope writes:

> What is now published, is only to be considered as a *general Map* of MAN, marking out no more than the *greater parts*, their *extent*, their *limits*, and their *connection*, but leaving the particular to be more fully delineated in the charts which are to follow. . . . I am here only opening the *fountains*, and clearing the passage. To deduce the *rivers*, to follow them in their course, and to observe their effects, may be a task more agreeable.

Maynard Mack explains the place of the *Essay* in the much larger work of four books Pope had in view: "The first book was to contain the *Essay on Man* as we now have it; the second was to treat of 'Knowledge and its limits'; the third, of 'Government; both ecclesiastical and civil'; and the fourth, of 'Morality'; in eight or nine of the most concerning branches of it; four of which would have been the two extremes to each of the Cardinal Virtues" (*Twickenham* 3: i, xi). This plan was the product of Pope's later years, though it probably arose in his mind in some relatively coherent formulation as early as 1726, and as early as the second decade of the century he was engaged in the sort of historical enterprise I have briefly assessed in relation to *The Temple of Fame*.

In taking account of his role as spokesman to an age, one must keep several factors in mind. Pope's being a Catholic in Protestant England was not merely a politically neutral fact (as it would be today), since Catholics were not allowed to reside in London or attend public schools and universities. Yet Pope's public expressions of religious conviction seem consistent with a Protestantism that was increasingly rational, anti-Puritan, and hostile to the claims of personal inspiration. Bolingbroke, Pope's mentor in the *Essay on Man*, clarifies Pope's position through the metaphor of so-called savages confronted by a clock:

> Carry a clock to the wild inhabitants of the Cape of Good Hope. They will soon be convinced that intelligence made it: and none but the most stupid will imagine that this intelligence is in the hand that they see move, and in the wheels that they see turn.
>
> (qtd. in Sambrook, *Eighteenth Century* 33)

The faith that rested on nature rested also on the idea that the religious person was essentially a social being, not an ascetic or fanatic, whose beliefs were compatible with a commitment to social and cultural authority. The essential purpose of the *Essay on Man* (itself a religious poem) may be defined as the effort to defend the integrity of God's creation and to understand the bond among human beings as predicated on love, the unifying principle of cosmic order sustained into the eighteenth century by the tradition of Platonic idealism. The *Essay* also modernizes the biblical story and modifies Milton's theme in *Paradise Lost*. Paradise in Pope's poem is, as I have indicated, not an objective but a subjective fact, a possession of the mind, akin to Miltonic "Christian liberty," serene in its fidelity to God and certain of its status in the world. In this context the hero is everyman, neither Adam nor Christ (or both Adam and Christ), and the heroic contest is internalized as the self's struggle with itself. It has been remarked, for example, that the proper use of individual freedom dominates the action of *Paradise Lost*. This being so, Milton offered Pope a pattern of internal conflict, a focus on the problem of freedom and choice within a Christian framework of universal order and design.

To raise this subject is to inquire into the bases of human identity from a behavioristic perspective. For Pope, the individual's goal is to create the total form of his or her identity, an enterprise aided by an agency called the ruling passion, a divine gift from God indicating the direction the individual personality should follow in the formation of character. To simplify the issue somewhat, the ruling passion provides an objective or goal for the self — doctor, scholar, politician, and so on — toward the achievement of which the self employs its various resources. The form of oneself that one is engaged in making requires the cooperative participation of self-love (distinct from pride), reason, and ruling passion, which occasions Pope's advice in the *Essay* that reason "treat this passion more as friend than foe" (2.164). Something may go wrong in this creative enterprise, however, since reason

(Pope's "weak queen" in the *Essay*) may be seduced by pride. When this occurs, reason is transformed into erring reason, which, together with pride, forms an entity opposed to self-love. The divine is then closed to the human imagination, and the new agency of selfhood (not named as such by Pope) creates the dark powers it then worships.

One can view the essay as "myth" — the assault by pride on reason being a restaging of the seduction practiced by Satan on Eve. The assault is, on one level, a violation of the female by the male intruder, a rape of sorts, and the challenge to self-love is presented at the deepest rung of instinctual response. The ruling passion falls under the suasion of pride and erring reason, and God's gift of this datum is corrupted and perverted from its legitimate and desirable ends. In these circumstances one now conceives of the Christian god as a tyrant who cruelly imposes his law on human beings and forbids them access to the instruments of his greater power. This substantially states the Satanic case and is echoed by the person so enlisted in his cause. It is Pope's explanation of the corruption of the will.

The *Essay on Man* is not a history poem (as is *The Temple of Fame*); rather its scope is theodicy (a defense of God's goodness and omnipotence in view of the existence of evil) and ethics. Its central concern is with the individual as a being domiciled in a middle kingdom, midway down the great chain of being extending from God to the lowest forms of life. We inhabit our kingdom with limited vision and limited knowledge, but we are, like all other creatures, perfectly suited (as perfectly suited as we *can* be) to the place we occupy. Newton's seventeenth-century discoveries of universal order were widely duplicated in various scientific works celebrating the divine design of the world and the benevolence of the Creator. Reason revealed the correspondence between religion and a cosmos ordered according to principles of immutable law. The optimism energizing the *Essay* is based on the evidence provided by nature, which everywhere testifies to the majesty of the providential (divine) plan. Yet nature itself can only imperfectly reflect divinity; this being so, it is subject to disorders of one kind or another (famine, flood, etc.). Yet such catastrophes may in some obscure way serve the good of the whole, and in any event human wisdom does not extend to the comprehension of God's purposes. It is surely arguable that the systematic exposition of universal order sustained in the analogical inquiries of the early eighteenth century offered Pope a context for his own ambition to assemble conventional and traditional wisdom in the service of a "science of Human Nature." It was not of course uncommon for other thinkers to analogize moral conduct with universal order or, for that matter, to bring various organizational patterns into relation with political structure.

To situate Pope politically requires some familiarity with the positions of Whig and Tory parties in the early years of the century. The essential points of Tory politics are based on a belief in the authority and political responsibility bestowed on an individual by real property (land) and thus on the necessary political relation between landed interests and civic life. This conviction was held by those who feared financial speculators and money manipulators, all those regarded as promoters of private appetite and false consciousness. The Tory view of individual identity was thus grounded on the idea that property existed in a precommercial past and that the lamentable drift of commercial history toward public credit and public debt sponsored an illusory notion of civic virtue and moral independence.

Conversely, the Whig position tended to accept credit as a measure of economic value and to ground personal identity on "a psychology of imagination, passion, and interest as the mainsprings of . . . the ego's pursuit of satisfaction and self-esteem, and [this position] was beginning to explore theories of how the diversities of passionate and self-interested action might be manipulated and coordinated . . . into promoting a common good no longer intimately connected with the inner moral life of the individual" (Pocock, *Machiavellian* 487). Clearly, each ethical argument was formulated on a different conception of human psychology, and the economic thesis was itself offered as a determinant of modes of conduct. The Whig position was the most threatening to traditional values, for it set forth an alternative conception of the self, involving a transmutation of ethical principles. "Private vices" could become "public benefits," as Bernard Mandeville proposed in well-known treatises published between 1714 and 1732. Self-liking was thus a construct of social valuation formed to promote the particular economic interests of the financial entrepreneur and commercial speculator, and the self was increasingly based on expedience and authorized by power, with the result that Whig-Tory debates not uncommonly took the form of contests between power and virtue. Excessive desire, fantasies of self-aggrandizement, and false consciousness were the consequences of power without virtue.

As a Tory, Pope makes his charge against the dunces in *The Dunciad* precisely in these terms, and the poem is a representation of minds enchanted by the goddess Dulness and obedient to her interests. *The Rape of the Lock* is an early depiction of Belinda so self-enchanted, and the goddess Rumour in *The Temple of Fame* is another manifestation of the ways a false consciousness is produced and perpetuated in the world. From a Tory perspective the power of credit was subversive, and insofar as credit assumed a quasi-literary or allegorical status in the imaginations of those who feared and opposed her, she was or could be invested with the characteristics of pride and erring reason. No distance separates the figure of Credit from that of Dulness; the two tend to merge as malign, demonic, destructive of the integrity of traditional values and civic virtue. The ground of authority in one department of human inquiry was therefore similar or related to authority in another. This is a distinctive (though not exclusive) feature of English Enlightenment thought, and its synthetic or analogical basis is a major component of Pope's intellectual vision.

For example, *nature* was (and remains) a key term in the lexicon of authority. It provides the basis for reason's edicts, a universal principle not subject to the contingencies of time or place. Ultimately, this ground encouraged or postulated an ordered hierarchical conception characteristic of both the universe (the great chain of being) and of society. It was also the basis for correspondences between part and whole in a properly organized (Aristotelian) aesthetic form. The same rational principles that determine correspondences between political and poetic order determine correspondences between political and cosmic order. Literature may thus, following this formulation, be said to be based on nature, which is what Pope means when, in the *Essay on Criticism*, he proposes that nature was "[a]t once the *Source and End*, and *Test of Art*" and "[o]ne *clear, unchang'd*, and *Universal Light*" (73, 71). The great writer, like Homer, is an embodiment of these principles, and in this way "*Nature* and *Homer* [are] the *same*" (135). That nature and Homer are the same reinforces the authority of literary tradition and insists on the continued viability and pertinence of the great classical authors. The objective status of nature is thus present permanently and expressively in classical literature and becomes a standard for present and future ages. The concept could also be adapted to serve as a regulating principle for literary kinds (from epic to epigram), so that each "kind" has its own *natural* characteristics and a decorum proper to its nature.

It is not really possible to separate such terms as *decorum* and *propriety* from *nature*, for nature as a regulating principle provides appropriate standards for an entire complex of human activities. In *The Rape of the Lock*, Belinda transgresses the bounds of female conduct and is repaid for her assumption of superiority by the mock-rape she suffers. At the end of the poem, presumably chastened, she is restored to a woman's true interests and sphere of behavior. Clarissa speaks the moral and enjoins the practice of "merit" and the proper employment of female "Pow'r." The advice is consistent with the natural (i.e., domestic and civic virtue proportioned to a woman's place in the great scheme of things) role of woman. Like *Windsor-Forest*, but differently, *The Rape of the Lock* is an exercise in the rejection of primitive forms of honor and the false ideal of virtue accompanying it (warrior societies of predator and prey). The Amazonic figure of Thalestris, who incites the women to war with the men, is rejected along with the idea of female honor she represents. One of Pope's best-known dicta, that self-love is social (*Essay on Man* 3.318), goes directly to the heart of his repudiation of primitivism and the false consciousness already associated, in another context, with the figure of Credit. It would not be difficult to chart the occasions of false consciousness in Pope's poems and to tabulate their underlying causes. We would find, I think, that the examples are recurrent and interrelated. That this is so defines the distinctive composition of a particular intelligence or imagination and is the primary means by which we gain entry into his works.

With this observation in mind, we may attend also to Pope's poetry of allusion, as it has been called, a richly referential literature, in which echoes of biblical, classical, and Renaissance literature are everywhere to be heard. Popian virtuosity may be regarded as a tour de force, but it is better to view it as consistent with a literary anthropology; that is, allusion provides a way of complicating and deepening the text, extending its referential range, and enforcing judgments by sustaining them at levels below the surface. A poetry of allusion summons the relevant aspects of the European tradition and employs them judicially. For example, in the *Epistle to Bathurst* various characters are summoned for praise or blame. They assume what scholars call a typological identity: that is, characters present in the poem are there as contemporary types of pagan or Christian forebears in mythology and literature. Many pagan heroes, among them Hercules, Achilles, or Aeneas, were regarded in the Renaissance as pre-Christian types of Christ. In *Bathurst*, Pope ridicules a financial speculator under the scriptural name of Balaam (Sir Balaam in the poem). The scriptural Balaam was a liar and false prophet, who agreed to sell out his gift and to curse the Israelites in exchange for gold and silver, although God prevented any such curse; Pope, however, focuses not on the outcome but on Balaam's intent and employs him as the antithesis to Job: "And sad Sir Balaam curses God and dies" (402).

Typology provided an immediate commentary on malign or virtuous behavior and sustained the relevant context by which appropriate judgment was rendered. The strategy suggests another way in which correspondence could be employed. Sir Balaam and his biblical prototype are alike despite the differences in time and place that separate them. A reader familiar with the biblical Balaam perceives the correspondence and understands the satiric point of Pope's characterization and the larger indictment of false prophet (i.e., financial speculators promising riches). If we follow the typological pattern throughout *Bathurst* we recognize that Cotta is the type of Mammon, Villiers of Satan, Kyrle of Christ; Blunt and Balaam are the opposites of Noah and Job. To condemn greed (the *Epistle to Bathurst* bears the subtitle *Of the Use of Riches*) Pope's ethical poem makes its judgments through the use of sacred history. History informed by the biblical perspective is analogous to nature informed by the divine (as in the *Essay on Man*). It is arguable — given the fact that Pope intended the *Epistles to Several Persons* as complement to the *Essay on Man* — that *Bathurst* builds out from the *Essay*, incorporating meanings and subjects not directly present in the *Essay*.

A poetry of allusion manipulated by a skillful cultural critic may indict by evoking familiar literary contexts. Thus, to take a more obvious example, Belinda's dream of desire resembles Eve's in *Paradise Lost*, and the similarity is intended to enforce the idea of comparable seductions, by Ariel on Belinda, by Satan on Eve. Employed in these ways, allusion both complicates and clarifies the text, providing it with something like a palimpsest (a text from which the writing has been partially removed to make room for another text). Imagine, then, texts below texts and you gain some idea of the complexity of a poem by Pope.

This observation may bear also on the function of wit in eighteenth-century discourse. As a key term, wit meant primarily the intellectual ability to recognize similarities amid dissimilarities (even as judgment, another important word, signified the perception of differences among like objects) and the lively gift of concise and apt expression to convey such perceptions (see David Morris's useful discussion of wit in this volume). In the following line from the *Essay on Criticism*, the words imitate exactly what they describe: "And ten low words oft creep in one dull line" (347). This is witty in the special sense that language provides an example of the thing it critiques in the act of making the critique, becoming thereby the thing to which it voices an objection (similarity in dissimilarity). It is equally witty in defining the baggage of Belinda's dressing-table ("Puffs, Powders, Patches, Bibles, Billet-doux" [1.138]) to include one item conspicuously inconsistent with the others. Note that small Bibles, prettily bound, could sometimes be found on a lady's dressing table, though possessing no more intrinsic value than the other objects surrounding it. Not to be aware of this tidbit of social history is to miss the moral edge of Pope's gently satiric catalog.

It should be apparent that Pope's poetry makes many and various demands on a reader, some of them vexatious (forgotten contemporaries may seem to offer only exercises in obscure identifications), but also part of what cultural criticism is all about. Similarly, and more interestingly, a reader must make an effort to understand the stages of Pope's career, the relation of each to the other, and the pertinent correspondences between works informing each stage. From 1711 to 1717 — the years that mark the inception of his career — he produced, in addition to the *Pastorals* and the *Messiah* (the former inspired by Virgil, the latter an imitation of him), six poems of major interest. *Windsor-Forest, The Temple of Fame*, and the *Essay on Criticism* assess political, cultural, and literary history and initiate for the young poet an encounter with public valuations. As historical discourse the three poems enforce conceptions of national identity (*Windsor-Forest*), the achievement of great men (*The Temple of Fame*), and the judgments of the great writers of the past (*An Essay on Criticism*). The *Essay on Criticism* advises us to "[h]ear how learn'd *Greece* her useful Rules indites" (92); *Windsor-Forest* surveys the present ordered state of England and then turns to historical retrospection: "Not thus the Land appear'd in Ages past" (43); *The Temple of Fame* begins with "The whole Creation open to my Eyes" (12) and proceeds to review the exemplars of heroic virtue drawn from the distant past. These poems were written long before Pope voiced (or perhaps even dimly conceived) the idea of an opus magnum, but they contribute to an elaborate version of historical review that clearly defines the educative role he early assumes.

The same years also witness the publication of *The Rape of the Lock*, *Eloisa to Abelard*, and the "Elegy to the Memory of an Unfortunate Lady." These poems have little in common with the poems of historical survey. At the center of each of these three works is a rebellious female; the poems explore the fate of desire subjectively and privately constituted, and thus the ravagement (mock in *The Rape of the Lock*), entrapment, and death to which the self is thereby exposed. At issue in *The Rape of the Lock*, *Eloisa to Abelard*, and the "Elegy" is the priority each heroine gives to a heroic identity (self-conceived) decidedly not consistent with the self-love that is social. The two "sets" of poems suggest that very early in his career Pope was already formulating (and completing) related inquiries: historical discourse in one "set" of poems, a presentation of heroic passion (love) in another. His pause in original composition in 1717 (following the first collected volume of his *Works*) indicates a resting point and a need for further study to fulfill larger ambitions (the years 1715 to 1726 are those of the *Iliad* and *Odyssey* translations and the Shakespeare edition). When he returned to the writing of his own poetry, as he did with the three-book *Dunciad* in 1728–29, he also began to formulate his plan for the opus magnum.

We should not and cannot read all the later Pope in the young poet, but it is of special value to notice that the poems of the period 1711–17 introduce themes and subjects that assume normative importance within the body of his works. Ripley Hotch, for example, speaks of Pope's use of the word *pride* in the *Essay on Criticism*, which "delicately establishes a connection between political rebellion, Adam's rebellion, and poetic rebellion that finally issues in the assault on heaven of 'Witt's Titans' " (480). Substitute Eve's rebellion for Adam's, and the connection between political and personal rebellion informs and determines the plot of *The Rape of the Lock*. Explore *The Rape* within the context of political reference, and it inevitably invokes subtextual references to contemporary public issues and the larger political context in which they exist. Pope's strategies enforce the proximity of shared areas of discourse, which are further emphasized by recurrent patterns of imagery, diction, and action. The familiar fiction of predator and prey, for example, designates a sustained concern with the exercise of power within related though dissimilar contexts.

Pope was writing at a time when new commercial relations threatened to swamp the older ideologies of civic and personal virtue, a time prior to the religious revival in the second half of the century and the renewal of spiritual fervor consistent with Methodism. He was also writing when the controversy involving the superiority of ancients to moderns, or moderns to ancients, was lively, and it is not hard to imagine on what side he is to be found. If, in fact, his views were to a large extent reactionary, they were no more so than Wordsworth's, though of course radically different. They were founded on the effort to review the history of Western civilization and literature and to take from them what was of continuing value in the formation of the modern citizen.

We can further grasp Pope's intellectual identity if something is said here about views not his own, though held by eminent thinkers of the age. Mandeville's *Fable of the Bees* (1714) argued that a commercial society is based on the self-seeking effort of individuals and that the restraints of religion or law are fictions proposed by those who would limit individual initiative and desire. The philosopher Thomas Hobbes put forth the view in his *Leviathan* (1651) and other works that the individual was essentially selfish and constantly at war with others. Fear of violent death is thus the chief motive underlying the creation of a government in which people surrender their natural rights and agree to live under the absolute power of a monarch. These deeply materialistic views are not consistent with each other except insofar as they share an unidealizing response to human motives. Against these positions may be enlisted those of Francis Hutcheson and Anthony Ashley Cooper, earl of Shaftesbury. Hutcheson was a professor at the University of Glasgow from 1729 until his death in 1746. His principal works are *An Inquiry into the Original of our Ideas of Beauty and Virtue* (1725) and *An Essay on the Nature and Conduct of the Passions and Affections, with Illustrations on the Moral Sense* (1728). He proposed that each person has an innate moral faculty and therefore a natural desire to do good, a conception that was developed initially by Shaftesbury and that is further indebted to the body of seventeenth-century thinkers known as the Cambridge Platonists. Shaftesbury's chief essays are collected in *Characteristicks of Men, Manners, Opinions, Times* (1711), in which he sets out the case for a moral sense and suggests that the harmony between society and the individual makes the general welfare identical with individual happiness. Ironically, a correspondence exists between Mandeville's notion of private vices and public benefits and Shaftesbury's idea of collective and individual good, but the authors' optimism is sustained by quite different conceptions of the relation between the individual and the collective.

Pope's own ideas move between these extremes, taking something from each but committed to neither. Generally speaking, his philosophical position is predicated on the belief that human identity is compounded of opposing forces or tensions within being; the individual bears responsibility for sustaining these tensions, for creatively and productively composing them and disposing them to particular goals: self-love is social. Microcosmically, this activity mirrors God's control of the opposing elements of which his universe is created. The ethical basis of human enterprise is thus patterned on the composition of the good that informs God's. Ethics is first of all theodicy, and while Pope believed that "Passions are the elements of Life" (*Essay on Man* 1.170), he believed also in a drama of conversion; that is, in the possibility of converting "passion into reason and rational egoism into socially desirable behavior" (Pocock, *Virtue* 113). This article of belief may be the single most important feature of early eighteenth-century ethical thought, almost an item of faith whereby the changes occurring in traditional modes of political and economic practice might yet be controlled so as not to issue in a self-love that was antisocial.

The Dunciad is best understood in this context and as the antithesis to the *Essay on Man*. It is an account of the state of mind precipitating a second and more calamitous fall of man, and though it has sometimes been dismissed by critics as nasty trifling, it is Pope's most ambitious prophetic poem and an experiment in apocalypse. (It is also the poem to which, late in life, he returned to revise and extend.) That such a work was possible for him should caution us about hasty conclusions as to the limitations of his imagination. *The Dunciad* dramatizes evil as the *Essay on Man* does not; the *Essay* accounts for moral evil by explaining its occasion: the human ability to do good would not be possible without the capacity also to do evil. *The Dunciad* has more to say on the subject, and within its own broadly satiric form it presents an image of the self possessed by the demonic goddess Dulness. It is the *Essay* inverted, for as the *Essay* speaks to the creative action that elevates the individual to full potential, *The Dunciad* addresses a nature whose origins have been obscured and whose reality is appropriately veiled. For all its local and topical satire, *The Dunciad* details the displacement of the divine that is at the heart of pride's usurpation of the role of self-love in the *Essay*. Moreover, *The Dunciad* echoes and restates the major preoccupations of many of Pope's works. The goddess Rumour in *The Temple of Fame* is a malign divinity, and Eloisa, ensnared by the "jealous god of love," is trapped in a way that resembles Colley Cibber's predicament as "hero" of *The Dunciad*.

Throughout his career Pope appears particularly alert not only to various manifestations of error and folly but especially to forms of human aggression. In *Windsor-Forest* his response to this subject arises from his engagement with history and with the pervasiveness of "blood" as a ruling principle. Belinda's militance in *The Rape of the Lock* and Eloisa's "rebel nature" neatly represent the ego attempting to fulfill its own dreams of desire. And the *Essay on Man* defines the self as the field on which warring impulses contend for mastery. At its most intense, Pope's poetry dramatizes the ego brimming over with the ambition to realize the possibilities that lie at the edge of perception, to become its own image of itself, to fulfill itself in various acts of transgression that constitute a raid on an imagined idea of self.

His poems are thus dramas of the individual realizing or subverting the place designed for him or her, and they commonly focus on the authority that may (or may not) be invested in such recurrent terms as *knowledge* or *honor* or *power*. He deploys an immense cast of characters in what is ultimately an eighteenth-century version of the human comedy and speaks for an idea of civilization vanishing even at the moment of its defense. His awareness of this fact gives special point to his later assumption of the Horatian persona, for the Latin poet, living just prior to the Christian era, had criticized his own age and yet enjoyed the friendship of Augustus Caesar as Pope could never have enjoyed that of George II. The *Imitations of Horace* (1730s) permitted Pope to set before the reader a portrait of the poet and the man, and nowhere in his own work is the social function of the satirist presented better or even as well. Also evident in these poems is the intimacy of self-portrait as Pope meditates on his function as satirist and contemplates retirement from active engagement with the follies of the world. He was about forty-five years old when the first imitations began to appear, and though he was to live for another eleven years, some of his closest friends, including John Gay, Dr. Arbuthnot, to whom he wrote one of his best-known epistles, and Lord Bolingbroke, the sage of the *Essay on Man*, were dead, dying, or removed from him. The attractions of retirement obviously appealed to him as, nineteen centuries earlier, such similar attractions tempted Horace to the Sabine farm, though for Pope the revised and enlarged *Dunciads* were tasks yet to be accomplished. One scholar has spoken of Homer and Horace as occupying different "symbolic zones" in Pope's mind (Rousseau, "On Reading Pope" 32): Homer the poet of an epic and warrior culture, of heroic deeds, and Horace the urbane critic of human folly. If this is so, it is certainly Horace who prevails and who offers Pope, in the last full decade of his life, the chance to dramatize the writer as observer both of himself and of the world.

Yet these remarks should not obscure the representations of the heroic in Pope's writings. *The Temple of Fame* is about the exemplars of heroic virtue, and, more modestly, such men as Bathurst and Burlington in the *Epistles to Several Persons* or Bolingbroke in the *Essay on Man* served Pope as contemporary examples of the possible forms of the good. A half century after Pope's death Wordsworth writes his own discourse of exemplary types, marginal figures such as leech gatherers, highland girls, wanderers of one sort or another. The difference is instructive, for it underscores the movement of the imagination from a confidence in the use of public individuals as exemplary figures to a reliance on the marginal to suggest the special truths of human identity. The Wordsworthian idea suggests that something of inestimable original value has been obscured or lost and requires recovery. The Popian idea is European, civil, bookish in the sense that our history as written is what matters, and Pope insists at all points that something is about to be lost but need not be.

In fact something was lost, with results so debilitating that English poetry did not recover imaginative energy until the later years of the century, when a new literary movement, Romanticism, arose, to a significant extent as a reaction to Pope and his age. Most of the major Romantic poets found Pope of limited use to them and largely antithetical to their own imaginative disposition of human life. His diction seemed artificial to Keats, his sense of human limitation distasteful to Blake. Modern criticism commonly argues that Blake's mediations between the claims of myth and of history are settled in favor of myth, and Wordsworth and Keats, despite the efforts to sustain their enterprise within the arena of public political discourse are frequently viewed as engaged in displacing the world inward and reconstituting it as a mental event. Pope cannot be so regarded; if anything, the special difficulty he poses for modern readers is the very presence of that world as composed of persons and places bearing public names and identities. To some, Pope's imagination may seem prosaic (it seemed so to nineteenth-century detractors). Yet it is worth remembering that on his five-acre home at Twickenham, just outside London, he built a grotto. The walls were decorated with sparkling stones and pieces of mirror, and falling water added to the illusion of a reconstructed and fantastic nature, so that when the interior was lighted it presented, as one visitor said, "an undistinguishable Mixture of Realities and Imagery." A modern scholar speaks of it as "a concrete metaphor of that cave of dreams, the poet's mind" (Sambrook, *Eighteenth Century* 161). Pope's poetry presents an equally curious mixture of the worldly and otherworldly. Dream visions, mini-allegories, fragments of mythology, malign deities of one kind or another, villains, fools, and the good combine to create a totality too various and comprehensive to submit to any of the familiar tag lines purporting to sum up his achievement.

Alexander Pope's work is really the last large-scale poetic vision of a premodern imagination in which elements of classical, medieval, Renaissance, and Enlightenment thought commingle. God and nature are still relatively stable categories; the traditional bases of civic virtue remain visible; Greece and Rome are the relevant models for civilization and indexes to learning; philosophical history is the great subject of the age. Pope's work is deeply invested in each of these contexts and unrecognizable without reference to them. Finally, it may be that what is most interesting about Pope is his participation in a culture's self-identity or discovery and formulation of itself. We are often told that poets are educators; that this is true is evident in the organization — the composition and structure — of a cultural ideal. Blake's desire to build Jerusalem in England's green and pleasant land is only a more compelling statement of a common recurrent desire: to build anew the city of humankind. Pope's special contribution to this enterprise must be the reason we continue to read him.

TEACHING SPECIFIC POEMS

Windsor-Forest in Historical Context

Charles H. Hinnant

I teach *Windsor-Forest* in several contexts: in a sophomore-level survey course on early English literature from Beowulf to Blake, in a course on eighteenth-century English literature intended for advanced undergraduate majors, and in a graduate seminar on Swift and Pope. Although I focus explicitly on matters of scholarly dispute only in the graduate seminar, I attempt to address the broad theoretical and historical issues raised by the poem in all three courses. Thus I usually begin every class by asking students to consider whether poetry is autonomous, detachable from its cultural context and thus from the ideological matrix in which it was produced. A useful point to make during this initial discussion is that the notion of cultural determination suggests, at the very least, that a poet may not be fully aware of the implications of his or her own texts. This point gives one the opportunity to frame a central question about the conclusion of *Windsor-Forest*. On the one hand, the poem ends by affirming a vision of a peaceful world in which "Conquest" will

> cease, and Slav'ry be no more:
> Till the freed *Indians* in their native Groves
> Reap their own Fruits, and woo their Sable Loves,
> *Peru* once more a Race of Kings behold,
> And other *Mexico's* be roof'd with Gold.   (408–12)

On the other hand, it is apparent that if we go beyond the repudiation of Spanish and Portuguese imperialism envisaged in these lines, as we are encouraged by the terms of the poem's concluding prophecy to do, we encounter something at odds with the poem's Arcadian vision. We encounter an awareness of coercion as well as consent and even a recognition that the "fair Peace" the poem celebrates does not stem from the kind of voluntary traffic between a multitude of equally prosperous nations that Joseph Addison, for example, celebrated in *Spectator* 69. In Addison's well-known essay, the spectacle of a universal mercantile economy is but one aspect of an ordered and harmonious universe in which all nations cohere and play equal roles. In *Windsor-Forest*, by contrast, the principle of universal mercantile amity derives from a violent hierarchy in which "a new *White-Hall*" shall "ascend!" where

> mighty Nations shall inquire their Doom,
> The World's great Oracle in Times to come;
> There Kings shall sue, and suppliant States be seen
> Once more to bend before a *British* QUEEN.
>   (381–84)

In a graduate seminar, one might pose this contradiction in terms of the debate between Laura Brown, who in her controversial Marxist study of Pope characterized the poem as imperialist, and critics like Howard Weinbrot ("Recent Studies") and James Winn, who responded to Brown by reaffirming a traditional humanistic reading, in which Pope is seen as celebrating a Tory peace that brought two decades of costly war on the Continent to an end.

It might also be worthwhile at this point to introduce to the advanced courses Paul Ricoeur's distinction between theories and practices of interpretation, or hermeneutics, associated with "suspicion" and those associated with faith. For Ricoeur, the "school of suspicion," initially linked to the names of Nietzsche, Marx, and Freud, is best understood as a persistent — even obsessive — attempt to point out the gaps and inconsistencies in a text; and contemporary critical movements concerned with deconstruction, ideology, and psychoanalysis may be its lineal descendants. One should bear in mind that if we are right in detecting a contradiction in the conclusion of *Windsor-Forest*, then Pope's poem is particularly suitable for the application of the tools of suspicion. Indeed, an application of such tools might be seen as taking at least two forms: the first, associated with the term *deconstruction*, could be characterized as formalist, since it examines instabilities and blind spots within the text of the poem itself. The second, linked to the term *demystification*, is cultural and historical; it would examine *Windsor-Forest* in relation to the poem's avowed purpose, a celebration of the Treaty of Utrecht of 1713. It would thus deal, among other topics, with the question of whether Pope was aware of the asientos, the controversial articles in the Treaty of Utrecht that gave Great Britain monopolistic privileges in the West Indian slave trade.

Such concerns can only be explored schematically in a classroom context. In advancing a possible deconstructive interpretation of *Windsor-Forest*, I find the best place to begin is with the description of the physical forest near the beginning of the poem:

> The Groves of *Eden*, vanish'd now so long,
> Live in Description, and look green in Song:
> *These*, were my Breast inspir'd with equal Flame,
> Like them in Beauty, should be like in Fame.
> Here Hills and Vales, the Woodland and the Plain,
> Here Earth and Water seem to strive again,
> Not *Chaos*-like together crush'd and bruis'd,
> But as the World, harmoniously confus'd:
> Where Order in Variety we see,
> And where, tho' all things differ, all agree.
>
> (7–16)

Almost all teachers of *Windsor-Forest* point out to their students that this passage embodies the classical *topos* of *concordia discors* — the notion that peace arises from a harmonious reconciliation of opposites — which is, in some way, contrasted to the violence implied in the phrase "*Chaos*-like together crush'd and bruis'd." But one might also ask students to discuss the implications of the reference to the Garden of Eden in line 7, the use of the conditional tense in lines 9–10, and the employment in line 13 of the verb *seem*. The best students will almost certainly be able to recognize that the allusion to Eden points to an integration of ideal with reality that is broken with the Fall and exemplified, later in the poem, by the hunter-tyrant Nimrod. In a postlapsarian world, any talk of a *concordia discors* will inevitably involve fragmentary discontinuity, and the paradigm, insofar as it is constructed from a classical metaphysics ignorant of the Fall, is likely to seem fallacious and blind to its own origins.

Evidence that Pope might have been aware of the distinction between prelapsarian and postlapsarian worlds can be found in Father Thames's invocation to "Sacred *Peace*!" in which the river god contends that "the shady Empire shall retain no Trace, / Of War or Blood, but in the Sylvan Chace" (371–72). Here hunting is seen as an edenic pastoral activity, implicitly opposed to warfare and violence, since it is aimed at animals, not human beings. Earlier in the poem, however, the "Sylvan Chace" is seen as a manifestation of the same violence that produced Nimrod's "Despotick Reign" (58). The classical deity Pan is perhaps the best symbol in the poem for this instability. He is associated at one point in the poem, students easily recognize, with pastoral "Flocks" (35), but he is also the god who pursues the female huntress Lodona when "It chanc'd, as eager of the Chace the Maid / Beyond the Forest's verdant limits stray'd" (181–82). Concentrating on the word *Trace* in the above passage will help students better understand the complex relation between hunting and violence in the poem. The *Trace* in this context is a trace of the memory that the "Sylvan Chace" seeks to repress. The "Sylvan Chace" has no knowledge of its origins in cruelty and blood other than this *Trace*, and even then it retains a trace of its memory of its origins only because it defines itself as a "Shady Empire," the opposite of the warfare and violence it has forgotten.

The aim of the discussion, then, would be to suggest that the economy of the *concordia discors* in *Windsor-Forest* requires that violence be banished from the system, that any recollection of its origins in postlapsarian conflict be erased. To indicate how the poem defines this process, one might ask students to discuss the Ovidian Pan-Lodona episode (171–218). Lodona's postlapsarian virginity and excess, her eagerness in the chase, are what trigger Pan's pursuit and produce a collapse of the distinction between hunting animals and human beings. A comparison of Pan with "the fierce Eagle" insists on the predatory, violent nature of his pursuit. But the metamorphosis of Lodona into the river Ludden, into a "silver Stream," leaves only a non-visual and nonverbal "trace" of the violence to which she has been subjected:

> The silver Stream her Virgin Coldness keeps,
> For ever murmurs, and for ever weeps;
> Still bears the Name the hapless Virgin bore,
> Still bathes the Forest where she rang'd before.
> (205–08)

In the discussion of these lines, students should recognize that what was once transparent has become opaque, transformed from a window into a "Glass," in which the "musing Shepherd" now "spies" only a peaceful landscape (211–18). The dark side of this "Glass," or mirror, becomes an apt symbol of the memory that has been suppressed. Because Pan's violence has been forgotten, it can now be seen as exteriorized and thus expelled, like the personifications of evil in lines 413–18, to "deepest Hell."

A careful discussion of this episode will probably lead students to decide that Pope was conscious of this dual process of effacement and exteriorization in *Windsor-Forest*. They are much less likely to be persuaded, however, that Pope was aware of the contradictions implicit in the poem's celebration of the Treaty of Utrecht. It is impossible, of course, to discuss any poem in relation to its historical context except in a preliminary way and without presuming some knowledge on the part of students of that context. To avoid having to lecture on the economic aspects of the Treaty of Utrecht, I find it useful to ask students to read a two-page excerpt from Christopher Hill's *The Century of Revolution, 1603–1714* summarizing the main issues involved in the treaty. Having absorbed this material, students will be much better able to participate in a discussion of the poem in its historical context.

To assist them in grasping the relation between the theme of hunting and actual historical events in *Windsor-Forest*, one might establish a series of broad parallels between, for example, the conquests of Nimrod and William the Conqueror and the land wars pursued by William III on the Continent. One can also trace a parallel, established both metonymically and metaphorically in the poem, between the peaceful pursuit of game in the edenic "Shady Empire" of Windsor-Forest and the peaceful pursuit of wealth and commerce through colonial trade. The ordered variety of the countryside is what permits its exploitation for peaceful purposes: the forest oaks provide both the shade necessary for hunting and the timbers essential for naval expansion and trade.

In the same way, moreover, that the peaceful activity of hunting erases its own origins and defines itself in opposition to a violence that it has exteriorized from itself, so the new policy of colonial expansion celebrated in the poem defines itself by its opposition, on the one hand, to the prolonged Wars of the Spanish Succession and, on the other, to the brutal practices of Spanish and Portuguese imperialism. Nor was Pope alone in glorifying and thus mystifying the practices of British imperialism. As long ago as the age of Elizabeth, propagandists were determined to undermine the Spanish empire and bring glory to England. A useful point to make is that in *Discourse of Western Planting* (1584), for example, the Hakluyt brothers contrasted planned English actions in Virginia with the barbarous cruelty of the Spanish in Latin America. In Pope's time, writers were much more likely to stress the benefits of free trade over a parasitic dependence on gold and silver forcefully extracted from ruined colonies. In projecting the outlines of a new and enlightened English imperialism, Pope was merely following in this tradition. Because he believed that the "Persecution" and gross barbarities of the Spanish and Portuguese conquests would be purged from this new imperialism, Pope was willing to affirm whatever was necessary to sustain the vision of a *Pax Brittania* in which "Earth's distant Ends our Glory shall behold, / And the new World launch forth to seek the Old" (401–02). Indeed, his poem may seem less mystified than writings like Addison's *Spectator* 69, in that it openly acknowledges that the aim of British policy is to make London the center of world trade.

This argument will not, of course, explain whether Pope was aware of the asientos at the time he was composing the poem. One ought to note to students that Pope never explicitly condemned African slavery in his writings and thus may have viewed blacks differently from Indians. Like many of his contemporaries, he may have regarded the Indian nations of Mexico and Peru as distinct political entities that deserved to regain their independence, while placing the Africans he encountered in the category of what Winthrop P. Jordan terms "individuals," persons who did not retain the quality of nationality and hence could be bought and sold.

A discussion that concludes by raising the issue of Pope's silence concerning the asientos can have considerable value in the classroom. It may help us, for example, understand why he appears to have sought to distance himself from certain aspects of the poem. Even though Pope's act in delegating the history of England to George Granville, the lord to whom the poem is dedicated (299–328), and the concluding prophecy to Father Thames (329–434) is not sufficient to undermine the speaker's commitment to the poem's political vision, it may partly explain the unease, exemplified in the famous whirring-pheasant episode (111–18), that many students have sensed in *Windsor-Forest*. It may also assist students in understanding Pope's subsequent abandonment of partisan myth and history. In advanced undergraduate and graduate courses, it is useful to organize Pope's poems in such a way that his celebration of British imperialism in *Windsor-Forest* is set off against the loss of faith in political and national symbols evident in several later poems. By comparing the conclusion of *Windsor-Forest* with the parodic prophecies of *The First Epistle of the Second Book of Horace*, "To Augustus" (395–403), and of *The Dunciad* (3.68–340); with the repudiation of political panegyric in *The First Satire of the Second Book of Horace*, "To Mr. Fortescue" (23–28); and, above all, with the attack on merchants and mercantile trade in *The First Epistle of the First Book of Horace*, "To Lord Bolingbroke" (67–72), and in *The Sixth Epistle of the First Book of Horace*, "To Mr. Murray" (11–13, 31–32, and 69–73), we may bring our students closer to recognizing the complex political tensions and shifts that occur within Pope's poetry.

Neoclassical Aesthetics
and *An Essay on Criticism*

Peter Walmsley

An Essay on Criticism appears in the Pope selections of several of the more traditional introductory anthologies, their editors doubtless recognizing that the poem provides opportunities to teach some of the rudiments of practical criticism. Students embarking on literary studies would surely benefit from heeding Pope's advice about reading from part to whole or from following the play of his exemplary lines on making sound the echo of sense. But the *Essay*'s sophisticated and highly allusive argument makes it more suited to the upper years of the curriculum, and students most often first encounter it in courses dedicated either to the eighteenth century or to the history of critical theory. I have taught the poem in both contexts, and the suggestions I offer here are most appropriate to the discussion possible in senior classes. At this level I can rely on students for careful reading and confident critical dialogue. As much as possible I limit my own contribution to raising questions that open problematic issues, directing attention to key passages, and suggesting points of contact with works students have seen previously in the course.

In their initial readings students usually enjoy the satire on Grub Street that opens the poem and seem to approve of the earnestness of the later portrait of the moral critic. They are less certain, however, about Pope's aesthetic argument, deterred by the flurry of abstractions, the ambiguity and unfamiliarity of the key terms, and the confusion as to whether Pope's subject is criticism or the writing of poetry. But at this stage of study, the *Essay* is, perhaps, most valuable for its statement of critical principles, not just for the understanding of Pope's poetry but as an occasion for broader reflection on the aesthetics of his age. That Addison and Johnson should both be so vigorous in their praise of the poem argues that Pope succeeded in articulating principles of central and lasting concern. So I teach the *Essay* as exemplary of the preoccupations and the complexity of neoclassical criticism, encouraging the class to connect Pope's thought with that of other theorists of the period, particularly Boileau, Dryden, and Addison. Those studying the eighteenth century thus have an opportunity to familiarize themselves with the critical commonplaces of the age, while those pursuing the history of literary criticism can consider the mixing of ancient and modern in neoclassi- . cism and even plot the origins of Romantic aesthetic thought.

To focus discussion on these issues, I ask my students to pay special attention to Pope's theoretical reflections early in the poem (lines 68–168). A few years ago, a student opened the class with her version of John Dennis's damning question — What *can* Pope mean by "Nature"? — and ever since I have done the same. Responses show that in urging us to "follow NATURE" Pope is not subscribing to a strict mimetic theory. A *"Universal* Light," nature becomes the *"Source"* rather than the object of art, the animating poetic intelligence attuned to the universal order rather than simply external sensory experience. Distinctions between art and nature are further blurred by the image of art as the invisible soul, or essence, informing a poem (68–79). The analysis of these lines prepares for discussion of Pope's neoclassicism in the strict sense: his conviction that "Nature" and Homer are the same and that the rules derived from ancient poetic practice are but *"Nature Methodiz'd"* (89). Students, rankled by the apparent pedantry of Pope's insistence on the authority of the ancient epic precedents, are quick to criticize the *Essay's* central tenets as narrow and restrictive. They point, in particular, to the lines celebrating Homer's works as establishing a closed and unattainable poetic standard. And Pope's story of Virgil's confining his epic visions and learning to copy the rules seems to demote the poetic act to a merely technical exercise (130–38). In the context of these objections, I ask about decorum in the *Essay* and read aloud from the famous passage on poetic numbers (337–83). Here Pope's preoccupations with technique and appropriateness, even while they are seen to work within his vision of the poetic whole, again serve to legislate strict external standards for the work of art.

From this point on, my questions and arguments are devised to challenge in different ways this perception of Pope's aesthetic as constraining and monologic. I begin this contrary reading by drawing attention to Pope's antithesis of wit and judgment (80–87). First I canvass the class for definitions of wit, of which the poem itself handily provides the full range — from the deft and entertaining conversationalist to human understanding in the broadest sense (Empson 201–02). Students of the eighteenth century will know the importance of wit for Dryden's comedy and will recognize that Pope's definition — *"True Wit* is *Nature* to Advantage drest" (297) — advertises its own departure from earlier emphases on conceit and analogical wordplay. But I suggest that in pitting wit against judgment here, Pope is evoking a conventional antithesis for his immediate purposes. Some recall how, at the end of Dryden's *Essay of Dramatic Poesy*, Neander argues that rhyme in drama helps the playwright's judgment in disciplining a luxuriant fancy (Adams 256–57). I also quote Locke, for whom Wit lies "most in the assemblage of *Ideas*, and putting those together with quickness and variety," while *"Judgment*, on the contrary, lies quite on the other side, in separating carefully, one from another, *Ideas*, wherein can be found the least difference" (2.11.2). Reading these two contrary mental energies as fundamental categories, one can determine a pattern in Pope's seemingly loose aesthetic diction. Writing *Wit* and *Judgment* on the blackboard, I solicit critical terms from the poem that might be listed under either heading. Under the assimilative powers of wit fall genius, imagination, invention, grace, and license, while judgment's analytic restraint encompasses rule, learning, understanding, care, precept, and precedent.

These categories are neither neat nor exclusive, but this process helps students recognize an underlying conflict in Pope's argument. Pope's poetic proceeds by difference; his verse continually pits a critical concept against its opposite. As always, Pope provides images to help illuminate his more abstract conceptions, and students find an easy access to the fundamental tension in his aesthetics by fixing on the image of Pegasus — "The winged Courser, like a gen'rous Horse, / Shows most true Mettle when you *check* his Course" (86–87). Here wit's energy is appropriately restrained by judgment's bridle, but this image is balanced by Pope's later admission that "*Pegasus*, a nearer way to take, / May boldly deviate from the common Track" (150–51). Pope does not establish a hierarchy of poetic faculties here but describes instead their mutual dependence.

In teaching critical theory, I always ask students to consider the politics of each theorist, not just the explicit social role of poetry for, say, Plato but such implicit strains as Sidney's anxiety about class in the *Apology*. My students of the eighteenth century will have just read *Windsor-Forest* and will be aware of the ambiguities in Pope's celebration of the new economic order, particularly the poet's tentative place in a landscape that, while the very heart of empire, is still a sylvan retreat. *An Essay on Criticism*, by contrast, clearly situates Pope in the public realm, anatomizing the bitter urban politics of Grub Street. To open this avenue for exploration, I turn attention to an image related to that of the courser — "For *Wit* and *Judgment* often are at strife, / Tho' meant each other's Aid, like *Man* and *Wife*" (82–83). With little prompting, students attuned to gender issues will remark on this feminization of poetic energies as it surfaces elsewhere in the *Essay*. Throughout the poem Pope adopts conventional imagery of the poet's need to give naked Nature her appropriate dress, but he also extends his motif of domestic conflict, likening the muse to an abused mistress (432) and wit to "The *Owner's Wife*, that *other Men* enjoy" (501; Rumbold 16). As elsewhere, Pope casts the imagination as female (Fairer, *Imagination* 82–112), connecting poetry with both the vulnerability and the dangerous instability of the feminine. For my eighteenth-century class, this association will prove important in future discussions of Pope's ironic self-images, particularly of the airy and unstable portraitist of the *Epistle to a Lady*. But more immediately, Pope's images of male oppression and female rebellion carry his poetics of contrariety into the social realm.

It is worth pointing out to students that, while Pope dismisses the petty envies of feeble critics, the questions of criticism's social role and its proper relation to poetry remain of vital concern. The critic is granted the power to determine the canon; new poetry lives or dies by the critic's decree. And Pope's social poetic becomes explicitly political in his traditional images of the state: "*Nature*, like *Liberty*, is but restrain'd / By the same Laws which first *herself* ordain'd" (90–91). *Liberty* — "*Britannia's Goddess*" in *Windsor-Forest* — is, of course, a word laden with political emotions. Self-restraining liberty was central to the common perception of the British social contract and thus to national identity (Brown, *Pope* 57–58). But *"Liberty"* here is a late substitution by Pope. Up until 1743 the line had *"Monarchy"* obeying her own laws. The two readings are not contradictory; rather they offer two views of the same British political virtues at work — rule of law and the conciliation of competing interests. Pope is all too conscious of how modern Britain differs from the heroic realm of the ancients, where kingly poets could "dispense with *Laws* Themselves have made" (162) and Aristotle ruled uncontested over nature and wit (652). But however much he longs for such outright poetic sway, Pope clearly offers an aesthetic of balance and restraint suited to his nation and his generation.

Within the context of these political concerns, it is now possible to locate the class's earlier discussion of Pope's veneration of the ancient epic as a source for modern poetic and critical endeavor. The contest between ancient and modern literature is as crucial to Pope as it was to Dryden. A sense of history pervades the *Essay*, so that, as Pope elevates the altar of the classics, he deepens the bathos of modern scribbling. Despite his warnings to those critics who only praise the art of one age or one nation, the *Essay* conveys a strong sense of the limited possibilities of modern poetry. As in *An Essay on Man*, Pope is quick to remind us of our awkward middle state in the cosmos since the Fall — "Nature" has "wisely curb'd proud Man's pretending Wit" (53). Our degeneracy is most evident in our shifting language. Pope worries that its continual decay effectively limits poetic fame to sixty years (480–93), and his anxiety is one students will recognize from Swift, whose Struldbrugs lose even the comfort of conversation. I try to impress on the class the urgency of Pope's project: that his critical maxims are designed for present application, stays against the inroads of time. Like Addison, Pope condemns excesses in the writing of the previous generation, the rank obscenity of the Restoration and the religious laxity of William's reign (530–51). At the same time, by repeatedly returning to Dryden and his works, Pope offers the hope that the poet may excel in the worst of times. We see Dryden managing to rise above a host of malicious detractors to stand as the Timotheus of his age.

I ask next why Pope concludes the poem with a history of critical theory. Responses recognize here again the importance of ancient precedent, of the attention given Aristotle, Horace, Quintilian and Longinus and the praise awarded Vida and Boileau for preserving ancient doctrine. And here too political and nationalist themes can make their reprise as Pope describes the balance of liberty and law in English poetry. Students familiar with Dryden's *Essay* will recognize the same resistance to the incursion of French literary theory, and particularly to a dogmatism more appropriate to "a Nation born to serve" (713). And lastly, by placing himself at the poem's end as the most recent participant in this critical tradition, Pope admits that his *Essay* is a collection of tried truths rather than an excursion in original thought. As in *The Dunciad*, Pope is not averse to creating a cento, striving not for novelty but for inclusiveness. If Pope presents his poem as suited to the temper of his age and nation, he also takes care to publicize his debts to ancient sources. So we end the class by exploring Pope's dialogue with these classics, especially the works of Horace and Longinus, placing Pope's thought in its larger historical context.

Pope begins his history of theory with Aristotle, the source of both the formalism and the "rules" of neoclassical criticism. But he willingly concedes the *Essay*'s more extensive debt to the *Ars poetica* when he moves on to praise Horace's steady judgment and lasting precepts (657–60). Students of critical theory looking back to Horace may discover many of the guiding principles of Pope's aesthetics, especially in Horace's accounts of decorum, of the integrity and internal harmony of the work of art, and of the importance of convention. Horace, ever ready to chastise poetic slovenliness and deflate affected inspiration, depicts poetry as a taxing discipline and advocates tireless revision (Adams 72). These attitudes find expression in the large role granted to poetic judgment in the *Essay*, and Pope would elsewhere claim Horace's advice to set a manuscript aside for nine years as a practical principle in his own career. But mention should also be made of both theorists' consciousness of the social functions of art. For it is from Horace that Pope learns that ethical thought is the origin of poetry. And while Horace's epistle is ostensibly a poet's advice to a poet, Horace, like Pope, never loses sight of the poem as public property, a commodity that lives or dies in the marketplace. So here Pope finds depicted the vital role for criticism that concerns him in the latter half of the *Essay*; he even finds models for his portraits of bad and good critics in Horace's babbling flatterer and rigorous Aristarchus (Adams 74–75). But Horace also provides an opportunity to reflect more generally on the style of Pope's *Essay*. Addison observed of the poem that "the Observations follow one another like those in *Horace's Art of Poetry*, without that Methodical Regularity which would have been requisite in a Prose Author" (Addison and Steele 2: 483). Pope himself has as much to say in the *Essay* about Horace's intimate and unmethodical style as about his precepts. In the ease and friendliness of his epistles, Horace exemplifies Pope's "Candour" (563), the critical virtue that verges on charity itself. If Pope's voice remains, perhaps, less intimate than Horace's (Brower, *Pope* 191), Pope attains nonetheless this same candor by the earnestness with which he offers his advice and the gentleness of his satiric excursions. Moreover, Pope finds in Horace's "graceful Negligence" a formal precedent for his expatiatory "essay," a genre that, like Dryden's dialogue, facilitates the exposition of a poetic of contraries.

But our final tour through Pope's gallery of critical forebears reinforces the theme that neoclassicism is neither so exclusive nor so dogmatic as it first appears. For Aristotle and Horace are joined here by Quintilian and Longinus, and the formalist tradition is thus balanced by these proponents of the affective and pragmatic powers of language. In his own notes to the *Essay* Pope frequently cites Quintilian, whose *De institutione oratoria* provides an authority for, among other things, Pope's admission that poetic license itself may be a rule (146n). And his placing of the rediscovered Longinus in his critical pantheon confirms the importance of the sublime in the *Essay*. If Pope owes such details as his "shapeless *Rock*, or hanging *Precipice*" (160) to the painting of Salvator Rosa, his understanding that such rugged disorder has an immediate access to the heart is surely Longinian (157). And when Pope uses the extended simile of discovering, as we climb, the alpine prospect of "*endless* Science," he clearly follows Longinus's rules for evoking astonishment — dramatizing a vividly felt encounter with the vast in nature (225–32). In the following lines Pope seems to justify this sublime excursion by giving "*Rapture*" precedence over cold correctness (236). And here Pope recognizes, with Longinus, that literature moves us not because of the perfection of its "parts" but because of its power to make a single, bold, and immediate impact on the mind, a power it shares with painting and architecture (245–52).

In discussing Pope's inclusion of the radical discourse of sublimity, we lay the ground for future readings in later English neoclassical criticism. Students in both classes will discover how the aesthetics of Addison and Burke are built on the competing critical categories of the sublime and the beautiful. For Addison the imagination effects a kind of possession of the beautiful object, resting well satisfied in the "Chearfulness" engendered by symmetry and order, while a scene of "*Greatness*" pleases as it eludes our powers of comprehension, its rude magnificence leading the mind from the sensible to the spiritual, from the world to God (Addison and Steele 3: 542–45). This contrast deepens into an "eternal distinction" for Burke, who feels the tragic emotion of terror before the obscurity of the sublime scene (Adams 310–11). Students can thus begin in Pope's *Essay* to comprehend one of the central conflicts of eighteenth-century poetic theory and recognize too how neoclassicism, by virtue of its exemplary intellectual candor, nurtures the seeds of Romantic aesthetics.

What the Sylphs Do:
Studying *The Rape of the Lock*

John Sitter

Before beginning *The Rape of the Lock* most teachers and many students
know that the poem we now read is a much expanded version of a poem
of two cantos and no sylphs. This remarkable fact is more often noted than
grasped. That those inhabitants of air who seem so inseparable from the
poem's entire atmosphere were lacking from 1712 to 1714 (the work was
expanded yet again in 1717 to include Clarissa's speech in canto 5) is worth
taking hold of as a way of asking what the sylphs do in, or to, or for the
poem we now have.

One can lecture on the question, and some of what follows offers a few
notes toward such a fiction. But the only way to grasp the question experi-
entially is to read the poem without, as well as with, the sylphs. If it is not
practical to have students read the text of 1712 (available in volume 2 of
the Twickenham edition and in Geoffrey Tillotson's paperback edition), the
first version may be reconstructed closely enough by assigning just these lines
of the five-canto work: 1.1–18; 2.1–46; 3.1–24, 105–34, 147–48, 153–78;
4.1–10, 93–140, 143–74; 5.1–6, 37–52, 57–88, 97–150.

Although this assignment may seem to vandalize a great poem, there is
considerable value in having students read the work in this manner before
reading the whole. Newcomers nearly always have trouble following the
"plot" of *The Rape of the Lock*. The primary reason they do is because as
soon as the scene has been set in the first eighteen lines of the poem they
run into Ariel's long explanation of the sylphs' existence; then, after a few
more paragraphs, they hit Pope's elaborate description of sunlight and sylphs
that plays along the Thames for nearly a hundred lines. Whatever its shortcomings, the 1712 version has the advantages of narrative clarity and direct-
ness. Without the sylphs, card game, and Cave of Spleen, which together
make up more than half of cantos 3 and 4, the mock-heroic human action
is easily followed from beginning to end. Moreover, the reader who follows
this shortcut will have already met about 40 percent of the lines from the
final version.

Once readers have compared the first and finished poems, it is useful to
begin simply by asking what major additions come in with the sylphs. The
six new scenes are these: (1) Ariel's speech to the dreaming Belinda (1.27–
114); (2) the dressing-table scene (1.121–48); (3) Belinda's sunny progress
up the Thames with her friends and a host of sylphs (2.47–72); (4) Ariel's
speech reviewing the sylphs' past roles, present assignments, and future
punishments for dereliction of duties (2.73–136); (5) the card game
(3.33–100); (6) Umbriel's journey to the Cave of Spleen (4.11–92).

A natural question to raise next is whether all these additions require the sylphs' presence. Only the first, third, and fourth actually do. By contrast, the three scenes always pointed to in accounts of the poem as mock-epic (the dressing table, card game, and Cave of Spleen) might have been constructed without a sylph in sight. The sylphs enter only the concluding four lines of the dressing/arming of the hero/heroine and only the first few lines of the long battle on the card table; in the journey to the underworld Umbriel functions primarily as observer, a role that might have been assigned to the muse or to a human-sized mortal, as in epic proper. This review leads, then, to the question of whether, in some more general way, all six of these new scenes are related to the sylphs' entrance into the poem.

The sylphs' minimal role at the dressing table suggests some answers. The action of the scene is nearly over, Belinda's "keener Lightnings" and "purer Blush" already achieved, before their literal entrance:

> The busy *Sylphs* surround their darling Care;
> These set the Head, and those divide the Hair,
> Some fold the Sleeve, whilst others plait the Gown;
> And *Betty*'s prais'd for Labours not her own.
>
> (1.145–48)

What the sylphs bring to this scene is magnification. Ariel's first speech had prepared thematically for the celebration of Belinda's beauty—"thy own Importance know" (1.35)—by establishing that "unnumber'd Spirits" hover around her (1.41). But the insinuation of the sylphs into the waking action in canto 2 picks up the hints of sylphic diminution in Ariel's speech (so many sylphs attending one human must be very small) and begins to make these hints visual.

Inevitably, miniaturization and magnification are reciprocal; as in the first part of *Gulliver's Travels*, the smallness of the attendant population magnifies the "real" protagonist's body and possessions. Even the game of Ombre in canto 3, which could have proceeded without the sylphs' help, is magnified by their comparative littleness ("th' Aerial Guard / Descend, and sit on each important Card" [3.31–32]). What was in 1712 a simpler mock-heroic comedy—little things treated in big language—grows more complex: little things are treated in big language but, surrounded by hosts of little spirits, become big after all. More than any other single effect, these paradoxical transformations make the poem an elusive compound of satire and celebration.

Like *Gulliver's Travels*, *The Rape of the Lock* uses big bodies and little bodies to illustrate the confusion of big and little questions, the need for a sense of proportion, for keeping things in perspective, for a sense of ethical scale. But both works also go further, using the play of perspective to defamiliarize the "real," thus making common things at once exotic and questionable. On one level, invisible quotation marks are put around every-day reality by means of extreme close-ups, as when familiar objects such as Gulliver's or Belinda's watch are seen through miniature eyes. On another level, Pope uses the sylphs to play with the question of visible versus invisible causes, and thus with the problem of causation altogether. What "causes" Belinda's full beauty is as mysterious as the source of Minta Doyle's aura in Virginia Woolf's *To the Lighthouse*: "Besides, she knew, directly she came into the room that the miracle had happened; she wore her golden haze. Sometimes she had it; sometimes not. She never knew why it came or why it went. . . . Yes, tonight she had it tremendously" (148).

If Betty is praised for labors not her own at the close of canto 1, the error is no more than Ariel had predicted. His first speech explains two common mistakes in attributing causes. When young women preserve their chastity, " 'Tis but their *Sylph*, the wise Celestials know, / Tho' *Honour* is the Word with Men below." And when they seem unsteady, "This erring Mortals Levity may call, / Oh blind to Truth! the *Sylphs* contrive it all" (1.77–78, 103–04). In one light, Ariel's mystifications are simple sarcasm: "honor" and "levity," not the sylphs, protect young women. The sylphs, after all, can do nothing once an earthly lover gains the heart. The host of sylphs, as Auden said of poetry, "makes nothing happen" ("In Memory of W. B. Yeats," line 36).

In another light, however, Ariel's remark is ironic rather than sarcastic, for what the sylphs make happen is much of the work's best poetry. How do the sylphs make poetry happen? Two ways have already been suggested.

First, they bring attention, not protection, to Belinda, magnifying and defamiliarizing her by introducing a rich visual scale into the work. Second, the sylphs are figures of paradox and equivocation. It is at once questionable whether they are "real" or imaginary, natural or artificial, male (as they appear now) or female (as they were originally). As paradoxical creatures who are, so to speak, originally derivative, they render equivocal any questions of origins and causes. More specifically their presence tends to complicate sarcasm into irony whenever causation is at issue.[1] Ariel's remarks about "Honour" and "Levity" do not simply affirm conventional explanations; rather, they require the reader to entertain the possibility that as explanations the abstractions "Honour" and "Levity" are as mysterious as sylphs: common sense and magic alike must posit invisible causes for visible effects. (The sylphs also suggest a playful solution to a large and related problem of eighteenth-century Newtonianism, "action at a distance."[2])

A third way in which the sylphs help the poetry "happen" is by becoming vehicles for the analysis of experience, both aesthetic and conceptual. This function is related to their sponsorship of the poem's visual scale and their role as equivocal causes, a connection best seen in the rich description of sylphs and sunlight in canto 2. There Pope takes apart the complex visual perception of light on the moving water by using the sylphs almost as individual light particles ("corpuscles" in the Newtonian world):

Some to the Sun their Insect-Wings unfold,
Waft on the Breeze, or sink in Clouds of Gold.
Transparent Forms, too fine for mortal Sight,
Their fluid Bodies half dissolv'd in Light.
Loose to the Wind their airy Garments flew.
Thin glitt'ring Textures of the filmy Dew.

(2.59–64)

These lines deserve the frequent praise "painterly" — Pope was in fact avidly studying painting at the time — not so much because they are "descriptive" as because they self-consciously call attention to the painter's subject — objects in light — and to light itself.

The analysis and new synthesis of perception accomplished so lavishly in this section is related to briefer instances of the analysis of concepts. We have already seen the sylphs embody two such fanciful "deconstructions" (and immediate reconstructions): what *seems* "Honour" or "Levity" to mortal conceptualization is actually sylphic contrivance, just as what seems Betty's labor at Belinda's toilette is really sylph power. A similar but more complex moment occurs just as the descriptive passage quoted above has set sail:

Soft o'er the Shrouds Ariel Whispers breathe,
That seem'd but *Zephyrs* to the Train beneath.

(2.57–58)

The mortals who think they have the right name for what they think they are experiencing are wrong both perceptually and conceptually. The joke is complex because (a) it suggests (not "seriously," of course, but then . . .) that a revived animism may come closer to doing justice to the aesthetic experience of a fine day than does a list of the day's meteorological ingredients, and (b) it allows Pope to call attention to the composition of this poetic scene as he is assembling its parts.

Pope uses the sylphs, in other words, to show how beautiful parts may be brought together as even more beautiful wholes. The mysterious attraction of unity is contemplated only half satirically as Belinda composes herself before the mirror. The face that she admires there may be her own, but it is essentially the same image Pope had used a few years earlier for the power of art:

'Tis not a *Lip*, or *Eye*, we Beauty call,
But the joint Force and full *Result* of *all*.
(*Essay on Criticism* 245–46)

The sylphs make it easier for Pope to write a narrative poem that contains not only beautiful objects but an analysis of beauty. By casting them as the agents of beauty that otherwise "seems" worldly, Pope deliberately lets the "seems" show in the poem. This function, then, is a fourth way in which the sylphs help make the poetry happen in the finished *Rape of the Lock*: they embody a metapoetic current of meaning that opens the process of aesthetic transformation to the reader and allows the work to become in large part a poem about poetry. Any mock-epic will of course display its own artistry somewhat self-consciously — and even the first version of this poem did so — simply by calling attention to its relation to other works of art. But the final, sylph-inhabited version of this poem goes beyond studied allusion to the study of illusion.

All four of these changes in the atmosphere of *The Rape of the Lock* tend to make it more a poem about beauty than an exposé of Beautiful People. By bringing magnification and extreme attention to all its objects, by complicating sarcasm and mock-heroic hyperbole into irony and equivocation, by providing a visual vocabulary for analyzing experience, and by deepening the poem's initial parody into metapoesis, the sylphs change *The Rape of the Lock* radically. They do not exactly steal the show, but they *show* the show.

This partial account of the sylphs' role has said nothing of satire and little about mock-epic, simply because it seems to me that students are usually too ready to affix such labels to any feature of *The Rape of the Lock* without looking further. Until recently, I did not regularly assign both versions of the poem to undergraduates. When I would tell students that it was first published without the sylphs and then ask why they thought Pope might have added them, invariably several would reply that the sylphs "increase the satire" and "make the whole thing more of a mock-epic." I would then usually find myself trying to complicate some of these stock responses by pointing out that the poem might be neater as a mock-epic with a few gods and goddesses than with all the diminutive creatures Pope came to imagine or that one could as easily argue that the sylphs make the human actors seem less responsible for their actions and thus less culpable. Having students make the comparison themselves leads at once to a more complex discussion of the poem and of poetry.

Neither this nor any other strategy I know, however, rids one of the perennial feeling of being a prosaic bull in a poetic china shop. But that sense of one's predicament as a reader is perhaps valuable as a sylph-made and more self-conscious version of the situation of the poem's unwitting "mortals."

NOTES

[1]Irony is a notoriously difficult term. In distinguishing it from sarcasm I rely on the relatively simple idea that sarcasm requires only two people, irony three. The

third party to an ironic statement need not be actually present, or even actual; but it is possible to imagine someone who wouldn't get the remark, which does not usually happen with sarcastic inversions.

[2]The problem, roughly, is how one physical body could affect another without touching it either directly or indirectly, through intervening matter; there was some speculation that gravity, for example, operated through a "subtle medium" of "aether." One might regard Pope's "Aerial Kind," some of whom dwell in the "Fields of purest AEther" (2.76–77), as connecting as well as insulating the poem's larger bodies.

Reading the *Rape* and *To a Lady* with Texts by Swift, Wortley Montagu, and Yearsley

Donna Landry

How does one teach Pope while questioning the canon? Would it not be preferable to forget him and substitute women and working-class writers in the study of eighteenth-century poetry? Because questioning the canon seems to require understanding something of the processes of canon formation, rather than simply replacing one canon with another, I think we should continue to teach Pope, whose *Rape of the Lock* remains the most highly canonical poem of the eighteenth century. One way we might teach him would be to read the *Rape* alongside *Epistle to a Lady*, Swift's "The Lady's Dressing Room," Mary Wortley Montagu's "The Reasons That Induc'd Dr. S[wift] to write a Poem call'd the Lady's Dressing Room" and "P[ope] to Bolingbroke," and Ann Yearsley's "Written on a Visit." I have often taught some combination of these poems as supplementary texts in a survey of English literature before 1800 based on volume 1 of the *Norton Anthology*.

Such a configuration establishes that Pope's poetry should be seen relationally, as socially embedded in a matrix of discourses. That Pope was interested in the "woman question" seems undeniable when we read the *Rape* and *To a Lady*. That his reworking of gender ideology took different forms from his friend Swift's is instructive. The fact that both Pope and Swift could be read as misogynist by an eighteenth-century contemporary, as Wortley Montagu's poems demonstrate, is significant but not definitive. Yearsley's homage to Pope suggests a possible countertradition of reception of his work by women writers. Investigating such contradictory evidence is important if we are to ground our feminism or revisionism historically, in the potential differences from, as well as continuities with, the present represented by texts of the past. Among the eighteenth-century versions of Pope in circulation we can identify at least two that suggest how widely different views of a writer could be: Pope the misogynist and condescending satirist of women and Pope the writer of ravishing verse some women writers wished to imitate.

Why is the *Rape* such a supremely canonical poem? There are many ways to answer this question, but one way is to suggest that canonicity depends on a text's particularly powerful figuring of what scholars have identified as representative values, representative of their period and also representative of great literature, which supposedly transcends its period. The values exemplified by the *Rape* might be categorized as follows:

1. The poem is ingenious in conception, complex in structure, and rich in its use of rhetorical figures and tropes.

2. The poem displays "neoclassical" preoccupations in its dependence on the epic; it is learned in its allusions but playful in its tone, embodying the gentlemanly ideal of "learning lightly worn."

3. In its governing structure and emphasis, the poem appears to subordinate political and social commentary to a psychosexual plot.

4. In this "heroi*comical*" poem, the fun is had at a woman's expense.

When the time has come to talk about Pope, I write this scheme on the board, drawing attention to its polemical tone, admitting that I am trying to be provocatively critical of the institution of literary studies within which we are working together. By this point in the course (Pope appearing three-quarters of the way through a syllabus that runs from Chaucer to the eighteenth century), students are used to preparing answers to discussion questions, so this time I ask them to make up their own about the *Rape*. What strike them as the most interesting and important questions to ask about each canto?

Pursuing these questions in discussion, we inevitably end up looking at those formal qualities familiar to readers who first read Pope through the lens of the "old" New Criticism. Chiasmus, zeugma, and periphrasis; parallelism and antithesis; the difference between "mock-heroic" or "mock-epic" and "heroicomical" and whether the target of satire seems more often to be epic conventions or eighteenth-century social life; how Clarissa's speech might be ironized by her role in the poem as Belinda's rival: each of these features contributes toward the poem's aesthetic complexity and rhetorical effectiveness. We also notice certain moments that open the text onto its cultural and political contexts (Belinda's dressing table as a repository of imperial commodities [Landa]; the connection between predatory femininity and the figuring of women as the chief consumers of the wealth of empire [Brown, *Pope* 8–28]; the question of English Catholic families and the marriage market [Rumbold 57–67]; the possibility of a Jacobite subtext or code in which "[t]he conqu'ring Force of unresisted Steel" [3.178] signals a buried idiom of resistance to the Whig conception of 1688 as securing British liberties, substituting for it the Jacobite reading of William III's accession as an act of conquest [Erskine-Hill, "Literature"]).

If the formal qualities illustrate the first two values of ingenious complexity and gentlemanly erudition, the politically inflected cultural contexts of imperialism and increasingly fixed gender ideology lay the groundwork for the second two values. All four kinds of value reinforce one another; the poem's aesthetic appeal is crucial to its ideological persuasiveness. Through reducing and sexualizing all power differences, a certain political mystification is produced: class largely disappears from the poem, and the misogynist tendency to blame a female for the presence of conflict comes to seem so "natural" that no one notices it as misogynist any more. The almost parenthetical passage about business as usual at the Exchange and about "Wretches" hanging "that Jury-men may Dine" (3.19–23) suggests a suppressed social narrative — about class conflict — quite different from the one we are given about "the war between the sexes." What if a number of Pope's readers took a covert, coterie, Jacobitical pleasure in recognizing the plot of the rape as "really about" William III's conquest of Britain in 1688? What might it mean that we have lost that dimension of the poem but not the gendered dimension, in which anatomical (or is it social?) difference "means" antagonism?

Especially if there is skepticism regarding the final point about the fun being had at a woman's expense, we look at Pope's letter to Arabella Fermor. Its sublime condescension regarding a projected female readership incapable of understanding what it reads but flattered by being represented at all usually leads effectively into discussing *Epistle to a Lady*, another poem addressed to a woman but at best equivocally complimentary. We observe the curious similarities between Clarissa's speech in the *Rape* (5.9–34) and the terms in which Martha Blount is praised in *To a Lady* (249–92). We discuss the gap between these terms of praise and Martha Blount's own circumstances, the seeming impossibility of offering a single woman as exemplary of femininity in this period, the need to provide her with a fictional husband and children, the ambiguity of "softer Man" as a name for "woman" (Pollak, *Poetics* 108–17) in a text in which even a woman says, "Most Women have no Characters at all" (2). We notice how the satire builds in intensity as we go higher up the social scale until we get to the queen herself (181–90), a different queen from Anne taking counsel and tea at Hampton Court, a "foreign," Hanoverian queen. The more power a woman has, the more Pope's rhetoric condemns her as unnatural and absurd; Caroline's foreignness adds xenophobic fuel to this fire. A single woman on a tight budget, however, especially if she is Catholic, fond of Pope, and critical of other women, is worthy of his poetic memorialization as compensation for the social power she lacks.

To clarify that gender ideology is culturally inescapable and that many of Pope's assumptions were shared by his contemporaries, we now turn to Swift, or rather return to him, since *Gulliver's Travels* preceded Pope on the syllabus. To the preoccupation with perspectives, spectacles (as instruments that enable one to see more and as shields against threatening possibilities), the voyaging mentality of the imperial subject and its connections with the scopic drive, and the relation of all these to the representation of grotesque female bodies in *Gulliver*, we can add Strephon's voyaging voyeurism in Celia's dressing room. The colonialist inventory of bodily functions and effluvia compiled by Strephon comes to seem grotesque because of the gap between the body's corporeality and the conventions by which the body has traditionally been represented. Whether this parody of the *blazon*, or anatomy of the beloved's attributes, is dominantly a critique of the philosophical tendency to glorify the mind at the expense of the body while representing women obsessively as if they had only bodies, as Ellen

Pollak suggests (*Poetics* 165), or dominantly a misogynist attack on female bodies and their dependence on mercantilist consumption, with the possibility of misogyny here being crucial to an antiimperialist critique, as Laura Brown argues ("Reading"), is textually undecidable. It is a matter for strategic reading, a case that foregrounds the multiple possibilities excluded, in historically specific, overdetermined ways, by every reading in the interests of producing *a* reading.

At this point the question of *women* readers presses (Modleski 135), and it seems to me to require a historical answer. In Wortley Montagu's satiric responses to Swift's and Pope's poetry, we have evidence of their both having been read as misogynists in their own time. Since this evidence exists, and since Wortley Montagu's poems powerfully exemplify what gendered table turning an upper-class woman poet was capable of, I think that, strategically speaking, reading Wortley Montagu has now become as indispensable to "reading" Pope as reading "Pope."

In "The Reasons" we are told that Swift wrote "The Lady's Dressing Room" because he was fed up after being defeated by his own performance anxiety on a visit to a prostitute:

> The Reverend Lover with surprise
> Peeps in her Bubbys, and her Eyes,
> And kisses both, and trys— and trys.
> The Evening in this Hellish Play,
> Beside his Guineas thrown away,
> Provok'd the Preist to that degree
> He swore, the Fault is not [in] me.
> Your damn'd Close stool so near my Nose,
> Your Dirty Smock, and Stinking Toes
> Would make a Hercules as tame
> As any Beau that you can name.   (63–73)

Turning the Swiftian rhythms and deflatingly comic rhymes back on their creator is a standard parodic technique, but Wortley Montagu represents the prostitute as able to defend herself in true Swiftian style. This character, parodying Swift's Celia, who so ignominiously shits, gets her own back by threatening to use Swift's poem as toilet paper. And Wortley Montagu uses the opportunity to impugn his advocacy of Irish causes as hypocritical; Swift comes across as typically English in his anti-Irish racism, as well as misogynist, penny-pinching, and impotent:

> I'll be reveng'd you saucy Quean
> (Replys the disappointed Dean)
> I'll so describe your dressing room
> The very Irish shall not come.

> She answer'd short, I'm glad you'l write,
> You'l furnish paper when I shite.
>
> (84–89)

With this example of aristocratic disdain for middle-class intellectuals like Swift and Pope in mind, we can read "P[ope] to Bolingbroke" as a gloss on how Pope's friendships with upper-class men seem inseparable from his desire for aristocratic identification (getting above himself, according to Lady Mary) and from a homosocial economy that excludes women (Sedgwick 1–27), though they remain necessary for securing dynastic futures.

Wortley Montagu makes "Pope" write his epistle to Bolingbroke in such a way that his class anxieties and sexual insecurities erupt in a perpetual crisis of masculinity and social identity. His sense of class inferiority is reinforced by his physical disabilities, and both are cast as the source of his writing. Bolingbroke embodies for Pope both the libertine and the aristocratic ideal, though he may be impotent and hypocritical — just like Swift. Women appear as mere counters in libidinal competition and exchange between men. In some lines from an early draft of this poem that were eventually suppressed, Wortley Montagu ventriloquizes Pope as writing:

> 'Tis known to all what Conquests you have gaind
> And I insinuate joys I ne'er obtain'd,
>
> . . . .
> Tell in what raptures our soft hours are spent,
> Tho me deform'd, and You thought impotent.
> And in the Midst of these Heroic strains
> We seek for Mistrisses in dirty Lanes,
> Even there superior, there it often happ'd
> My Lord was pox'd, when I was only clapp'd.
>
> (59–60, 63–68)

Even venereal diseases can distinguish a lord from the son of a linen merchant, it seems. Wortley Montagu's vilification of Pope may owe a great deal to their personal feud, but ideologies of class and gender exceed merely personal boundaries, and I would argue that Wortley Montagu's writing is fueled more by her recognition of the connections between Swift's and Pope's politically ambitious literary ventures, their status as middle-class intellectuals, and their reworking of conventional misogyny, often at upper-class women's expense, than it is by purely personal pique.

By the time Ann Yearsley publishes "Written on a Visit" (see app.) in 1787, Pope, who died in 1744, has become a classic of the national literature, a poetic monument even if his style is no longer fashionable and an inspiration for women poets aspiring to the marketplace. Tourists visit Twickenham's "leafy shades, where Pope in rapture stray'd" (2), looking for inspirational traces. This poem is only one of many by eighteenth-century women poets paying homage to Pope and hoping to be able to "soar, full-pinion'd with the buoyant maid" — Pope's muse — in order to match him in writing ravishingly beautiful verse (Landry 43–55).

Yearsley is the "milkwoman of Bristol," hence her pen name Lactilla, an arch recognition of the plebeian status that polite readers would be bound to read into her poems. We should notice that she feels intoxicating inspiration for a brief moment during her visit: "*Rule*! what art *thou*? Thy limits I disown!" (37), only to return to the fold of "Precept" two stanzas later. Somehow the day trip to Twickenham cannot sustain the writing of the working-class female tourist and poet; Pope's groves remain Pope's groves, and not Lactilla's:

> Farewel, ye groves! and when the friendly moon
> > Tempts each fair sister o'er the vernal green,
> Oh, may each lovely maid reflect how soon
> > Lactilla saw, and sighing left the scene.
> > > > > > (49–52)

The irony of this conclusion is that Yearsley hopes that her poem about failing to imitate Pope will be read by other women writers and remembered. She assumes that subsequent generations of "fair sisters" in search of a muse will be drawn to the scene of Popian inspiration. Yearsley will have achieved something powerful enough to constitute a kind of immortality if those women think of how Lactilla, as well as Pope, once traversed this terrain, if only to abandon it abruptly as inhospitable. This homage to Pope is not unambiguous; Yearsley wishes to stress that she "soon" saw through the Popian mystique as an appropriate model for her own poetic production. Yet her assumption that a female tradition of admirers of Pope's verse continues to exist this late in the century suggests that simply dismissing Pope as misogynist, even with Wortley Montagu as evidence, is an insufficiently nuanced historical response to the question of how Pope was read.

However oddly it may strike us now, both Pope and Swift served as enabling models for women poets throughout the eighteenth century (Landry 43–55, 81–89, 110–19, 249–51; Doody, "Swift"). By the last quarter of the century, when Yearsley was writing, Pope had become one of the most accessible and popular, not fashionable and elitist, poets, available in cheap editions and consequently widely read by an emerging lower-class reading public. When class and gender are both brought to bear on his texts, Pope's misogyny does not disappear, but it becomes complicated by both his contradictory class position (aristocratic identification, middle-class status) and the class identifications and statuses, as well as gender, of his readers.

Thus it seems to me that knowing something about how Pope was read should condition, though not entirely determine, how we read him now. Not forgetting Pope but refiguring him as the intersection of multiple discourses of production and reception in which gender and class are crucial: that is one way of circumventing the potential reductionism of simply substituting one canon for another.

APPENDIX

Written on a Visit
by Ann Yearsley

DELIGHTFUL Twick'nham! may a rustic hail
    Thy leafy shades, where Pope in rapture stray'd,
Clasp young-ey'd Ecstasy amid the vale,
    And soar, full-pinion'd, with the buoyant maid?

Ah! no, I droop! her fav'rite Bard she mourns;
    Yet Twick'nham, shall thy groves assist my song;
For while, with grateful love my bosom burns,
    Soft Zephyr bears the artless strain along.

Through Maro's peaceful haunt with joy I rove:
    Here Emma's spotless lamb forgets to bleat;
Nor heeds her native lawn, or woolly love,
    But gently breathes her thanks at Beauty's feet.

Emblem of whitest Innocence! how blest!
    No cruel mastiff on thy heart shall prey,
Nor sanguine steel e'er rend thy panting breast;
    But life, with happy ease, still glide away.

Far be the hour that must demand thy breath;
    For, ah! that hour shall claim my Emma's tear;
E'en Maro's manly eye shall grace thy death;
    Nor will the pang Lactilla's bosom spare.

But hence, Melpomene! to cells of woe;
    I would not now thy melting languors own:
Here Friendship bids exulting Rapture glow;
    While Sorrow, list'ning, stills her deepest groan.

Protected thus from ev'ry barbed dart,
    Which oft from soul-corroding passion flies,
I own the transport of a blameless heart,
    While on the air the pow'rless fury dies.

Hail! steady Friendship, stubborn in thy plea!
  Most justly so, when Virtue is thy guide:
Beneath your mingled ray my soul is free,
  And native Genius soars with conscious Pride.

See, Maro points the vast, the spacious way,
  Where strong Idea may on Rapture spring:
I mount! — Wild Ardour shall ungovern'd stray;
  Nor dare the mimic pedant clip my wing.

Rule! what art *thou*? Thy limits I disown!
  Can thy weak law the swelling thought confine?
Snatch glowing Transport from her kindred zone,
  And fix her melting on thy frozen line?

As well command the hoary Alps to bear
  The Amaranth, or Phoebus-loving flow'r!
Bid the Behemoth cut the yielding air,
  Or rob the Godhead of creative pow'r!

Yet, Precept! shall thy richest store be mine,
  When soft'ning pleasure would invade my breast;
To thee my struggling spirit shall resign;
  On thy cold bosom will I sink to rest.

Farewel, ye groves! and when the friendly moon
  Tempts each fair sister o'er the vernal green,
Oh, may each lovely maid reflect how soon
  Lactilla saw, and sighing left the scene.

"La Nouvelle *Eloisa*": Pope outside the Period

Anne Williams

Pope specialists praise *Eloisa to Abelard* for its technical virtuosity, its psychological subtlety, and its ingenuity in adapting the heroic epistle tradition. While all these dimensions are indeed admirable, such acclaim ironically slights those qualities Pope's eighteenth-century audience most appreciated — its Gothic, romantic sensibility and the passionate intensity that risks, but never falls into, sentimentality. These are the qualities, however, that still make the poem one of Pope's most teachable outside the context of "the eighteenth century." It seems particularly appropriate to allow this poem about transcending boundaries to ignore some institutional ones.

This essay describes three unconventional contexts in which I have used *Eloisa to Abelard*: a course in the lyric, a course in the later Romantics (Byron, Keats, and Shelley), and an introduction to feminist literary theory. Often my students find Pope's language difficult and are unprepared to appreciate his skill with the heroic couplet. Thus before assigning the poem I spend some time introducing this form, and in the course on lyric poetry (where acquiring a certain amount of technical knowledge is one aim) I have students write ten lines on a subject of their choice in heroic couplets. On assigning the poem, I briefly recount the story of Eloisa and Abelard and also hand out a set of study questions for students to ponder while they read. Sometimes I ask for written answers; more often I tell groups of four or five students that they will be responsible for leading class discussion on a particular question. (Sample questions are included in the appendix.)

Pope as Lyric Poet

Elsewhere I argue that *Eloisa to Abelard* belongs to a tradition of the "greater lyric" that flourished throughout the eighteenth century in ostensibly non-lyric genres (Anne Williams 24–37). Whether or not one agrees that *Eloisa* is such a poem, this proposition offers an opportunity to talk about the concept of genre, the nature of poetic influence, and the function of allusion. Throughout this course I emphasize the importance of recognizing genre as a signal of poetic intention (and hence a dimension of meaning) as well as a context for critical reading.

Having defined Pope's ostensible genre, the "heroic epistle," I first ask students to consider which aspects of the poem this context accounts for and which it does not. (In considering the dramatic monologue, one can use *Eloisa* as a basis for a similar assessment.) By asking this question, I hope to get students to see that Pope follows the "rules" in giving us a historical woman writing a letter to her beloved in a moment of stress; the formula does not, in contrast to some genres (e.g., the sonnet), determine

anything but situation. But while there are no specifically formal require-
ments, the poem's "radical of presentation" (Frye, *Anatomy* 247) is fundamentally lyric; a letter, especially to a lover, demands at least an imitation
of self-expression, pushing the poem toward a lyric mode.

I then ask students to consider the poem's obvious debt to a poem unre-
lated to the heroic epistle, Milton's "Il Penseroso." (We have already discussed
this work, emphasizing the way Milton uses "objective correlatives" — how
he paints the portrait of a mind through its perceptions.) Specific echoes
provide a point of departure. How does Eloisa's view of the "pensive" differ
from Milton's Penseroso? What about her view of "Black Melancholy"? What
is the difference between Milton's "forget thyself to marble" (line 42) and
Pope's "forget my self to stone" (24)? I then ask students to think about the
phenomenological experience implied by the two poems: what is Eloisa's
sense of time, space, matter, and movement in contrast to that of Milton's
speaker? "Il Penseroso" implies that the self is a landscape to be explored.
Eloisa, however, portrays the self as enclosed, a "claustrophobic" space with
dark corridors and troubling secrets from the past. When teaching this course
at the graduate level, I ask students, who have been introduced to Bloom's
theory of poetic influence, to speculate about *Eloisa* as a rewriting of "Il
Penseroso."

Eloisa's concluding fantasy of death has perhaps been more problematic
than any other aspect for critics reading in the context of Pope or of "neoclassical" poetry. From the perspective of the Renaissance love lyric, however, Eloisa's resolution is far from puzzling — it is virtually conventional.
Eloisa has been indulging in the lover's casuistry so familiar in Donne — the
gesture of the speaker in "The Sunne Rising," for example, who declares
(and somehow "realizes") the idea that his love appropriates the entire world.
As in "The Canonization," Eloisa makes herself and Abelard saints of love,
and their tomb in the Paraclete a shrine for pilgrims, who will pray and
be redeemed by the example of their lives. One study question requires
students to look for ways that Eloisa's imagined paradise after death restores
her paradise lost: for instance, Eloisa and Abelard are reunited (though in
the tomb); they also survive in the spirit of other lovers and the sympathetic
poet; the lost communion of soul with soul is restored. In fact, the poem
concludes by affirming the power of Eloisa's imagination to transform and
transcend reality, a faith in the creative capacity of the imagination more
familiar among the Romantics than anywhere else.

Pope as Early Romantic

Reading *Eloisa* as a lyric emphasizes its historical antecedents; using the
poem in a course on the Romantics focuses on the poem's connections with
subsequent tradition. I begin a course in the later Romantics by studying this poem for two reasons: first, it exemplifies the eighteenth-century

"romanticism" and "Gothic" in the diction and meter that critics such as Wordsworth were to reject; second, it offers a revealing context in which to read Byron in particular. As Byron commented, "If you search for passion, where is it to be found stronger than in the Epistle from Eloisa to Abelard?"

The Giaour, for instance, one of the earliest of the "oriental tales," is now generally praised for its formal experimentation. (Byron's "broken tale" forces us to piece together numerous points of view.) But the hero, who has taken refuge from the world in the cloister, has much in common with Eloisa. Not only is he alienated from the people he lives among, but he also dwells primarily in memories of a tragic, forbidden love about which he feels no guilt, only regret at the loss of that love. Fed and torn by passion, like Eloisa, he "want[s] no Paradise, but rest" (*Giaour* 1270). The Giaour's love is the overwhelming, all-consuming value of life; true passion is worth any price.

Like Pope, Byron uses certain poetic devices to suggest the conflict within his protagonist. Byron fully exploits the possibilities of the paradox and the couplet (though his couplets are tetrameter ones). The many affinities between the two poems suggest (surprisingly) that Pope's Eloisa may have been an important model for the Byronic hero, who (like her) is always torn between love and duty, past and present, and whose overwhelming passion for one woman is a redeeming, if tragic, experience. Eloisa and the Byronic hero act in the interest of love, not law; or rather their love *is* their law. This "feminine" side of the Byronic hero may help suggest why Byron's female readers found this character so sensationally appealing.

Critics tend to agree that between 1812 and 1816 Byron's heroes move from being formula characters of popular fiction to increasingly serious representatives of the human condition. "The Prisoner of Chillon" develops Pope's implied concept of the self as an inescapable, fatal prison. Eloisa and the prisoner actually have many points in common; it is interesting to observe, however, that the space identified with the enclosed woman is one of erotic turmoil; the male imprisoned self is characterized by an absence of emotional ties (though he refrains from killing mice and spiders). And though the poem implies that relationships might provide a saving grace, the prisoner is bereft of them. Finally, Byron's debt to *Eloisa* has its satiric, ironic dimension. As Lawrence Lipking points out (44–47), Donna Julia's letter of farewell to Don Juan at the end of canto 1 (192–98) is a comic allusion to Eloisa's passionate letter. Since allusiveness is so important in Byron's satire, I have found that giving students one context that the poem plays against helps them appreciate its wit and complexity—a dimension otherwise absent from their reading.

Pope as Female Impersonator

Byron's use of *Eloisa to Abelard* suggests that the poem exemplified "feminine sensibility" for him. But like Samuel Richardson's Pamela or Clarissa,

Eloisa may be more interesting as a male fantasy of the female than as a realistic portrait. What appears convincingly "feminine," feminist criticism emphasizes, is less a reflection of "reality" than a cultural artifact. In different ways, Peggy Kamuf, Ellen Pollak (*Poetics*), and Ruth Salvaggio demonstrate this notion at work in eighteenth-century literature. Thus *Eloisa to Abelard* offers a particularly interesting opportunity to examine such cultural assumptions, since it is an utterly conventional exercise (in adapting the heroic epistle Pope chose a genre that demands the creation of a convincing woman) and an utterly successful one (generations have felt that he succeeded).

Thus I have also taught *Eloisa to Abelard* in an undergraduate course on feminist literary theory. I begin by spending about a third of the term on the concept of gender as a cultural construct and on an examination of the ways that unconscious assumptions about male and female shape the plot, imagery, and other aspects of men's stories about women in the Western tradition. After looking at some crucial texts that establish or manifest gender roles (such as the story of the Fall in Genesis) and at Aristotle's paradigm from *Metaphysics* A3, I present Pope's text as a poetic act of "female impersonation." That is, since Eloisa is an "imitation" of "womanliness," what do her character and behavior imply about conscious (and unconscious) conceptions of the "female"? (Following the Pythagoreans, Aristotle suggested that reality could be divided into ten pairs of opposites: male/female, limit/unlimited, odd/even, one/plurality, right/left, square/oblong, at rest/moving, straight/curved, light/darkness, good/evil [Maclean 13].)

Early in the course I introduce my students to the idea discussed by French theorists Luce Irigaray and Hélène Cixous that seeing the world in pairs of binary opposites is a patriarchal habit of mind. I first ask them to point out some of the ways that Pope organizes the poem around binary principles. Such elements include the very nature of Eloisa's conflict as Pope imagines it — "the struggle of nature and grace, virtue and passion" — and even the use of the heroic couplet. Thus one may also see the poem's conclusion as Eloisa's rejection of this way of thinking; her ultimate comforting fantasy is not a choice of one or the other alternative; it entails both and neither: she both is and is not reunited with Abelard, and so on.

Then I ask students to look for ways in which the imagery of the poem, as well as Eloisa's behavior, conforms to cultural expectations about the "female" as exemplified by Aristotle's paradigm, the "line of evil" (as the list headed by the terms *female, dark,* etc., was called). Such an analysis reveals that the poem associates Eloisa with darkness, passion, irrationality, a set of disordered priorities — "just like a woman," she is more concerned with the personal and concrete than with the abstract, with this world more than the next, with love more than law. Pope portrays her behavior as "hysterical" in a sense — dominated by dreams and fantasies. What he seems to find most interesting about his heroine is her range and depth of emotion, her capacity to suffer, her role as victim of her own "natural," "feminine" sensibility.

Finally, I ask students to consider a hypothesis suggested by various readers through the centuries: that these letters are forgeries — written not by Héloïse but by a man, perhaps by Abelard himself. I ask for intuitive reactions to this proposition, which invites the introduction of a second main theme I am concerned with in this course: reader response. Do elements in this portrait of Eloisa seem characteristic more of a man's fantasy of a woman than of a woman herself? On the one hand, Pope defines his heroine as a woman driven by love and worshiping a man (the historical Eloisa led the busy life of a highly successful abbess); at the same time, however, she is an extremely strong, assertive character and fascinating in those very qualities that are most feminine and "other" in relation to the patriarchal standards she subverts.

Reading *Eloisa to Abelard* from new perspectives not only offers fresh insight into the poem itself but also introduces students to a superb poet they may have avoided out of the vague prejudice that Pope is "hard" or "boring." Most important, it may provide an experience of great poetry's power to communicate human experience, exemplifying Eloisa's credo that words "live, they speak, they breathe what love inspires, / Warm from the soul, and faithful to its fires" (53–54).

APPENDIX

Study Questions on Eloisa to Abelard

1. General questions designed to foster a close reading of the text before class (I usually include these, no matter what the specific class):
   a. Think of as many reasons as you can why the heroic couplet is a particularly appropriate form for this poem. (e.g., How does it reflect Eloisa's basic dilemma?)
   b. Choose one couplet in the poem that seems to you particularly to exemplify Pope's skill in transcending the limits of this highly restrictive form. Be prepared to explain your choice to the class.
   c. Find three different levels of irony in the poem and be ready to talk about them. Possibilities include verbal irony, irony of situation, dramatic irony, cosmic irony.
2. Questions relevant to genre, especially the lyric.
   a. What does Eloisa have in common with the speaker of "Il Penseroso"? How is she different? (Consider the poems' mood, tone, relative emphasis on sense perception, feeling, and fantasy.)
   b. Compare and contrast the structures of the two poems.
   c. What attitudes and ideas does Eloisa share with the speaker of "The Sunne Rising"?
   d. Some critics have been concerned with the "heretical" or "blasphemous" nature of Eloisa's attachment to Abelard. Explain how her

attitude is conventional in terms of Petrarchan conceits. (Consider Donne's "The Canonization" and "The Relique.")

    e. List as many ways as you can in which the state Eloisa imagines for herself after death fulfills her implicit standards of "paradise."

3. Questions related to Pope as Early Romantic.
    a. How does Pope use setting to create a psychological portrait?
    b. What does Byron's Giaour have in common with Eloisa? (Consider his history, current situation, character.)
    c. How does Eloisa foreshadow the values of the Byronic hero?
    d. Compare the notion of selfhood implicit in *Eloisa* with that in *The Prisoner of Chillon*.
    e. How is our reading of Donna Julia's letter of renunciation (*Don Juan* 1.192–98) enriched by a knowledge of *Eloisa*? Comment on the satirical function of the allusion.

4. Questions related to feminist literary theory:
    a. The opening lines suggest that Eloisa's psychological condition is virtually identified with her convent. What might one infer about the conditions of the "female" interior?
    b. Find as many aspects as possible in which Eloisa manifests characteristics of "the line of evil" in the Aristotelian paradigm. (Consider the setting of the poem as well.)
    c. To what extent do the opposing pairs "nature and grace, virtue and passion" conform to the culturally "male" and "female"?
    d. How might the resolution of the poem subvert patriarchal structures? (Consider theme, setting, etc.)
    e. Some have argued that the famous letters on which Pope based his poem were in fact written by Abelard (or some other man). What is your intuitive response to this hypothesis? Does this poem seem to you to show an authentically feminine sensibility (versified by Pope) or a male fantasy of suffering womanhood? Why or why not?
    f. According to this poem, what do women want?

Timon's Villa Revisited: Pope's Architectural Criticism in the *Epistle to Burlington*

Douglas Murray

Alexander Pope resolutely grounds his poetry in the world of objects, of "mutton" and "chicks" (*Horace, Satire* 2.2.144), of "Puffs, Powders, Patches, Bibles, Billet-doux" (*Rape* 1.138). Matthew Arnold, who expected a certain vagueness and cloudiness in verse, infamously concluded that such passages could not be called poetry. Our students have different expectations: they have perhaps become accustomed to the specificity of modern poetry, to red wheelbarrows, white flannel trousers, peaches, carbuncles, and jars in Tennessee; they have certainly become adept at reading the intensely visual imagery of MTV. They have been primed to use their eyes, and so had Pope.

Many of the visual images in Pope's verse derive from the arts. In the *Epistle to a Lady*, Pope conducts his readers through a portrait gallery, and *The Rape of the Lock* alone provides a nearly comprehensive survey of the decorative arts in early eighteenth-century England. Such attention to the visual arts is hardly surprising since Pope, in his mid-twenties, spent a year or so in the London studio of the minor portraitist Charles Jervas, developing his skill in sketching and painting (Mack, *Life* 226–30). He numbered among his friends many of the artistic figures of his day, for example, the portraitist Godfrey Kneller and the architects James Gibbs and William Kent. Pope employed Gibbs and Kent when he had amassed enough money to improve his villa at Twickenham (Mack, *Garden* 16, 283). Fortunately, the modern teacher of Pope can turn to Morris Brownell's excellent and comprehensive *Alexander Pope and the Arts of Georgian England*, which addresses relations between Pope and the architecture, sculpture, painting, decorative arts, landscape gardening, and music of his time.

Of course, Pope's poetry is not great only because it recalls the English artistic heritage. It is great because of the thematic, ideological implications of Pope's visual imagery. To assist students in unraveling such implications, I offer the following commentary on one of Pope's finest poems about the arts.

Pope's *Epistle to Burlington* (1731), the fourth of the *Moral Essays*, is too often read simply as a document in the history of the English country house. Of course, the poem does ground itself in art history, but it is also an exercise in symbol making and symbol reading, exemplifying how Pope's nimble mind unites worlds, here the worlds of architecture and politics. I wish to argue that this poem offers riches to undergraduate readers, to those enrolled in surveys either of English literature or of eighteenth-century literature. To teach the poem, I suggest beginning in art history, using books and slides to illustrate the two estates described in the poem, Timon's villa and Burlington's Chiswick. Then readers should consider the ways of life and the ideologies that the structures in the poem suggest. By this time, students become adept in the interpretation of structures, a skill that I invite them to practice in their own time and place.

Two builders preside over the poem. At the beginning and the conclusion of the *Epistle* (23–64, 177–204), Pope praises Richard Boyle, the earl of Burlington (1695–1753), who was building his villa at Chiswick, just east of London, at the time Pope was writing the *Epistle*. The other builder is the fictional Timon (99–176), who in the poem has built a luxurious but tasteless "Villa" (99), in reality a great country house or palace. It is essential to use photographs and, preferably, slides to illustrate the real and fictional estates. With the use of magnifying lenses and a light board, it is possible to make fine slides from books and magazines. Consult art and photography departments or local photography stores for assistance. Even though printed photographs are under copyright, slides may be legally made for instructional purposes. The notes to this article indicate where clear photographs and useful floor plans can be found.

It is also essential to teach architectural and gardening terminology. I provide a handout that lists and defines some of the terms used in the poem: "Pilaster" (33), a slice of a column, ornamenting a wall; "rustic" (34), the rough stone facing on the ground story of a building; "Front" (34), a facade; "Quincunx" (80), a group of five trees forming a square, one at each corner, one in the middle; "Espaliers" (80), trees trained to grow on walls; "Parterres" (87), flat, geometric arrangements of closely cropped plants; "Alleys" (97), walks or roads formed by trees on both sides; "Down" (106), expansive grassland; and topiary (119–20), shrubs pruned to geometric or other artificial shapes.

The first of the poem's builders is the earl of Burlington, the primary English disciple of and publicist for the Italian Renaissance architect Andrea Palladio (1508–80). Hence, illustration of Pope's ideal in the poem must introduce not only Chiswick House but also the villas of Palladio in the Veneto, that portion of the northern Italian mainland controlled by Venice. Instructors should certainly show students the Villa Rotunda, Palladio's most influential and emulated domestic design and the model for Burlington's Chiswick. As other pertinent examples of Palladian-influenced villas, the instructor might illustrate Thomas Jefferson's Monticello and Pope's own house at Twickenham, whose modest size and symmetry proclaim its architectural allegiances.[1]

Palladian villas are comfortable and certainly large enough for a reasonable establishment, but not particularly pretentious or showy. As the art historian John Summerson writes, the classical and Palladian villa's "accommodation is necessarily modest and its character therefore more in the nature of a retreat than an advertisement of its owner's standing or ability to entertain" (551–52). The villa is surrounded by practical farm buildings — stables

and the like — reminders that the villas were administrative centers for working farms. In fact, Venetian authorities encouraged the wealthy citizens of
Palladio's time to construct rural estates with the expectation that villa farms
would produce food for the Venetian republic. The Palladian villa achieves
dignity through proportion and organization rather than through expensive
building materials; construction budgets were amazingly low, the villas
generally being built of local brick or stucco, sometimes with lines drawn
on facades to suggest stone. Other features of the villas include moderate
size, porticos, symmetry, clear articulation or separation of levels, and clever
and harmonious combination of shapes (often rectangles and ovals). A
favorite English manifestation is the so-called Palladian window — in three
parts, with an arched central section.

One facet of Palladianism that the instructor must emphasize is the historical, re-creative component. Palladio saw himself engaged in that historical project dear to the Renaissance and Enlightenment: imitating and
updating the achievements of the classical world. Specifically, the owners
and builders of Palladian villas believed that they were, in their own times,
recapitulating the unpretentious but capacious life that Horace celebrates.
Horace's Sabine farm provided the poet and his readers with an image of
plain living and high thinking, of the unselfish and responsible use of wealth
(*Satire* 2.2; *Epistle* 1.3, 4, 5, 7, 14). Pope honors and underlines the Roman
lineage of Palladianism in the subtitle of his poem: *Occasion'd by his*
[Burlington's] *Publishing Palladio's Designs of the Baths, Arches, Theatres,*
&c., of Ancient Rome.

Pope's message in the *Epistle* is more than merely the endorsement of
a single style. I hesitate to turn a poem bristling with images into a few
guidelines, but I see Pope providing three chief bits of advice to builders.
First, don't construct bigger houses than owners can use, for use alone justifies expense. As Pope writes in the first lines of the *Epistle*, physical possessions should be not hoarded and cataloged but rather enjoyed and tasted
(1–12). Burlington's achievement, Pope writes, was to show that Roman
buildings were "glorious, not profuse, / And pompous buildings once were
things of Use" (23–24). Second, Pope warns builders against thinking they
are being classical just because they have copied a few elements of Palladian
design (I am reminded of Samuel Johnson's comment in *Rasselas* that "No
man was ever great by imitation"). Pope makes considerable fun of those
who, mindless of implication, "Load" a church with "Theatric state" (29)
or who hang noble ornaments on a "patch'd dog-hole" (31–32). The third
and most memorable component of Pope's advice is this: in all planning
and building, "Consult the Genius of the Place" (57). Here Pope revives
the Roman belief in local deities — guardians of particular places, whose
wishes must be consulted before any building project proceeds. He tells
builders to cooperate with surroundings, not to attempt to surmount or over-
power them. Some readers would limit Pope's advice to the visual and the

aesthetic, but references to weather (35–36, 111–12) suggest that the poet was concerned with all the givens of a site. In nonmythological language, Pope advises builders to take full recognition of climatic, horticultural, and topographical realities. Do not, Pope implies, adopt Palladian features if they are inappropriate to the English climate. Thus Pope makes fun of those who follow designs that might provide comfort enough in sunny Italy but not in drafty England: such builders "call the winds thro' long Arcades to roar, / Proud to catch cold at a Venetian door" (35–36).

There was no single model for the poem's deficient estate, Timon's villa. As James R. Aubrey argues, "Timon" is best understood as a composite figure. But illustrating Timon's tasteless villa is easy. Simply find photographs of large eighteenth-century estates in which the owner overbuilds and overgilds and does not take into proper consideration the givens of the property. When I teach the *Epistle to Burlington*, I illustrate and discuss five country houses. Each is a possible source for Timon's villa and illustrates something about its impudent tastelessness. What follows is not an exhaustive list; I encourage other travelers and researchers to discuss other estates.

1. Houghton, built by Robert Walpole. This structure, with its symmetry and Palladian windows, is consciously and stylishly Palladian.[2] But it misses the essence of the "villa," for its scale is vast and it was not built to enable its owner to experience rural contentment and practice hospitality. Rather, it was a house designed to consolidate its owner's power. Walpole spent only a few months each year there, and he entertained lavishly, not to cement friendships but to impress political allies and cement political relationships. We are reminded of Timon in Pope's poem, who in greeting his guests "advances with majestic mien, / Smit with the mighty pleasure, to be seen" (127–28).

Houghton provides a superb example of not consulting the genius of the place. Walpole's estate lies in flat and windy Norfolk, inhospitable even by English standards. As Lord Hervey wrote to the Prince of Wales in 1731, Houghton had "no water: absolutely none for ornament and all that is necessary for use forced up by art" (Hervey 70–71). Ignoring the site's realities, Walpole planted forests, dug out pools — which would not stay full during the dry summers — and tore down an old village to enlarge the park (Mack, *Life* 207). Thus, Houghton well manifests Timon's ostentatious "Impudence of wealth" (*Horace, Satire* 2.2, 117).

2. Blenheim, seat of John Churchill, the first duke of Marlborough. Of all the English country houses, this is perhaps the easiest and, for the purposes of teaching the *Epistle*, the most profitable to illustrate.[3] Teaching Blenheim also provides a rationale to introduce students to John Vanbrugh (1664–1726), its architect and a dramatist and courtier. Pope knew Blenheim Palace well. He visited it in 1717 and called it "a great *Quarry of Stones above ground*" (*Correspondence* 1:432), a phrase recalled in the *Epistle*: "Lo,

what huge heaps of littleness around! / The whole, a labour'd Quarry above ground" (109–10). Blenheim is, of course, a palace in the country, not a villa at all. It was by far the most expensive house of its era, costing about £300,000, with the government providing £240,000 (Brownell 380): hence the appropriateness of Pope's line, "What sums are thrown away!" (100). Blenheim well exemplifies the gargantuan scale of Timon's structure: "his building is a Town, / His pond an Ocean, his parterre a Down" (105–06). Of all English houses, Blenheim most resembles a town, as its floor plans demonstrate (Girouard 160). The grounds used to include an immense parterre, at 2,500 by 2,200 feet (Brownell 382) among the largest in Europe, justifying Pope's use of the word "Down" (106). A generation after Pope, when new styles of natural gardening had become fashionable, the gigantic parterre was seeded into an immense lawn by the famed gardener Capability Brown. Some idea of the original complexity of Blenheim's parterres can be glimpsed in the "Italian Garden" on the West Front, replanted in the early twentieth century in the early eighteenth-century style that Pope satirizes (N. Nicolson 216 and overleaf).

The Brobdingnagian scale of the house and garden at Blenheim occasionally led to comic effects, as when Vanbrugh's great bridge, suited for multiple Roman legions, was made to cross a tiny rivulet downhill from the house. Later, Capability Brown dammed the stream and gave the bridge a river worthy of traversing; the nickname "Capability" clearly suggests Brown's talent for consulting — or at least finessing — the geniuses of places.

3. Chatsworth, home of the duke of Devonshire. The chapel there is the work of, among others, Antonio Verrio and Louis Laguerre (Aubrey, "Timon's Villa" 340–41) and thus recalls Timon's place of private worship:

> On painted Ceilings you devoutly stare,
> Where sprawl the Saints of Verrio or Laguerre,
> On gilded clouds in fair expansion lie,
> And bring all Paradise before your eye.
> (145–48)[4]

4. Burlington's own Chiswick House. It is possible to detect some unexpected satire of the poem's dedicatee. My argument runs as follows. Chiswick House closely resembles Palladio's Villa Rotunda, the significant difference being locale. Vicenza, with only 87 rainy days a year and an average daily high temperature of 63° F. (17.3° C.), contrasts with wet, overcast Chiswick, receiving rain 164 days a year, with an average daily high of 57.5° F. (14.2° C.) (*National Geographic Atlas* 236–37). One might argue that, in simply relocating a design made for one climate in another, Burlington has not consulted the genius of the place. It used to be argued that this meteorological consideration was unimportant, for scholars believed Chiswick House

to be not a structure for daily use but rather a pavilion for entertaining, a mere appendage to an older structure, now destroyed. But T. S. Rosomon has learned that, while the older portion housed at least seven principal rooms as well as ample servants' quarters, the Palladian portion contained two well-organized suites of apartments, one a study and dressing suite for Lord Burlington, the other a three-roomed bed- and dressing-room suite for Lady Burlington (Rosomon 677, 667–75). Thus, the Palladian portion was put to domestic use. Contemporary accounts and inventories indicate that this Palladian wing was used daily through the eighteenth century, even during winter, with we know not what inconvenience (664). The Red Closet, in which the Earl kept his desk and presumably transacted much business, lacked a fireplace and was lit by only one window, and that under the portico. To be sure, proud homeowners can put up with inconveniences, and Lord Burlington probably thought Palladian splendor ample compensation for a little English chill, just as Pope must have simultaneously found solace, inspiration, and dampness as he sat writing in his famous grotto, built into a clammy Thames riverbank a few miles from Chiswick. Perhaps both men, like Timon, were proud of colds caught in tasteful surroundings (35–36). But in their sager moments, Burlington and Pope must have recognized that they themselves had not always consulted the genius of their places.

5. Cannons, home of James Brydges, the duke of Chandos. Less than ten days after the publication of the poem, spoken and printed gossip had suggested the original of Timon to be Brydges. Pope himself denied in conversation, correspondence, and print that he intended the duke of Chandos, whom he personally liked, as Timon (Mack, *Life* 498–99). Although in the poem Pope probably never writes specifically of Chandos, some of the duke's immense expenditure did alert the poet to wastefulness in general; for example, a thousand window sashes at Cannons were gilded (Dunlop 1950). This estate is, alas, the most difficult to illustrate since it was pulled down within thirty-five years of its construction in 1715.[5]

After students have visualized Timon's and Burlington's houses, Pope would not want them to stop thinking about his poem, which concerns more than mere "taste" and architecture. In Pope's cultural heritage, architectural images often suggest ways of thinking and of being. The Bible depicts the Kingdom of God as a structure with Christ as "cornerstone" (1 Pet. 2.6–7; Eph. 2.20–22); heaven itself is "house" of "many mansions" (John 14.2); believers are enjoined to envision themselves as "temples" (1 Cor. 3.16; 6.19) and as houses "not made with hands" (2 Cor. 5.1). Such familiar metaphors encouraged George Herbert to allegorize the structural components of the English parish church in *The Temple* (1634). The same metaphors suggested Dryden's comparison, in *Absalom and Achitophel* (1681), between the English state and a building where

> If ancient Fabricks nod, and threat to fall,
> To Patch the Flaws, and Buttress up the Wall,
> Thus far 'tis Duty. . . .
> To change Foundations, cast the Frame anew
> Is work for Rebels who base Ends pursue.
>
> (801–06)

Seventeenth-century country-house poems, such as Ben Jonson's "To Penshurst" (1616), often had politicized structures, as Alastair Fowler argues.

Thus, Pope's readers would have expected more than mere architectural commentary, and Pope does not disappoint. In criticizing Timon's villa, he suggests larger implications, specifically criticism of the Whig oligarchy of the mid-century: Pope condemns the wastefulness of the Whigs, their proud attitude that they controlled, rather than cooperated with, the countryside, and their ignorant notion that by simply copying a few Palladian details they had constructed a Palladian villa. And, of course, Pope condemns a nation ruled by an *elite* so wasteful, proud, and essentially ignorant. But Pope is doing even more in *Epistle to Burlington*: the large stately home built by Timon becomes Pope's symbol of Britain. The early eighteenth century saw the British Empire come into being, an empire based on foreign expansion, foreign domination, foreign trade, and a failure to use creatively the English countryside and the English peasantry. Both the immense new stately homes and the new British empire were gaudy, pretentious, proud, out of proportion with the surrounding countryside, and too large, too unwieldy (in the long run) to be kept going.

If Timon's villa is Pope's symbol for the new order, the Palladian villa becomes his symbol for an alternative England, a road not taken. The country, Pope implies, should have constructed itself just as good architects might construct Palladian villas in England. The nation should consult ancient models, ultimately deriving from republican Rome, mediated through the Renaissance. When appropriate, it should modify them to fit local conditions. Finally, it should build for use, not for status.

Pope's poem — simultaneously architectural and ideological — provides impetus for students to read their own surroundings. And it suggests many splendid essay topics for late-twentieth-century students. What, for example, do modern bank buildings wish to suggest about modern banking practices? Why all the glass? Why the open work spaces? What virtues are suggested and promoted by the typical American suburb? Students can also turn their attention to their campuses. Does their college or university English building, for example, suggest anything about how their society regards the study of literature? What about other buildings on campus? My own college has just dedicated a sparkling new School of Business, a building that is, in theory, the east wing of an older complex but that in reality dwarfs the late-nineteenth-century structure. The new portion self-consciously proclaims its harmony with the old by adopting the original building's color scheme and including a few oversize Ionic columns. The new building houses five left-over faculty members from the School of Music, but they are not allowed to play musical instruments in their offices. It is tempting to read this new structure as an accidental self-portrait of American business, which always claims to act in accord with traditional American values — hence the gestures toward older architecture — but which does pretty much what it wishes and which allows the arts only so long as artists make no literal or figurative noise. Such an interpretation, of course, requires speculation and creativity and therefore horrifies the cautious. But Pope expected his readers to see simultaneously the architectural details of his own culture and the ways of life they represented. Surely he would smile if he thought he could encourage readers two centuries later to make similar interpretative leaps.[6]

At some point in teaching the *Epistle*, instructors might like to discuss the well-publicized architectural criticism of Prince Charles. In the last decade, Charles has become increasingly outspoken about architecture. His similes are memorable and often quoted: he compared a proposed modern addition to the National Gallery in London to "a wen on a well-loved face"; commenting on the undistinguished tall buildings around St. Paul's Cathedral, Charles said that trying to catch a glimpse of Wren's master-piece was rather like trying to look at the Mona Lisa with a team of basket-ball players obstructing one's path of vision. A clear statement of Charles's architectural credo is contained in his book *A Vision of Britain* (a portion of which was reprinted in *Architectural Digest*). Margaret Anne Doody once suggested in conversation that the prince is using architectural language to make political and social commentary. The prince's pronouncements serve the same functions as Pope's *Epistle*: they suggest what has gone wrong with Britain and provide an alternative vision of what could be, all expressed in symbolic code.

The prince's situation is more complex than Pope's, since members of the British royal family are not supposed to voice political opinions. Charles and his mother must have them — they were rumored to have detested Margaret Thatcher. By opposing modernism Charles was opposing Thatcher's policies. I suggest that Charles opposes modern building in Britain for three reasons: its primary concern is with short-term cost effectiveness, it does not grow out of the valued traditions of British architecture, and it does not consult the tastes and opinions of the people who will live and work in its structures. These charges were often leveled against Thatcherism, known for its short-term cost effectiveness, for its breaks with British traditions, and for its lack of concern for ordinary Britons. These charges Prince Charles — and his mother — would perhaps have liked to have made public against the former prime minister's policies, but the discretion of office prevents open commentary.

Charles is a student of the eighteenth century. One of his favorite ancestors is that much-maligned monarch George III. Charles lives in an eighteenth-century Palladian structure, Highgrove. Charles's *Vision of Britain* contains references to and reproduces illustrations from the works of the eighteenth-century architect William Chambers. Charles has learned from the eighteenth-century poet Pope that architectural language is ideological language and that a building represents a way of life; a good building suggests, sustains, promotes, and images a good way of life. If Pope and Prince Charles have their way, we and our students will continue to look at buildings and ponder their antecedents and the ways of life they promote, and we will read buildings as images of the societies that produce them. It might at first seem strange to import contemporary images into a discussion of an eighteenth-century verse epistle, to speak of Pope in the same breath as we speak of modern princes, politicians, bricks, plate glass, steel girders, and floor-plans. But Pope is, after all, a poet not afraid of contemporary and topical details, a poet for whom the general resides in the specifics, the important in the parochial. He could have made a poem out of modern architectural squabbles but does not need to have, since *Epistle to Burlington* has already taught us how to perform our own readings of contemporary buildings.

NOTES

[1]For illustrations of and information about Chiswick House, see the duke of Devonshire's article in *Architectural Digest*; Jackson-Stops, *Treasure Houses* 215, 218; Rosoman; and other art history texts. For large, clear photographs of Italian villas, see Wundram, Pape, and Marton (which also provides useful floor plans) and Lauritzen and Wolf. Ackerman gives a good introduction to Palladio and his work. For information on which villas are open to travelers (for those who will take slides on location), see Lumsden. For eighteenth-century prints of Pope's now-vanished villa, see Brownell; Mack, *Garden*. For surveys of English Palladianism, see Richards 139–47 and Summerson.

[2]Houghton is illustrated in Jackson-Stops and Pipkin 57, 120, and 121; and Jackson-Stops's *Treasure Houses* 430.

[3]For illustrations of Blenheim, see Jackson-Stops and Pipkin 34, 53, 88, and 232 (floor plan); and N. Nicolson 214–23.

[4]For illustrations of Chatsworth, see Jackson-Stops and Pipkin 28, 52, 221, 222; and N. Nicolson 185–93.

[5]The best source for Cannons is Dunlop's article, which reprints eighteenth-century drawings and a twentieth-century artist's reconstruction.

[6]I have sidestepped the issue of whose intentions a building expresses. Does a structure manifest the will of its architect, of the patrons who footed the bill, of those who use the building, or of the society that passively allows the building to be built? This question recalls current debates among literary critics over authorial intention and is the subject of many an unwritten essay.

Pope, Martha Blount, and the *Epistle to a Lady*

Rachel Ann Miller

On a first reading of the *Epistle to a Lady*, students frequently complain of Pope's sexism. By what right, students demand, does Pope take it on himself to satirize all women? By what right does a man presume to say what women are really like, what they want, and what is best for them?

My first teaching experience with the *Epistle to a Lady* was at Mills College, a women's liberal arts college in Oakland, California. Although the students in my seminar were only vaguely familiar with the genre of antifeminist satire, they were, on principle, opposed to a tradition that relegated women to subordinate and silent roles. As we took up *To a Lady*, I was neither surprised nor alarmed at the intensity of student response. What did bother me was the way in which the poem was arraigned and indicted without consideration of evidence. From the outset of the discussion, it was assumed that the poem fit snugly into some antifeminist niche. Pope was alternately branded a male chauvinist and a misogynist. The bipartite structure of the poem, with its concluding, complimentary portrait of the ideal lady, was largely ignored or dismissed. As the discussion continued, it became increasingly clear to me that several students had altogether missed the dramatic presence of the lady in the gallery tour. While many students expressed interest in the historical women behind the satiric portraits, only one inquired about the historical identity of the lady. It was as though the lady to whom the epistle is addressed had disappeared from the poem.

My goal in teaching *To a Lady* is not to persuade students that the poem is or is not antifeminist. My goal is to channel the intensity of the student response into a close reading of the text. I stress what I take to be two of the neglected elements of the poem — the lady and the theme of friendship.

I begin by asking students to define the structure of the poem, this to emphasize the pattern of blame and praise. Some students discover two major sections (satiric portraits, lines 1–248; tribute to the lady, 249–92); others, three (portraits, 1–198; analysis of "Ruling Passion," 199–248; tribute, 249–92); still others, four (portraits, 1–156; the lady's defense of women and the poet's rebuttal, 157–198; analysis, 199–248; tribute, 249–92). The point is not to reach a consensus but to draw attention to the concluding portrait of the lady, which "balances" the satiric portraits. Invariably, students will object that there are 248 lines of attack or analysis and only 44 lines of praise.

I find it helpful to place the poem within the literary tradition of Horatian epistle and to draw a distinction between Horatian epistle and Juvenalian satire. Students will need to decide for themselves whether *To a Lady* "deviat[es] sharply from the antifeminist satires to which it has wrongly been linked" (Weinbrot, *Pope* 189). I provide background information on the genres: the epistle addresses a friend or educable *adversarius*, seeks to reform folly, and presents an ideal or norm; Juvenalian satire lashes vice, seeks to punish offenders, and excludes the norm. To demonstrate the difference, I read aloud to the class passages from Dryden's translation of Juvenal's sixth satire on women. Students appreciate the more moderate tone and structure of Pope's poem. The discussion of genre also alerts students to the presence of the lady in the poem not only as norm or ideal but also as friend or *adversarius*.

> Ah Friend! to dazzle let the Vain design,
> To raise the Thought and touch the Heart, be thine!
> (249–50)

So begins the concluding portrait of the lady, to which we now turn.

One of the first things that students notice about the portrait is the apparent contradiction regarding the lady's marital status. The lady is a married woman and mother, who "Sighs for a Daughter with unwounded ear" (260). But she is also a single and childless woman, who shines in "Virgin Modesty," much as does the moon or the moon goddess, Diana (254–55). She is dependent on a man, whom she must obey or artfully manage:

> She, who ne'er answers till a Husband cools,
> Or, if she rules him, never shows she rules.
> (261–62)

But she is also an independent woman, secure from spousal constraint:

> Ascendant Phœbus watch'd that hour with care,
> Averted half your Parents simple Pray'r,
> And gave you Beauty, but deny'd the Pelf
> Which buys your sex a Tyrant o'er itself.
> (285–88)

Students should note the paradox that Pope establishes in these lines. It is the financially dependent woman (the woman without a dowry) who achieves independence or autonomy. Students should also note the pun in the phrase "Mistress of herself" (268). Whether married or single, the ideal lady is even-tempered; the single woman, however, is also a free agent, morally and legally free to make her own decisions, which include choosing her own friends.

Why does Pope develop the contradiction about the lady's marital status? Does Pope present one portrait (with an inherent contradiction) or two alternative portraits? Which portrait best suits Pope's friend and addressee, Martha Blount?

In the text I use, the one-volume Twickenham edition, the selected annotations tell my students that Martha Blount (nicknamed Patty) was one of Pope's oldest friends, that she was Catholic, that she had had smallpox (in 1714), and that she was single. I provide considerably more biographical information.

Pope met Martha and her sister, Teresa, when he was living at Binfield and the Blounts were at nearby Mapledurham. Martha was seventeen; Pope and Teresa were both nineteen. Initially, Pope may have been attracted to the more dominant sister, Teresa, for whom he composed "Epistle to Miss Blount, on Her Leaving the Town, after the Coronation." In his letters, however, Pope developed "a teasing flirtation with both sisters" (Rumbold 113). He wrote to Teresa in 1714: "My *violent* passion for your fair self and your sister has been divided with the most wonderful regularity in the world. Even from my infancy I have been in love with one after the other of you, week by week" (*Correspondence* 1: 258). Although the flirtation continued for three or four years, Pope "increasingly abandoned the postures of courtship for the confidence of friendship" (Rumbold 64). "You will both injure me very much," Pope wrote to Martha and Teresa in 1714, "if you don't think me a truer Friend than ever any Romantic Lover, or any Imitator of their Style, could be" (*Correspondence* 1: 252).

It was with Martha that Pope developed a lifelong friendship. Martha was, by all accounts, a gentle woman, tender, "soft," and compassionate. Like Pope, she loved to read, she appreciated nature, and she prefered retired life to town life. She was also economically dependent, having been left dowry-less by her father's will in 1710, which accorded Mapledurham to Michael, Martha's brother. Pope offered Martha financial and emotional support. It was Pope, for example, who pressed Michael to pay Martha the allowance stipulated by the will. He even persuaded Michael to settle an annuity on her. In later years, when Pope came to believe that Teresa was mistreating Martha, he repeatedly urged her to set up an independent household. Martha ultimately did so in 1745, when she moved into the London house that Pope had purchased for her shortly before his death. In his will, Pope left her £1,000, his personal belongings, and a life interest in his estate.

Students usually ask if Pope and Martha's relationship was sexual, and I answer that, to the best of my knowledge, it was not, although there were rumors that Pope had secretly married Martha or taken her as his mistress. Even Pope's family and friends did not know for sure. Magdalen, Pope's stepsister, endorsed the secret-marriage theory, while Teresa apparently spread rumors of an affair. Pope denied them, while professing his true friendship for Martha. It may be that the rumors tell us more about the "assumptions of the age" than they do about Pope and Martha's relationship (Rumbold 46).

As we return our attention to the text, students readily identify those passages that refer to Martha Blount and those that do not. We then attempt to account for the discrepancy between the fictional and the historical lady.

I offer several theories for class consideration. Pope protects the lady by concealing her identity (Ehrenpreis, "Cistern" 119). By doing so, he honors the feminine ideal of privacy and anonymity that the poem recommends. Or, Pope "effaces" the historical Martha Blount to fulfill a "socially sanctioned feminine ideal" (Pollak, "Pope" 480–81). According to this view, a conservative Pope locates woman's proper role in marriage and motherhood. Or Pope presents two ideal ladies, in order to weigh the benefits of the married state against the benefits of the single state.

Intrigued by the unconventional relationship of Pope and Martha Blount, many students are willing to entertain the last theory. Students notice that the single woman primarily occupies the first, third, and fourth verse paragraphs of the concluding portrait; that she is addressed in the second person; that she is awarded the poet, with whom she enjoys an intimate friendship; and that she is characterized by her good sense and good humor. The married woman occupies the second verse paragraph of the portrait; she is referred to in the third person; she is awarded a sister and a daughter, whom she loves, and a husband, whom she charms; and she is characterized by restraint, patience, submission, and disguise. The underlying assumption is that she is caught in a power struggle with her "Husband," or "Tyrant" (216, 288). She must either relinquish her autonomy or rule without showing she rules. Pope sympathizes with the plight of the married woman. He celebrates the escape of the single woman.

Is Pope merely paying a gallant compliment to Martha Blount? Offering consolation to a spinster? Or is he serious in suggesting that the single woman is, in certain respects, better off than the married woman?

To address these questions, I ask students to draw up three lists tracking the textual references to husbands, lovers, and friends. The first list (husbands) usually includes Arcadia's countess; Fannia, "leering on her own good man" (9); Papillia, "wedded to her doating spark" (37); Philomedé, "Chaste to her Husband, frank to all beside" (71); Flavia, "Say, what can cause such impotence of mind? / A Spark too fickle, or a Spouse too kind" (93–94); Simo's mate; Atossa; and the veterans. Sometimes it also includes Cloe, Queen Caroline, and the duchess of Queensberry.

The second list (lovers) significantly overlaps with the first, including Fannia, Philomedé, Atossa, Cloe, and the veterans. This list also includes Rufa, Sappho, Narcissa, and Calypso. We notice the satire on female lust and infidelity. By "Pleasure," after all, Pope specifically means sexual pleasure. But we also notice the power play in the relationships and how it is the women who dominate the men. Women dominate by indifference (Cloe), infidelity (Philomedé), longevity (Atossa), obstinacy (Simo's mate), and sexual allure (Calypso). Women become "Tyrants" (227). Men become uxorious husbands (Fannia's "good man," Papillia's "doating spark," Flavia's "Spouse too kind").

The third list (friends) includes Silia, "The Frail one's advocate, the Weak one's friend" (30); the nameless woman who claims that "she's honest, and the best of Friends" (104); Atossa, "By Spirit robb'd of Pow'r, by Warmth of Friends" (144); Cloe, who, "when she sees her Friend in deep despair, / Observes how much a Chintz exceeds Mohair" (169–70); beauties, "Old and friendless grown" (227); and veterans, "Young without Lovers, old without a Friend" (246). Pope exposes false friendship (Silia and Calista; the nameless woman who takes a lover with whom she pretends to be just friends). He implies that true friendship can exist only among individuals of the highest moral caliber. And he differentiates between short-lived sexual passion and enduring friendship.

Students are usually surprised at the number of references to friendship, which leads us to consider whether the poem recommends friendship as an alternative to marriage. Students must decide for themselves the following questions. Does the typical married woman become a tyrant in order to "avoid becoming [a] victim" (Jackson 93)? Does the ideal married woman become a victim and dissembler? Does the friendship between the poet and the single lady enable the lady to maintain her autonomy? Does the friendship enable the poet to escape the "futility of sexual warfare" (Jackson 91)?

The lesson that I have outlined does not intend to "vindicate" Pope or the *Epistle to a Lady*. Recent feminist criticism has persuasively identified misogynistic elements in the poem (Nussbaum, "Pope's 'To a Lady' "; Pollak, "Pope"; Smith). The lesson does intend to encourage students to think carefully about the text before drawing any easy conclusions. Such a lesson might go on to discuss the role of the lady as *adversarius*. (I begin by asking students to locate the dialogue between the poet and the lady—whether direct, indirect, or implied dialogue.) The lesson might conclude with a discussion of the lady as norm or ideal. (I focus on the androgynous ideal of the "softer Man.")

I no longer teach at a women's college, but I find that my students still approach Pope with prejudice and preconception. Recently I asked a student why he had branded Pope a misogynist. The student replied that he had been reading about Pope's public and private feud with Lady Mary Wortley Montagu and that from this he had assumed that all Pope's relationships with women were disastrous. Now, Lady Mary plays only a small role in the *Epistle to a Lady*, occupying the Sappho portrait and, perhaps, parts of Flavia. My feeling is this: students should be informed about Pope's feud with Lady Mary Wortley Montagu, particularly in regard to *The Dunciad* and the *Epistle to Dr. Arbuthnot*; but students should also be informed about Pope's lifelong friendship with Martha Blount and the significance of that friendship for the *Epistle to a Lady*.

Pope's *Arbuthnot*: Context, Text and Questions for Discussion

Howard D. Weinbrot

The guidelines described here are drawn from teaching *An Epistle . . . to Dr. Arbuthnot* to both undergraduate and graduate students. Either group needs historical and literary contexts — including politics, genre, and biography; a sense of the symbolic and thematic importance of the Pope-Arbuthnot dialogue; guidance in the structures of the poem, so that movement becomes metaphor; and particular passages for students to read aloud and analyze. Such dramatic reading makes plain the urgency and energy of Pope's poem and engages students in their own education.

At first, however, the instructor needs to be armed with enough information to encourage and answer questions like the following. Who was Alexander Pope and why were some contemporaries so angry at him? Why should Great Britain's prime minister and his aristocratic allies care what a poet says? Why should a poet care what the prime minister says? What in particular made Pope so angry that he wrote a public letter to an eminent physician, hoping to convince him that Pope should continue to write dangerous satire? Who was that physician, and why does Pope want us to know and respect the announced name, while he masks his enemy Lord Hervey behind the name Sporus? The following capsule information may help guide the student and the instructor through history to the poem and its maker.

Historical and Political Contexts

As a young man, Pope used apparently innocent genres — pastoral, georgic, mock-heroic, and sublime emotional lyric narratives. He nonetheless aroused extreme hostility. He was a successful Catholic in an Anglican country; hunchbacked, four foot six, perennially ill, and more likely to find an early death than immortality; so proud and confident that he translated Homer and edited Shakespeare; so shrewd regarding sales of his work that he became one of Britain's first financially independent, self-supporting writers; and so aware of his achievement and potential that by 1717 he had already issued his collection of works, as if seeking comparison with the ancients. Life was made harsher for Pope when he published *The Dunciad*, in which British literary culture in general and many named poets in particular were labeled worthless. By then it was clear that Pope's political sympathies were closer to the defunct Stuarts than to the post-1714 Hanoverian dynasty. Pope was especially hostile to the dramatic changes being wrought by the powerful and corrupt prime minister, Sir Robert Walpole, who governed from April 1721 to January 1742 and who found Pope and most other distinguished men of letters in opposition to him.

Though Walpole was from an old Norfolk country family, he knew that the days of little agricultural England were numbered. Commercial, trading, City-based financial interests soon would be permanent, and they required peace even with traditional enemies like Spain and France. The outcome of war was uncertain and inhibited enriching and, the argument went, civilizing trade.

Walpole helped further his policies through bribery with cash, titles, jobs, and often unsavory allies in aristocratic or literary circles. Indeed, he regarded the world of letters as useful only if it furthered his political ends. Noisy satire could be threatened or legally suppressed, and its poets or printers arrested. Pope represented the ideal of poetry as a traditional apolitical (though actually highly political) moral force that drew authority from the enduring values of the past and of the land. Walpole saw poetry as an adjunct to government policies that drew authority from wealth, contemporary financial centers, and commercial expansion.

Given Pope's numerous enemies, many were willing to take up verbal cudgels on their own or on Walpole's behalf. Lady Mary Wortley Montagu and John, Lord Hervey, savaged Pope and his family in their *Verses to the Imitator of Horace*, a bitter response to Pope's Horatian imitation *Satires* 2.1 (to Mr. Fortescue), in which Lady Mary was rudely treated. They called Pope an "angry little monster," "odious," "A puny insect," "hated by Mankind," marked by God "on [his] Back, like Cain," "accursed," and "No more for loving made, than to be belov'd." With such personal and political attacks, Pope needed to have respectable friends and allies and to demonstrate that he could win over those not hitherto persuaded by anger or by gold.

Dr. John Arbuthnot was just such a person. He had been a physician to Queen Anne between 1705 and 1714; he was an eminent man of letters and part of the Scriblerus group of Pope, Swift, and Gay, which from 1713 to 1714 satirized abuses in human learning. As a distinguished physician he was respected throughout the political spectrum and had a professional interest in keeping his frail patient alive and away from dangerous activities like satirizing Walpole and his chums. By implication, if Pope convinces Arbuthnot that his cause is right, he convinces us and other open-minded readers. And again by implication, Arbuthnot and others would, in their own right, have condemned Sir Robert Walpole and his world as unfit, and certainly as unfit to judge Alexander Pope.

The Adversarius, *Apologia, and Epistle*

The *adversarius* in Pope's second dialogue of the *Epilogue to the Satires* makes comments and raises perversely useful questions: "none but you by Name the Guilty lash" (10); "where's th'Affront to you?" (157); "what's that to you" (163); "How hurt he you?" (165). Pope finally squashes this uncomprehending voice of corruption by affirming that he is his brother's keeper, with a "strong Antipathy of Good to Bad" (198). Hence

> When Truth or Virtue an Affront endures,
> Th' Affront is mine, my Friend, and should be yours.
> . . . .
> Mine, as a Friend to ev'ry worthy mind;
> And mine as Man, who feel for all mankind.
> (199–200, 203–04)

This sort of conflict is familiar in satire. At least from Horace in Augustan Rome, the satirist was forced to write an apologia, an answer to questions thrown back at the imperfect satirist: what business is it of yours, and who gives you the right to criticize others? Pope urges that for all his admitted flaws, he cares deeply about the ravages of evil, has an inner drive to expunge or resist it, and sees the intimate connection between parts of fragile culture. An attack on any innocent virtue, or poet, is an attack on all. Alas, however much he tries to keep quiet, he will be affronted, and so he must respond on his own behalf and on behalf of a beleaguered world in which satire replaces ineffectual law. Thus in the "Advertisement" to *Arbuthnot* he insists that he publishes this poem because his enemies attacked "my *Person*, *Morals*, and *Family*." Pope can take care of himself; his aged or dead parents need help to defend their honor. What decent son would not take action in such a case? In so characterizing himself, Pope also reinforces the good character of the satiric speaker — sometimes called his ethos or persona and always positive enough to gain the reader's respect and attention.

This brief discussion suggests several ways to approach *Arbuthnot* and much other formal verse satire. Let us ask ourselves, and then our students, some of the following questions. Why does the satirist have to write satire? What or who is the satirist attacking in the poem? What or who is the satirist praising, and how do these relate to one another? What is the image the satirist gives him- or herself to justify the satiric role? What image does he or she give to the adversarius or interlocutor or other person acting in the poem? Who is that other person, and what does he or she represent, especially if identified by name or political affiliation? Assuming that the poem includes a dialogue, how do the satirist and adversarius relate to each other? Does either change? If so, how and why? If not, what inferences can we draw? How much does the satirist speak, how much does the adversarius speak, and what symbolic value is there in these approximate proportions?

The word "Epistle" in the title allows us to ask students what sort of expectations we have when one friend writes to another. The answers are likely to include the following: colloquial diction, plain dealing, and an assumption of intimacy that allows one to speak personally to a sympathetic audience.

When the recipient of the letter also is named, well known, and highly respected, we may draw another set of inferences — including the letter writer's own distinction. Ask students what they think of someone who could write intimately to, and be read respectfully by, say, a head of state, a major entertainer, or some other important figure the students might know and respect. The private epistle allows judgments about the character of the speaker, based in part on the depicted relationship with the person to whom he or she is writing.

Students, however, probably will observe that this private letter has been made public, since readers like themselves obviously have been engaged with it for about 260 years. Here we can guide them toward awareness of author-audience complicity. Pope has allowed us to read his mail, to see what a good sort he really is, and through such shared intimacy he has moved us to his side in the dispute the poem chronicles. The epistle is both to Dr. Arbuthnot and to us as readers. We briefly become Arbuthnot, see Pope's point of view, and presumably are moved to respond as approvingly as Arbuthnot finally does. The privilege of reading Pope's mail makes us part of his world, as Pope manipulates us for our pleasure and his rhetorical purposes. He is, after all, writing an apologia and needs to have our approval, which he probably gains as we become surrogate Arbuthnots.

Themes and Structures

Arbuthnot's function as a doctor also supplies Pope with an essential metaphor and device of poetic structure — inversion of the healing role. Ask students to trace images, acts, and needs for healing, to note changes as the poem proceeds, and thereby to characterize one of Pope's major themes. As the poem begins, for example, Pope is attacked by the mad, vain, omnipresent, insectlike poets infecting the larger Walpole world and Pope's smaller world at his home in Twickenham. He asks his doctor friend for a *"Drop* or *Nostrum"* to remove "this *Plague,"* or he is done for: "If Foes, they write, if Friends, they read me dead" (29, 32). So long as Pope allows the infection to remain untreated, so long will he be defensive, endangered, and in need of Arbuthnot's mediating skill.

As the poem develops, Pope begins to reverse the medical role and take command. He lectures Arbuthnot regarding the poison of insects (105–06), he ridicules his own illness and deformity (116–17, 121–24), he suggests his stoicism in the face of illness (133–34), he transfers illness to his enemies (181–82, 224), and he concludes with two formidable excursions into his own role as doctor. By attacking vice, most notably in the portrait of Sporus, Pope becomes his own, his family's, and his nation's satiric doctor. He is on the offensive, seeking to destroy the dangerous "painted Child of Dirt that stinks and stings" (310). By the end of the poem he even assumes Arbuthnot's "prolonging" role (27). Pope cares for his aged mother and will

With lenient Arts extend a Mother's breath,
Make Languour smile, and smooth the Bed of Death.
                    (410–11)

Earlier Pope calls himself "the Being [Arbuthnot] preserv'd" (134); as healer Pope asks "Heav'n, to . . . preserve my Friend" (415).

Pope's change helps highlight Arbuthnot's change. We recall that in an apologia the satirist needs to move the audience, which here is Arbuthnot as the representative of other fair-minded readers, like us.

Isolate each of Arbuthnot's remarks, have them read by consecutive students, and then ask what has happened to Arbuthnot along the way and how Pope has moved him, and us, in that direction. Here are the lines that Arbuthnot speaks, together with comments on them. Note that this method requires a textual emendation, since most texts wrongly, in my judgment, give the final couplet to Pope, who is asked to approve of himself. If Arbuthnot speaks the lines, they are a brilliant conclusion to Arbuthnot's dialectic.

1. 75–78. Even when Arbuthnot dissuades Pope from being a satirist, he implicitly acknowledges the need for satire: it is dangerous to speak truth to power. Look out or they'll get you.
2. 101–04. Arbuthnot again subverts himself, for he is agitated while urging calm, and he again shows the need for satire: don't name exalted rogues or they will harm you.
3. 305–08. While dissuading Pope from satire, Arbuthnot has become a satirist, when he calls Sporus "that mere white Curd of Ass's milk." As Pope becomes more the doctor, Arbuthnot becomes more the satirist and does some of Pope's work, as Pope does some of his.
4. 360. Arbuthnot now merely asks a leading question rather than offer his usual aggressive negative.
5. 389. This other question is muted and politely directed toward the poet's genealogy. Arbuthnot shifts focus from defending Pope to allowing Pope to defend his family.
6. 418–19. The last lines in the poem should be Arbuthnot's. "Thus far was right" is the response Pope wants from Arbuthnot and from us in an apologia.

There are three other aspects of structure that I have found helpful in teaching *Arbuthnot* as a heterogeneous but coherent poem. One is temporal structure. The poem clearly ends at about the same chronological time that it begins. The long central passage from lines 125–333, however, is a mazy movement through biographic and symbolic time. Students can see that Pope begins as a child (127) and ends as a powerful adult attacking the hateful Sporus (333). Within these lines he also moves from childhood's early days, from being a poet in a nurturing community with a great continuing tradition, to the world of Atticus's greatness tainted by neurotic selfishness, to the more dangerous world of Bufo, the patron who destroys by withholding support, to the world of Sir Robert Walpole's puppet Sporus. As we move from past to present, we move from Stuarts to Hanoverians, from integrity to corruption, from a childhood Eden to Sporus as Walpole's serpent threatening the crown's integrity. This temporal progress makes plain why Pope must be a satirist—for himself and for his nation.

Temporal structure can be reinforced by the structure of satiric portraits. Ask the students to read consecutively the portraits of Atticus, Bufo, and Sporus. They are likely to hear the increasing anger, danger, and need for engagement against evil.

Finally, ask them to discuss why so much of *Arbuthnot* concerns literature as it relates to politics. Don't name queens, ministers, or kings, Arbuthnot says; Sporus is a creature of Sir Robert's court; rotten poets are everywhere. The world that Pope describes reflects Sir Robert's commercial, moral, and political values; poets reflect those values and become his literary emblems. Thus one dim poet asks Pope to rewrite a miserable play for him in exchange for a share of the profit (65–68). Another is incapable of shame in his wretched verse (89–94). The venomous Sporus

> . . . spits himself abroad,
> In Puns, or Politicks, or Tales, or Lyes,
> Or Spite, or Smut, or Rymes, or Blasphemies.
> (320–22)

The undiscriminating energy of evil ("In . . . or . . . or . . . or . . . or . . . or . . . or . . . or") is the agent of the man who pulls the strings, Sir Robert Walpole, for "as the Prompter breathes, the Puppet squeaks" (318).

The portrait of Sporus, in fact, is one of the two sections I recommend for special analysis, generally after a student has read the earlier, muted, melancholic portrait of Atticus. We already have seen some points that suggest themselves: the about-face Arbuthnot makes as he too becomes a satirist in the world of such evil, the about-face Pope makes as he abandons any lingering notion that he can be detached from his world, the image of Sporus as an agent of Sir Robert and of the devil himself (319, 330), and Sporus as a bad poet who also exemplifies bad government. Some other points require attention, though, for they suggest how Pope turns private quarrels into urgent public matters.

We recall that the *Verses to the Imitator of Horace* asserted that Pope lacked sexual manhood. This claim was an important tack for Lord Hervey to take, since as a homosexual or bisexual he gave Pope an easily exploited opportunity. Sporus is either "Master" or "Miss," "one vile Antithesis," and a subhuman "Amphibious thing" (324–26). No wonder, then, that Pope chose the name Sporus for Hervey: Sporus was the castrated male whore of the Roman emperor Nero. Here, however, the able student will see the connection between the public and the private. Pope clearly is getting even, but he also is making a political statement: Walpole uses Lord Hervey politically as Nero used Sporus sexually. Each abuses power and offends morality. Similarly, by twice alluding to Sporus as the diabolical toad or serpent at Eve's ear, Pope also alludes to Lord Hervey's influence with Queen Caroline. The problem of Sporus no longer is Pope's own; it becomes the nation's and the world's, as we sadly see, played out before us, the fall that is imminent unless Pope breaks the blasphemous monster on the torture wheel as he might a common criminal.

Another section for separate study is the comedy of lines 115–24, depicting the flatterers who praise Pope's presumed literary achievement. Reading aloud suggests the humor of the passage, its role as a perverse vision of the classical past, and its characterization of the literary world Pope resists. For Pope's flatterers, the classical tradition is a series of unconnected, chronologically warped personal quirks or acts — Horace's cough, Alexander the Great's raised shoulder, Ovid's long nose, Virgil's posture, and Homer's death. Aberration and illness replace awareness of poetry's continuum. As usual in Pope, these lines also serve a double function, for they soon contrast with the vibrant English literary tradition of Pope's youth. Garth, Walsh, Congreve, Swift, and others demonstrate the proper role of literary tradition — a severe but nurturing family that improves and loves without self-interest. It also is one from the Stuart past, not from the Hanoverian, Walpolian present.

These are among the ways to teach Pope's *Arbuthnot*: supply such political and literary context as you think appropriate; focus on the poem's role as a private epistle that engages us publicly; deal with Arbuthnot's role as a doctor and how it allows Pope to develop themes of personal and national health; discuss the dialogue form, in which Arbuthnot gradually changes; suggest ways in which the poem's temporal structure and sequence of satiric portraits and linking of bad art and bad government are related; examine specific passages, like "Sporus" and the contrasting literary traditions, always supplying relevant information (who Sporus was, for example) and drawing students into their own education by having them read portions of the poem aloud. In my experience, reading Arbuthnot's responses is extremely effective. Since all students know about doctors, the "theme" and role of health in the poem also offer productive discussion. "Sporus" sometimes puzzles students, since they are frightened by Pope's anger; but this section is an excellent point of departure for discussions of the character of the speaker, the need for Pope's anger, and the role of his parents. If you read students portions of Lady Mary and Lord Hervey's *Verses*, they will well understand why Pope was so grumpy. Whichever combination of questions the teacher uses, the experience is likely to be good for those on both sides of the desk. *Arbuthnot* is a compelling poem and a pleasure to teach and learn.

Horace in Modern Dress

Peter J. Schakel

If Pope's Horatian imitations aren't the hardest works in English literature to teach, they have to be close. Everything about them is foreign to students near the end of the twentieth century — Pope, Horace, imitation, the couplet, the eighteenth-century figures and events referred to in them. Yet the imitation is the most characteristic of eighteenth-century forms, quintessentially "neoclassical": students who can reach an understanding and at least some appreciation of them touch the literary heart of Pope and his contemporaries. This essay is intended to encourage and assist teachers, particularly in survey courses, to spend an hour, or even half an hour, on the imitation, using Pope's *First Satire of the Second Book of Horace*, a short, accessible, and teachable example, to introduce the form.

The initial difficulty facing students is to understand the nature of imitation. They assume that creative must mean wholly new, original, and personal; thus a creativity based on witty restatement of earlier expression is virtually a contradiction in terms. The imitation as a form involves specifically such restatement, and contemporization, of classical poems. John Oldham, in 1681, described his own imitations as "putting *Horace* into a more modern dress," that is, "making him speak, as if he were living and writing now. I therefore resolved to alter the Scene from *Rome* to *London*, and to make use of *English* names of Men, Places, and Customs, where the Parallel would decently permit" (Oldham a1v).

The impulse of students is to confuse such paralleling with parody, with which they are very familiar. Every Saturday night they see, live or in reruns, "Deep Thoughts," parodying syrupy messages from Christian cable-television networks, or "All My Luggage," in which a woman's paroxysms of anguish over her missing suitcases mock the sentimentalism of the soap opera *All My Children*. There is, therefore, precedent for their expecting works that borrow the form of other works to be parody: invariably someone will ask if a mock-epic is making fun of the epic form itself.

Finding a current near equivalent to help students separate imitation from parody and grasp the intent of imitation is difficult, but some sense of what is involved might perhaps be communicated by reference to film, a medium most students understand well, particularly some mid-career works of Woody Allen. Allen provides an interesting parallel to Pope because of his films' rich use of allusion, verbal, of course, but also visual — to expressionist painters, to Bergman and Fellini, to Shakespeare (Benayoun 91–94).

In *Stardust Memories*, for example, Allen, a filmmaker in his forties suffering from an artistic mid-life crisis (Benayoun 94), "imitates" Fellini's $8\frac{1}{2}$, a film exploring that theme. (Although students may not have seen either film, they do understand "film talk" and probably will follow the points being made.) Allen's film is not a remake of *8½*; it does not just use the earlier work as an inspiration and starting point; and it is too sympathetic in the handling of *8½* to be a parody. Allen, struggling with directions for his career, could find comfort — and defense of his struggling — in the fact that a great predecessor faced the same struggle, just as Pope found comfort in Horace and their common defensiveness about using satire. *Stardust Memories* is a new work modeled on an earlier one — sequences in structure are clearly identifiable, visual scenes are recognizable, themes echo clearly. One can understand, enjoy, and appreciate *Stardust Memories* without having seen *8½*, but familiarity with the earlier film enriches and deepens the experience of the later one, as Horace's poems do for Pope's Imitations.

The parallel is not exact, however, partly because it lacks equivalents for the various satiric possibilities the imitation provided eighteenth-century writers. The imitation permitted irony or pointed comment by omission of lines the classical writer had included or by inclusion of lines the classical author had not written. It permitted satiric undercutting of contemporaries by substituting them for — and thus comparing them to — bad Romans or by holding them up to a standard of good Romans that they could by no means reach. It also permitted praise of contemporaries by placing them parallel to good and famous Romans.

These strategies make clear that considering — and teaching — a poem as an imitation requires treating it in tandem with the poem it imitates. It is usually helpful to point out that the Latin poem or line references to it were published with the imitation or, better still, to bring in the Twickenham edition of the Imitations and show how original and imitation appeared on facing pages. Apart from the Horatian context, it is simply another original poem, not an imitation. So one must begin with Horace and with Horace's poem. Most students will need to be told that Quintus Horatius Flaccus was a Roman author of the first century BC, regarded as second only to Virgil and admired especially for the formal beauty of his odes but recognized also for his *Sermons*, or "talks," satires and epistles enlivened with conversation and anecdote lightly ridiculing human follies and endorsing such values as moderation and friendship.

The first satire of Horace's second book of *Saturae* is a graceful, low-keyed defense of satire as a form and of Horace himself as a satirist. It is written as a dialogue and addressed to the distinguished lawyer Trebatius, friend and adviser to Augustus Caesar. Students should, of course, read Horace's poem as well as Pope's — the Loeb Classical Library edition provides a reliable, clear prose translation. For students unaccustomed to following an argument in poetry, a brief outline on the board or in a handout can be helpful for understanding Horace's poem, and Pope's:

HORACE.   People criticize me for writing satire. Some say my satires are too harsh and vindictive; others say they are weak and shallow. Tell me what I should do.

TREBATIUS. Just stop writing — rest.

HOR. That would be best; but I cannot sleep.

TRE. Try exercising or drinking wine in the evening, or write only poems praising Caesar's heroic deeds and victories.

HOR. I'm no good at epic poetry with all its war scenes.

TRE. Then praise Caesar's personal qualities.

HOR. I will at the right moment; but if I time things wrong I might offend him.

TRE. Better risk that than get people angry at you because they think your satires are attacking them.

HOR. Other people do what comes naturally to them — dancing when drunk, training horses, boxing; why shouldn't I? I love to write poetry, as Lucilius [the earliest Roman satirist] did. I, like him, am an open, honest person, loyal to Rome though an outsider. I would rather not use my satiric weapon, but when I am injured, beware: I will strike back. People when attacked strike back with the weapons most natural to them or most effective for them, just as animals do. Writing is my weapon, so whatever lies ahead for me — a long, peaceful life or early death, wealth or poverty, Rome or exile — I must write.

TRE. You risk being killed by some "great friend" if you do.

HOR. Lucilius dared to write satires exposing evil, despite dangers, and he didn't lose his friends. They recognized that his purpose was to defend virtue. He would go off alone with virtuous friends like Scipio and Laelius to laugh at evil deeds and people. Though I am not as great as Lucilius was, yet I have mingled with the great, and if jealous people try to deny that, they will break their teeth biting against my solid name.

TRE. Granted all that, still you need to be careful. There are laws against writing bad, libelous poetry.

HOR. Yes, against bad verse; but I write good poetry, which even Caesar approves of.

TRE. Oh, in that case, the charges against you will be laughed at and dismissed.

Horace's defense of satire, in sum, rests on the claim that satire is natural and essentially harmless and that his work is justified by the precedent of Lucilius.

With Horace as background, students can proceed to Pope's poem prepared to understand it more readily. Pope's imitation follows closely the outline and even much of the language of the original. But the challenge is to notice and account for the differences, for it is in them, not in the similarities, that the creativity of imitation lies. "Every point in Pope has been inspired by Horace, and yet every point is different" (Stack 33). The differences here will be fairly subtle, and recognizing them often depends on knowledge of contemporary detail unfamiliar to students. Footnotes may help, though the frequency of notes required in most of Pope's imitations will force a fragmented and disconnected reading. Walking students almost line by line through a portion of the poem, then sketching the argument of the remainder seems to me the best way to help them absorb the richness and flexibility of Pope's achievement.

Reading aloud the opening fifteen or twenty lines can be helpful: students tend to puzzle out couplets a line or two at a time and thus miss the structure of the sentences and the flow of thought. They also don't hear the sounds, especially the brilliant conversational rhythms of this satire, illustrated well in the opening five couplets, with their parenthetical insertions, repetition of "there are," marvelous handling of half lines, and use of a periodic sentence to emphasize "Advice" at the beginning of a line, with a strong caesura punctuating it.

The divergences from Horace in these lines are mostly additions: students will note the inserted wit of "(I scarce can think it, but am told)" and "without a Fee," the use of specific names — Peter, Charles, Lord Fanny — where Horace generalized, and the irony in "Tim'rous by Nature, of the Rich in awe," which the preceding lines already have shown to be unfounded. But students will not feel the satiric sting of the lines without glosses — from footnotes or the instructor — to make clear that it would be almost impossible to say anything too rough about Peter Walter (a ruthless money dealer, who became rich by supplying funds at excessive rates of interest) or Francis Charteris (a notorious profligate, who gained riches through gambling and usury) (*Twickenham* 4: 392, 353). It may be apparent that "spins a thousand such" undermines Lord Hervey's "talent" by mocking the mechanical weaving responsible for his production of vapid (and venomous) verse — often aimed personally at Pope; but students may not recognize that "spins" also identifies Lord Fanny with the spider in Swift's *The Battle of the Books* and thus with the *"Dirt and Poison"* attributed to modern writers (Swift, *Tale* 232).

The light, humorous tone underlying these satiric jabs at figures whom Pope attacked more harshly elsewhere continues in the witty, self-satiric lines that follow. The genial self-mockery in line 13 — "I nod in Company, I wake at Night" — can be clarified by reference to Johnson's *Life of Pope*: "When he wanted to sleep, he 'nodded in company'; and once slumbered at his own table while the Prince of Wales was talking of poetry. . . . One of his constant demands was of coffee in the night" (Johnson 198–99; also 199n1). Pope's willingness to poke fun at himself, one of the most endearing qualities of the poem, intensifies in the following lines as he modifies Trebatius's advice to Horace to fit his own physical condition. Pope pointedly omits the line urging vigorous physical exercise as preparation for sound sleep, for Pope, "scarce able to hold himself erect" until he was laced into a bodice of stiff canvas, could hardly swim across the Thames thrice (Johnson 197).

But the same physical infirmity creates self-irony in the detail Pope substitutes: "Why, if the Nights seem tedious – take a Wife." Pope was not, of course, an attractive candidate for marriage: legend has it that Lady Mary Wortley Montagu (the Sappho of lines 83–84) burst into laughter when he made a declaration of love to her (Mack, *Life* 553–55). Beyond his appearance, Pope most likely was sexually impotent. Slander of the day did include stories of Pope visiting bawdy houses and needing to be cured of gonorrhea, stories that Pope did not repudiate (Mack, *Life* 292–93), probably because a reputation for profligacy would, understandably, be preferable to a reputation for incapacity. When, in lines 17–18, he counsels, "Or rather truly, if your Point be Rest, / Lettuce and Cowslip Wine" (both were believed to induce sleep, and the former was thought to counteract sexual desire), he is attempting either a pathetic affirmation of his sexuality or, more likely, a conscious self-satire of his unmanly figure.

The divergences from Horace gradually shift from self-satire to literary and political satire of others. Pope pointedly alters Trebatius's advice to Horace – "tell of the feats of Caesar, the unvanquished" – to Fortescue's urging Pope to "write CAESAR's Praise" (21): if George II was unvanquished, it was in large part because Walpole's policy of "peace at any price" prevented George from notable "feats," and that policy was part of what the opposition – Pope included – held against Walpole. Similarly, where Trebatius urges Horace to write "of [Caesar] himself, at once just and valiant," Pope omits those tributes and substitutes references to the royal line: "Let *Carolina* smooth the tuneful Lay, / Lull with *Amelia*'s liquid Name the Nine" (30–31). Such political satire is at the same time literary, for only adulatory works are rewarded in this regime. Trebatius's general encouragement – "many a reward for your pains will you gain" – becomes Fortescue's specific promise in line 22: "You'll gain at least a *Knighthood* [like Richard Blackmore, whose awkward and endless epics are parodied immediately below], or the *Bays* [a reference to the appointment of Pope's enemy Colley Cibber as poet laureate]."

Deeper implications of the political and literary satire soon become evident. In reply to Trebatius's encouragement to praise Caesar, Horace answers that he certainly will, at the right moments. Horace identified himself with the political establishment; his patron was Maecenas, friend and supporter of Caesar. In Caesar he had a ruler who appreciated good literature, even wrote poetry himself – thus in the final lines of his poem Horace moves from the issue of legality and claims instead that he composes not "ill verses" but "good [well-written] verses," of which Caesar would approve – and Trebatius says Horace then has nothing to fear.

Pope uses the Horatian structure and fabric but quietly alters the argument to an "unHoratian defense of the satirist who is seen set up *against* or even *above* an overt social order" (G. K. Hunter 399). Pope pointedly refrains from saying he will praise George and emphasizes instead the way the English court of his day differs from the Roman court of Horace's: "Alas! few Verses touch their nicer Ear; / They scarce can bear their *Laureate* twice a Year," that is, to hear the New Year's and birthday odes required of the laureate (33–34). Unlike Caesar, George has no appreciation of literature: "Why will not my subjects write in prose?" George is reported to have asked—thus the irony in line 152: "Such as a *King* might read." And Pope unobtrusively alters Horace's use of "just" as an adjective characterizing Caesar to an adverb defending George's scorn for poetry: "And justly CAESAR scorns the Poet's Lays, / It is to *History* he trusts for Praise" (35–36). George's "just" dismissal of poetry is, presumably, because of its supposed reliance on "fictions" in contrast to the "truths" of history, on which he will rely; for Pope, the dismissal of poetry for whatever reason is ironic, but the deeper irony is that George's faith in what the truths of history will tell of him is most likely misguided.

As Pope's situation is different from that of Horace, so too are the grounds of his defense of himself and of satire: Pope turns "Horace's claim that satire is harmlessly natural into a defence of it as socially necessary" (G. K. Hunter 397). Despite the emphasis thus far on the king, Pope's deeper concern is Walpole, the power behind the throne, and the corruption that has permeated society during his tenure. In the opening lines Pope mentions specific names of corrupt men associated with Walpole, as if the pervasive corruption compels him to speak out. Such compulsion also appears in the reasons Pope cannot sleep. Horace's explanation was simply that he wrote because he could not sleep. Pope adds, tellingly: "Not write? but then I *think*, . . . Fools rush into my Head, and so I write" (11, 14).

The contrast between Horace's defense of satire as natural and Pope's as necessary also appears in Pope's handling of Fortescue. Horace's Trebatius is a fairly innocuous interlocutor, posing gentle questions, mildly taken in by Horace's shift from libel to artistry in the final lines. Both were comfortably part of the social order and Horace does little more than adulate Trebatius by including him in a skillful poem. Pope similarly honors his close friend Fortescue by putting him in the place of the notable Trebatius, but their relations to the English court do not parallel those of Horace and Trebatius to the Roman court. Fortescue, unlike Pope, was a member of the court party, worked as Walpole's private secretary, supported Walpole in Commons, and received political appointments from him (Pope, *Twickenham* 4: 360). Pope builds into the imitation a tension between the two speakers, the one defending the figures at court, the other compelled to attack and expose them. Thus Fortescue urges Pope, "Better be *Cibber*, . . . [than] / Abuse the City's best good Men in Metre, / And laugh at Peers that put their Trust in *Peter*" (37, 39–40). He earnestly warns Pope of the penalties for libel, pulling down a law book and pointing to the relevant statutes (143–49), and his concern is alleviated only when Pope implies that what he writes will not prove objectionable to Walpole: "Indeed? / The Case is alter'd—you may then proceed" (153–54).

The effect of that tension is reflected in a shift from the light, self-mocking irony of the opening dialogue to the increasingly serious and intense tone underlying Pope's defense of satire. Horace, arguing that the need to write satire is inborn (Weinbrot, *Pope* 212), uses general, mythical comparisons, in a light tone: Castor's liking horses and Pollux's liking boxing are as harmless and natural as liking to write satire. The corresponding lines in Pope are more personal, specific, and cutting: "Each Mortal has his Pleasure: None deny / *Scarsdale* his Bottle" (45–46). Scarsdale's pleasure is not just inborn and harmless — nor is satire, despite Horace's claim. The following lines (57–68), which have no precedent in the original, account for Pope's satire not as his particular "Pleasure" but as a response the age requires: Pope is forced by his situation to "expose" the "Vice" of his age (58, 60).

The greater, and increasing, intensity of Pope's tone can be seen if one compares the passages where Horace refers to Lucilius with the corresponding passages in Pope. Lucilius was central to Horace's defense of satire as a part of a tradition Horace could fit into and the ideal exemplar of that tradition. Such a tradition and ideal were much less important in Pope's defense of satire. Horace mentions Lucilius three times: the first mention — referring to Lucilius's works praising Scipio — Pope entirely ignores. For the second he quietly substitutes Shippen and Montaigne — the former was known more for his integrity and his willingness to suffer for telling the truth than for his pedestrian satires (Pope, *Twickenham* 4: 385; Weinbrot, *Pope* 213), the latter, who was not a satirist, was valued for his plainspokenness. For the third mention Pope again does not provide an equivalent figure, but he himself echoes Lucilius's outspokenness, in the sharpest passage of the poem. Pope too will "Brand the bold Front of shameless, guilty Men" and "Dash the proud Gamester in his gilded Car" (106–07). But Lucilius is not the ideal. Lucilius had powerful friends like Scipio and Laelius to go to for protection; Pope does not. The friends he mentions in the corresponding lines are the earl of Peterborough and St. John Bolingbroke, a chief "out of War" and a statesman "out of Place" (126).

Pope supplies no equivalent to Lucilius, Jacob Fuchs argues, because he "becomes his own exemplar" (67). His defense of satire emerges through creation of a heroic figure — physically weak, lacking powerful friends, but a lone voice of good in a threatening age. The threats are abundant: slander, hard words, and libel, if not poison or hanging (81–84), from those close to and associated with "the mean Heart that lurks beneath a Star" (108), a direct reference to Walpole (Weinbrot, *Pope* 219–21). Pope does acknowledge being part of a satiric tradition, but he is superior to others in it like Boileau, Dryden, Horace, and Lucilius — partly because they lived in times when satire was understood and accepted while Pope does not, partly because they were "pension'd" or "Laureate" or friends of Maecenus and Scipio and therefore less free to tell the truth than Pope, who is "Un-plac'd, un-pension'd, no Man's Heir, or Slave" (116). He, therefore, must "strip the Gilding off a Knave" (115 — echoing Horace but also, perhaps, Swift's

"Digression on Madness" [*Tale* 173–74]). But he will do so not out of malice but "arm'd for *Virtue*" (105). In the poem's climactic line, Pope applies to himself a line Horace used to characterize Lucilius: "To VIRTUE ONLY and HER FRIENDS, A FRIEND" (121). The timid and uncertain Pope who in the opening lines hesitantly sought advice from Fortescue has, in the course of the poem, emerged as courageous and defiant, willing to stand alone against evil in a corrupt and dangerous era. He is, in the end, decidedly unlike the Horace in the original poem, and this fact sums up the teacher's challenge: conveying simultaneously the Horatian and un-Horatian qualities in a Popian poem to students unfamiliar with both Pope and Horace.

"Teach the Aphorisms": *An Essay on Man*, Madison Avenue, and "Nature"

Brian McCrea

And Malt does More than Milton Can
To Justify God's Ways to Man.
— A. E. Housman, *A Shropshire Lad*, 1896

What's more natural than Natural Light!
— Commercial for Anheuser-Busch's Natural Light Beer,
circa 1985

In his 1983 Clark Library lecture, J. Paul Hunter argues that modern criticism has been particularly unsympathetic to literary works that are "openly didactic" (15). Hunter's goal is not to restore now obscure didactic works to the canon but rather to suggest that our disdain for mere moral instruction has led us to "divorce" the eighteenth-century writers whom we continue to teach (Pope, Swift, and Fielding are his examples) from "the highly charged didactic field in which their works were conceived" (16). Instead we have looked for "irony," for what I elsewhere have called "requisite formal complexity" (123), and thus, Hunter believes, we have narrowed the critical enterprise.

Of course, when Pope writes, "Whatever IS, is RIGHT" (*Essay on Man* 1.294), he leads even his most sympathetic interpreters to shy away from discussing his values or his ideas. Pope's moral appears so unappealing, even so false, that most commentators have focused on the formal features of his verse—the antithesis and balance of his couplets—or have shown that Pope does not know or does not mean what he is saying. A. D. Nuttal typifies the latter approach when he notes that Pope's "lines seem clearer than they really are" (58). David Morris takes perhaps a more helpful approach. While admitting that Pope "was incapable of the sustained conceptual thinking that distinguishes Locke and Berkeley and Hume" (*Alexander Pope* 156), Morris traces Pope's lack of precision to his "aphoristic style" rather than to his confusion or uncertainty. As Morris brilliantly reminds, Pope wrote his *Essay on Man* in a style very different from his earlier works (a style that temporarily misled Pope's contemporaries). The aim of this style— like the aim of all great poetry—is to help the reader "see the world anew" (175). Thus from an unenlightened perspective, "Whatever IS, is RIGHT" is, indeed, a complacent and simpleminded sentence. From the perspective of universal hierarchy and order that Pope attempts to re-create, the statement makes perfect, if unglossable, sense. According to Morris, Pope attempts "the great Augustan miracle of reconciling philosophy to the language of sense" (177), and much of the ambiguity and difficulty of the *Essay* is owing to the differences he must overcome rather than to the "penury" of "his Knowledge." Morris begins his chapter on the *Essay* by reminding us just how impressed Pope's late contemporaries Voltaire and Kant were by his achievement. He then suggests that we accept Pope's aphorisms instead of rendering them ironic, ambiguous, or equivocal. The aphorisms take their rise from paradox and discord but briefly, through Pope's great art, transcend them.

While such judgments defy quantification, I believe my teaching of Pope has improved in the years since Morris's book appeared, precisely because I no longer feel compelled to apologize for, to complicate, or to render ironic Pope's aphorisms. This is particularly true of one of Pope's slipperiest terms — "Nature." If, in the vein of W. K. Wimsatt ("What to Say"), we "explicate" Pope's famous couplet "All Nature is but Art, unknown to thee; / All Chance, Direction, which thou canst not see" (*Essay on Man* 1.289–90), we make the couplet, seemingly so forceful and clear, infinitely elusive. In an admittedly "incomplete" catalog, Arthur O. Lovejoy lists eighteen "senses of nature as aesthetic norm" (" 'Nature' " 70) in the seventeenth and eighteenth centuries. And he warned his readers in 1927, "To read eighteenth-century books . . . without having in mind . . . a map of the meanings of 'nature' is to move about in the midst of ambiguities unrealized" (69). Critics of Pope who followed Lovejoy have not failed to heed his warning. In the 1950s and 1960s, New Critics traced the ambiguity, the ironic tension with which Pope uses the word;[1] even in the 1980s, in a purportedly Marxist and feminist rereading of Pope, Laura Brown finds in the *Essay* "a sliding definition of nature" (*Alexander Pope* 66). Brown, in effect, uses the ambiguity of Pope's "nature" to add political spin to her close reading of Pope, arguing that his shifts "enable" the poem to move between vindication and subversion of the social status quo.

To rouse in my students a feeling that all this philosophizing in verse is somehow relevant to their lives, I take an approach to the *Essay* that initially seems more simpleminded than Lovejoy's or Maynard Mack's or Brown's but that, I trust, is critically defensible in the context of Morris's work on Pope's aphoristic style. I ask my students to consider how totally different Pope's assumptions about nature (whatever they may be) are from those with which we, at least as consumers, operate. In the first reading of the *Essay* that I offer to the students, I take at face value Pope's description of "Nature" as hierarchical, as organized along a "Vast chain of being" (1.237). I then ask them to consider the implications — social, political, ethical — of Pope's model. However "sliding" the word "Nature" may be for Pope, the standards for human conduct he derives from it are, I argue, quite clear. For Pope the great philosophical injunction "Know . . . thyself" (2.1) translates into a command to determine and fill one's place in a larger order. From his description of "Nature," Pope extrapolates an ethics that values submission and modesty (2.43–52) and demeans not only vanity but ambition as well (4.277–308).

Usually, by the time we reach "ambition" something like a learning experience begins for my students. They can see that Pope uses this word, and a host of others ("pride," "liberty," and even "self-love" among them), with very different connotations than we do. Put most simply, Pope understands these words pejoratively, while we, all good postmodern readers, use them positively. When Pope claims that Heaven has given man "knowledge measur'd to his state and place" (1.71), that God "kindly" blinds all species such "That each may fill the circle mark'd by Heav'n" (1.85–86), he brings into question the "proud Science" (1.19) that is at the heart of the great American research university. He also brings into question the motives of both professors and students, all of whom hope to accrue power (admittedly of varying sorts) by gaining knowledge. By reading Pope in this relatively straightforward way, I present him to my students, not as an Augustan conservative, but as a writer who subverts some of our happiest notions about ourselves by taking a radical (in the sense of a departure from the usual or traditional) view of our nature. This aphoristic Pope threatens our epistemological and ontological assumptions to a greater degree than William Wordsworth does, or even, perhaps, Jacques Derrida. He is strikingly different from us, and the differences are unsettling enough to be instructive.

All of which brings us (my class and me) back to "Nature." At the beginning of our study of the *Essay* (I usually give three hours to it), I ask the students to look for that word, particularly in its adjectival form, in the mass media. We spend the final class period on the *Essay* adding up the uses that contemporary advertisers find for "natural" and then testing nature in the commercials against nature in Pope. We have found that nature is everywhere in contemporary advertising; indeed, only the phrase "new and improved" is used more frequently than the word "natural." While the word occurs in expected places — commercials for breakfast cereals — it is particularly popular with advertisers for cosmetics and shampoos. The materials for our contemporary Belindas' "sacred Rites of Pride" (*Rape* 1.128) unfailingly claim to be "natural." And in those commercials for beer that do not employ superannuated athletes or the American flag, the appeal to nature is pervasive. Anheuser-Busch's Natural Light Beer, with its erstwhile claim "What's more natural than Natural Light!" can stimulate, in the light of Pope's *Essay*, all manner of interesting student analysis — both of Pope and of us.

We begin by noting that the slogan, on its face, is preposterous. We can all agree, if regret, that no stream where beer flows like water has ever been found. Some of us can report on brewery tours we have taken — the huge stainless steel tanks, the long conveyor belts, the blindingly fast bottling and stamping machines — and establish that beer is a "made" thing, a product of labor and art. How, then, does the slogan work? Here, of course, responses vary, but the thread common to all is that we assume the natural is equal to the good. The advertiser uses this formula — natural = good — to create in us a positive association with the product.

If I am lucky, the question I ask at this point starts us on the way back to Pope: Why is the natural equal to the good? I have had classes get side-tracked by this question into discussions of purity and truth in labeling. But I also have had classes in which the students (incipient, if unwitting, Words-worthians) point out that the natural self is the best self, the self that endures apart from social restrictions and historical limitations. It is the self beyond the ordinary self, the self that does great deeds and dreams great dreams. By associating their products with this "natural" self, the advertisers suc-ceed in selling them.

Here Pope becomes an interesting, even monitory figure. Students can begin to see how his version of nature, with its spheres within a larger order and its emphasis on boundaries, differs from ours. For Pope knowledge of nature is difficult because that knowledge instructs us in our limitations and failings; for us knowledge is power because knowledge expands and enables our better nature. Knowledge, instead of placing us within a whole and subordinating us to it, offers us mastery of the whole.

At this point, class is out, and I sometimes have the happy, if dangerous, feeling that I have succeeded as a teacher because (1) I have brought my students to think about an important word that they tend to use sloppily and superficially and (2) Alexander Pope has been a helpful, even crucial figure in their self-study. To achieve this end, I must resist the temptation to deconstruct or to repoliticize Pope. By limiting myself to a didactic read-ing of Pope that grants him his aphorisms — a reading that in taking him at face value risks portraying him as a complacent rather than as a radical figure — I find that Pope can become a much more relevant and challenging figure than he is when I trace his ambiguities and "dislodge his work . . . from its personal battlegrounds, from its force and feeling" (J. P. Hunter 15).

The great drawback to my approach, of course, is that it may leave "ambiguities unrealized," particularly for those students who want only a clear sense of what the poem is about for the final examination. This risk, for me, is outweighed by two advantages that I did not anticipate when I started to "teach the aphorisms." First, my lectures are much less cluttered than they were when I was busy showing the different senses of "Nature" in the poem in order to show that Pope did not really mean, "All Nature is but Art, unknown to thee; / All Chance, Direction, which thou canst not see; / . . . Whatever IS, is RIGHT." Rather than cover every reference to nature, I now can focus on eight to ten verse paragraphs that are par-ticularly and tellingly aphoristic.

Second, this approach can activate my students' considerable skills as media critics and thus free me from relying on their less impressive abilities as literary critics. Most students come to my class to fulfill an area requirement

(". . . before 1800 . . .") for their English major, and their interests lie in film, literary theory, and, sometimes, modern literature. By asking them to use the *Essay on Man* as a context for contemporary electronic media, I free them to use their televisions, VCRs, even, in one case, their camcorders. A group in my most recent class produced an interesting video, one counter-pointing lines from Pope with scenes and audio from an array of advertisements. I am not sure how sophisticated their reading of Pope was. In one instance, they superimposed his couplet "All are but parts of one stupendous whole, / Whose body, Nature is, and God the soul" (1.267–68) on a shampoo commercial in which a gorgeous model, riding on a beautiful horse, hair blowing wild and free, claimed of the product, "All natural, it gives my hair the look I love." As I watched the video, I convinced myself that learning was, indeed, taking place. At the end of the show, I was less concerned that the students limn Pope's rich ambiguity; I was happy that they could see his couplets as instructive, even important. Of course, I have only just figured out how to put the date and time on the movies I make with my camcorder, so perhaps I was overawed by my students' technical expertise. Still, the episode left me feeling good enough to treat myself to a Natural Light for a job well done — by me and by my students.

NOTE

[1]A summary of criticism of the *Essay on Man* in the 1950s and 1960s is neither possible nor appropriate here. But I would note that Mack's introduction to the Twickenham edition of the *Essay* (1950) assumed a central role in studies of Pope. In that introduction, Mack described Pope as attempting to reestablish Renaissance principles of order in nature, most particularly "degree" (xliv). Mack emphasized Pope's debts to Milton and his fundamental differences with Bolingbroke — supposedly the philosophical source of the poem. Whatever its intent, Mack's work suggested ambiguities in the poem that previously had gone unnoted. Instead of reflecting neoclassical optimism, the poem now was seen to reflect Renaissance versions of the Fall of Man (1). Mack described Pope as having a "double attitude" toward the passions (xxxviii) — they are both a disease and a divine force. Mack thus cleared the way for readings of the *Essay* that emphasized its religious diction, even though the poem itself makes no mention of Christ, his incarnation, or his passion. And Mack also suggested the need (soon fulfilled) for readings of the poem that would emphasize the complexity and the ambiguity of its philosophical vocabulary. According to Mack, Pope's explanations of evil are based on traditional views (xxxii) rather than on the Enlightenment views of Bolingbroke or Leibniz. This placed the *Essay* in the philosophical context outlined by Lovejoy, with all its attendant "senses" of the ways in which the term "Nature" may be used.

The *Dunciad* and Smart Students:
Learning the Importance of Dunces

Deborah J. Knuth

Teaching *The Dunciad* can be a daunting prospect: the forbidding format, the harsh tone, the devastating treatment of some of the objects, the "occasional" nature of many of the allusions, the confusion of editorial annotation with Pope's own mock-notes — all these might seem reasons to omit the 1729 or 1743 *Dunciad* from an undergraduate syllabus, letting Pope's satire be represented by the smoother, more self-contained *Rape of the Lock* and, say, the engaging *Epilogue to the Satires*. But I want to argue that the very difficulty of teaching *The Dunciad* offers many opportunities that can make it the virtual centerpiece of a course in Restoration and eighteenth-century literature and an indispensable part of a general course on the satiric mode. Even in a British literature survey course, excerpts from *The Dunciad* offer an excellent test case for how we think about engaging undergraduate literature students with satire and with the eighteenth century.

If our lectures ever have a tendency to echo our own undergraduate classes, it is the generalizations we may find ourselves repeating. The received wisdom about satire is that it reinforces "norms," "corrects" "abuses," and, especially in the "age of Pope," "rises above" its transitory subject matter to make an "enduring statement" about the value of a particular stance in politics, religion, or art — and about the value of literature itself. Whether or not we feel compelled to say these things in an introduction to British literature or in a period survey, many of us teach from anthologies that do say them, and *The Dunciad* gives us an opportunity to appreciate how partial an account of satire they convey.

The many idiosyncrasies of *The Dunciad* defy any simple set of "norms" that are being upheld against some sort of challenge. And if we try to suggest that this poem's message transcends its transitory subject matter, Pope has built in subversions to this grand claim. In fact, only by wallowing in the particular can we ever get a general sense of the poem. However much the power of the verse reifies some of the dunces — authors appear in the 1729 "Index of *Things*" in the poem — many remain distinct and lively historical figures. The 1743 version begins with a piece of mock-criticism, an essay "Of the Hero," by "Richardus Aristarchus," where Pope's mock–Richard Bentley pompously notes that "it is not every Knave, nor (let me add) Fool, that is a fit subject for a Dunciad," and the text often gives enough detail to send the reader, intrigued, to the notes to find out who a particular dunce may be. Collected at the foot of the page are not only Pope's notes, of course, but also those of "Scriblerus," "Bentley," "Anon.," "Theobald," and others, all (different) voices of the poet, simultaneously complicating the meaning of *The Dunciad* and mocking any scholarly attempts to understand poetry in general. The point is hardly to tell students to ignore the notes; nor (worse!) should one order a text — there are many — that omits them. To engage students with this particular literary product we need only turn them loose on it. Their detective instinct and their interest in popular culture can easily lead them to become scholars of either of its significant (1729 or 1743) versions. The fact that the poem is, after all, a parody of a scholarly edition of a poem demystifies scholarship: its veil becomes less a protection of the holy of holies than a suit of emperor's clothes. Whatever students have been reading earlier in the semester, whether a *Norton Anthology of English Literature*, paperback editions of individual poets, or "full dress" standard editions of Dryden and Swift, *The Dunciad* gives them an opportunity to laugh at the convention of footnotes, at the portentous language of scholarly debate, and even at their professors. They'll have to laugh at themselves and at Pope, too, as well as with him, because their own pedantic researches will reveal that by the poem's own definition even Pope is something of a dunce.

We need to be certain we aren't letting our students understand satire too simply: identifying the two "sides" to an issue and then lining up with the satirist against the Philistines, Whigs, Dissenters, virtuosi, "scribblers," and so on. Reading Pope's poem, including his notes, with care should make clear that understanding this satire — and any satire — invites detective work, really another name for scholarship. So the student must ask, What's the real story? Why is Pope bothering to attack these guys, anyway? How has he tried to get me to agree with him? What kind of research must I do to check Pope's footnotes before accepting his apparent judgments? Who's committing and who's correcting "abuses"?

I assign students, individually or in groups, to pursue the stories behind one or two dunces each, starting their library research with James Sutherland's notes in volume 5 of the *Twickenham Edition*. This edition supplements Pope's notes with further notes and a biographic appendix — a catalogue raisonné — of dunces at the back. J. V. Guerinot's *Pamphlet Attacks on Alexander Pope 1711–1744* is another important basic source. The Augustan Reprint Society has made some of the more famous attacks widely available; most indispensable is probably Colley Cibber's "Letter from Mr. Cibber to Mr. Pope."[1] But some students will also be studying Theobald's contributions to Shakespearean editing, Cibber's autobiography and dramatic works, Richard Blackmore's epic poems, Lady Mary Wortley Montagu's correspondence, Edmund Curll's publishing policies, or the literary career of Eliza Haywood. How deeply students pursue their subjects depends on the level of the course, but even in a fairly basic course the poem can be divided up among the class, with individual students becoming relative "specialists" on their assigned topics. The resulting oral reports will juxtapose "facts" with the poetic portraits to show how and why Pope tries to enlist us against the dunces, but the reports should also portray objectively the achievements — many of them considerable — of the dunces. Other students can comment on *Peri Bathous, The Memoirs of Martinus Scriblerus*, and parallel Scriblerian satires from the syllabus, such as *The Beggar's Opera* and *Gulliver's Travels*, as they relate to the poem. One student can make a study of the revealing prose apparatus of "Advertisements" and essays "Of the Poem" and "Of the Poet Laureate," and so on.

From their researches students will discover how slippery the idea of norms can be even in an age that often seems easily defined. Of course, that recognition must be Pope's as well, and it is the source of the poem's energy. On the most obvious level, the poem displays Pope's concern not only that "such as *Chaucer* is, shall *Dryden* be" (*Essay on Criticism* 483) but that his own age is already witnessing a shocking shift in standards, which is accelerating the obsolescence of his work and that of his cultural peers — Handel, for example (*Dunciad* 4.45–70). But when Pope attacks contemporary translators of Homer, editors of Shakespeare, fiction writers, and epic poets, he may well be substituting self-interested treatment of his rivals for the role of the impartial prophet crying in a cultural wilderness. Students need, at least, to gather the information that will help them consider this possibility. Simply to have the class compare the first few pages of Theobald's *Shakespeare Restored* (1726) and *The Dunciad Variorum* (1729), preferably in facsimile, should arouse their interest in this project.

Another way to encourage students to think about this poem is to call on their broad knowledge of contemporary culture and to ask how they reconcile this interest with their academic work. My sense is that most students live almost completely bifurcated lives, finding no analogy between their passionate out-of-class focus on sports, music, television, and other media and the material they encounter in the classroom. Professors can become increasingly out of touch with the undergraduate generations and their successive subcultures, but *The Dunciad* can be used profitably to mesh these two worlds and also to instill in our students an analytic stance toward the popular culture they so avidly consume. Assign them an exercise in imitation, asking them to write a prose prospectus (or even a verse paragraph) of a section of a modern *Dunciad*, in which they mock several specific personalities or aspects of the popular culture (a talk-show host, a music video, romance fiction, soap operas) from a conservative or pedantic stance.[2] The process of thinking this way should enlist them in imaginative sympathy with Pope, condemning things with which he was in some ways obsessed. They will come to appreciate the appeal and perhaps the limitations of the satiric stance, with its easy and superior tone. And perhaps, as they come to think more skeptically about their nonacademic pastimes, volumes of cat humor will be less in demand at the campus bookstore.

If we use our study of *The Dunciad* to raise questions of the tension between elite and popular culture, moreover, we can invite students to consider questions of community values in the twentieth century as well as the eighteenth. In 1990, several well-publicized grants by the National Endowment for the Arts made artistic taste the subject of political debate in Washington. At the same time, results of several obscenity trials suggested that the conservative trust in legally termed "community standards" may not be of much help in distinguishing artistic monuments from ephemeral trash. In the cases of both Pope and the contemporary monitors of government support for the arts, it cannot be denied that there is a political complication to aesthetic judgments and that consensus is not easy to achieve. Seeing how anxiety about these distinctions persists over time, students can better appreciate that a society partly defines itself through its public vision of what is — and what is not — art.

The Dunciad can introduce issues of artistic quality within academe as well, especially if students feel that some of the dunces are unfairly excluded by Pope and by us from the literary canon. Pope's use of Militonic imagery to transform the dunces into a satanic threat can then be analyzed with full awareness of its multiple irony, including the historical and literary dilemma that prevents Pope from following Milton in writing an epic poem free from the prefix *mock*. Only when these multiple approaches show students the subtle conflicts of meaning in the satire can we extract the full value of studying *The Dunciad* as a fulcrum between ancients and moderns, before the syllabus proceeds to the novel, that latter-day literary counterpart (and opponent) of the epic poem.

Which *Dunciad* should an instructor assign? When Pope seized the initiative by producing a "scholarly" edition of his own poem as he wrote it, he ensured that editors as well as students and teachers would remain in an uncomfortable relation to the poem ever after. Choosing an edition is particularly complicated if one uses an anthology. The *Norton Anthology* prints only bits of book 4; the *Oxford Anthology* volume on the Restoration and the eighteenth century, only book 4, without notes. If one uses either, one can duplicate a packet of handout materials. But even many editions of Pope omit a significant number of Pope's notes, an essential part of the poem; vigilance is needed when one orders.

Should one teach the 1729 *Dunciad Variorum*, more integral as a work than the much-revised four-book version of 1743? My classroom emphasis on the parody of scholarship in the poem may work especially well with Theobald as the central figure, and the easy availability of the earlier, three-book poem, with all its notes, in the reduced Twickenham version edited by John Butt would seem to make it attractive in a Restoration and eighteenth-century poetry course. But I suspect that most of us, educated from the perspective that, as Margaret Doody (*Daring Muse* 191) insists, "we need Book IV," would prefer to include it, and hence only the four-book version. I teach both *Dunciads* in their chronological places in the syllabus, and my choice shows the shift in Pope's emphases as his career evolved. Only in Aubrey Williams's Riverside edition is the four-book version available with readily accessible annotation, however, and his version abridges the notes considerably.

Whatever decision you make, ask the students to comment on it at the end of the semester. What changes would they recommend in next year's syllabus, and why? The more we make undergraduates partners in the scholarly enterprise, the more considered and valuable their responses.

NOTES

[1]The William Andrews Clark Memorial Library in Los Angeles has recently begun to collect titles associated with *The Dunciad* and plans to publish an annotated bibliography, which will serve as an additional resource.

[2]Nason's *A Modern Dunciad* could be placed on reserve, but it is not precisely a version of the assignment I suggest. In fact, it requires so many footnotes itself, since the world of contemporary poetry is elite rather than popular, that it might defeat the pedagogical spirit of my argument.

CONTRIBUTORS AND SURVEY PARTICIPANTS

Carol Nevin Abromaitis, *Loyola Coll.*
Martin C. Battestin, *Univ. of Virginia*
Fredric V. Bogel, *Cornell Univ.*
M. Elaine Dolan Brown, *New York Inst. of Technology, Old Westbury*
J. Douglas Canfield, *Univ. of Arizona*
Martha C. Carpentier, *Seton Hall Univ.*
David Fairer, *Univ. of Leeds*
Oliver W. Ferguson, *Duke Univ.*
Janet Ruth Heller, *Grand Valley State Univ.*
Charles H. Hinnant, *Univ. of Missouri, Columbia*
Wallace Jackson, *Duke Univ.*
Carey Kaplan, *St. Michael's Coll.*
Thomas G. Kass, *St. Anselm Coll.*
Deborah J. Knuth, *Colgate Univ.*
Donna Landry, *Wayne State Univ.*
Brian McCrea, *Univ. of Florida*
Carey McIntosh, *Hofstra Univ.*
Rachel Ann Miller, *Univ. of California, Davis*
David B. Morris, *Kalamazoo*
Douglas Murray, *Belmont Coll.*
Elizabeth Nelson, *St. Peter's Coll.*
Martha Rainbolt, *DePauw Univ.*
G. S. Rousseau, *Univ. of California, Los Angeles*
Peter J. Schakel, *Hope Coll.*
John Sitter, *Emory Univ.*
Edwin Stein, Jr., *Whitman Coll.*
Albrecht B. Strauss, *Univ. of North Carolina, Chapel Hill*
J. Harlan Underhill, *Greenhills School*
Peter Walmsley, *McMaster Univ.*
Howard Weinbrot, *Univ. of Wisconsin, Madison*
Anne Williams, *Univ. of Georgia*
Donald J. Winslow, *Boston Univ.*
Deborah Baker Wyrick, *North Carolina State Univ.*
R. Paul Yoder, *Duke Univ.*

WORKS CITED

Abbot, Edwin. *A Concordance to the Works of Alexander Pope*. New York: Appleton, 1875.

Abrams, M. H., et al., eds. *The Norton Anthology of English Literature*. 5th ed. Vol. 1. New York: Norton, 1986.

Ackerman, James S. *Palladio*. Rev. ed. Harmondsworth, Eng.: Penguin, 1974.

Adams, Hazard, ed. *Critical Theory since Plato*. New York: Harcourt, 1971.

Addison, Joseph, and Richard Steele. *The Spectator*. Ed. Donald F. Bond. 5 vols. Oxford: Clarendon–Oxford UP, 1965.

Aden, John M. "Pope and Politics: 'The Farce of State.'" Dixon, *Alexander Pope* 172–99.

———. *Pope's Once and Future Kings: Satire and Politics in the Early Career*. Knoxville: U of Tennessee P, 1978.

———. *Something like Horace: Studies in the Art and Allusion of Pope's Horatian Satires*. Nashville: Vanderbilt UP, 1969.

Adler, Jacob H. *The Reach of Art: A Study in the Prosody of Pope*. Gainesville: U of Florida P, 1964.

Allen, Robert J. "Pope and the Sister Arts." *Pope and His Contemporaries: Essays Presented to George Sherburn*. Ed. James L. Clifford and Louis A. Landa. New York: Oxford UP, 1949. 78–88.

Altenbernd, A. L. "On Pope's Horticultural Romanticism." *Journal of English and Germanic Philology* 54 (1955): 470–77.

[Anon.]. *A Popp upon Pope: or, A True and Faithful Account of a Late Horrid and Barbarous Whipping*. . . . London: printed for A. Moore, 1728.

Arnold, Matthew. "The Study of Poetry." *The Works of Matthew Arnold*. Vol. 4. London: Macmillan, 1903. 1–41. 15 vols.

Atkins, G. Douglas. *Quests of Difference: Reading Pope's Poems*. Lexington: UP of Kentucky, 1986.

Aubrey, James R. "Timon's Villa: Pope's Composite Picture." *Studies in Philology* 80 (1983): 325–48.

Auden, W. H. "A Civilized Voice." Rev. of *Alexander Pope*, by Peter Quennell. *New Yorker* 22 Feb. 1969: 128–40.

———. "In Memory of W. B. Yeats." *The Collected Poetry of W. H. Auden*. New York: Random, 1967. 48–51.

Ault, Norman. *New Light on Pope*. London: Methuen, 1949.

Austin, J. L. *How to Do Things with Words*. Cambridge: Oxford UP, 1975.

Barnard, James, ed. *Pope: The Critical Heritage*. London: Routledge, 1973.

Barthes, Roland. *S/Z*. Trans. Richard Miller. New York: Hill, 1974.

Bateson, F. W., and N. A. Joukovsky. *Alexander Pope: A Critical Anthology*. Harmondsworth, Eng.: Penguin, 1971.

Battestin, Martin C. *The Providence of Wit: Aspects of Form in Augustan Literature and the Arts*. 1974. Charlottesville: UP of Virginia, 1989.

Bedford, Emmett G., and Robert T. Dilligan, eds. *A Concordance to the Poems of Alexander Pope*. 2 vols. Detroit: Gale, 1974.

Benayoun, Robert. *The Films of Woody Allen*. Trans. Alexander Walker. New York: Harmony, 1986.

Berry, Reginald. *A Pope Chronology*. Basingstoke, Eng.: Macmillan; Boston: Hall, 1988.

Bloom, Harold, ed. *Alexander Pope's* The Rape of the Lock. New York: Chelsea, 1988.

Bogel, Fredric V. *Acts of Knowledge: Pope's Later Poems*. London: Associated UP; Lewisburg: Bucknell UP, 1981.

Borck, Jim Springer, gen. ed. *The Eighteenth Century: A Current Bibliography*. Ns 1–11 (1975–85). New York: AMS, 1978–90.

Boyce, Benjamin. *The Character-Sketches in Pope's Poems*. Durham: Duke UP, 1962.

Bracher, Frederick. "Pope's Grotto: The Maze of Fancy." *Huntington Library Quarterly* 12 (1949): 140–62.

Brooks-Davies, Douglas. *Pope's* Dunciad *and the Queen of Night: A Study in Emotional Jacobitism*. Manchester, Eng.: Manchester UP, 1985.

Brower, Reuben Arthur. *Alexander Pope: The Poetry of Allusion*. Oxford: Clarendon–Oxford UP, 1959.

———. *The Fields of Light: An Experiment in Critical Reading*. New York: Oxford UP, 1951.

Brower, Reuben A., and Richard Poirier, eds. *In Defense of Reading: A Reader's Approach to Literary Criticism*. New York: Dutton, 1962.

Brown, Laura. *Alexander Pope*. Rereading Literature 1. Oxford: Blackwell, 1985.

———. "Reading Race and Gender: Jonathan Swift." *The Politics of Difference*. Ed. Felicity Nussbaum. Spec. issue of *Eighteenth-Century Studies* 23.4 (1990): 425–43.

Brownell, Morris R. *Alexander Pope and the Arts of Georgian England*. Oxford: Clarendon–Oxford UP, 1978.

Bruffee, Kenneth A. "Peer Tutoring and the 'Conversation of Mankind.'" *Writing Centers: Theory and Administration*. Ed. Gary A. Olson. Urbana: NCTE, 1984. 3–15.

———. "Social Construction, Language, and the Authority of Knowledge: A Bibliographic Essay." *College English* 48 (1986): 773–90.

Bruns, Gerald L. *Heidegger's Estrangements: Language, Truth, and Poetry*. New Haven: Yale UP, 1989.

Byron, George Gordon, Lord. *The Complete Poetical Works*. Ed. Jerome J. McGann. Vol. 3. New York: Oxford UP, 1981.

Callan, Norman. "Pope and the Classics." Dixon, *Alexander Pope* 230–49.

Chapin, Chester. "Alexander Pope: Erasmian Catholic." *Eighteenth-Century Studies* 6 (1973): 411–30.

———."Pope and the Jacobites." *Eighteenth-Century Life* 10 (1986): 59–73.

Charles, Prince of Wales. *A Vision of Britain: A Personal View of Architecture.* New York: Doubleday, 1989.

———. "A Vision of Britain: Architecture in Crisis." *Architectural Digest* Oct. 1989: 32–34, 43–50.

Cibber, Colley. *An Apology for the Life of Colley Cibber, Comedian, and Late Patentee of the Theatre-Royal.* 1740. Ed. Byrne R. S. Fone. Ann Arbor: U of Michigan P, 1968.

———. "A Letter from Mr. Cibber to Mr. Pope." 1742. Augustan Reprint Society Publication 158. Introd. Helene Koon. Los Angeles: William Andrews Clark Memorial Library, 1973.

Cixous, Hélène, and Catherine Clement. *The Newly Born Woman.* Trans. Betsy Wing. Theory and History of Literature 37. Minneapolis: U of Minnesota P, 1986.

Claridge, Laura. "Pope's Rape of Excess." *Perspectives on Pornography: Sexuality in Film and Literature.* New York: St. Martin's, 1988. 129–43.

Clark, David Ridgely. "Landscape Painting Effects in Pope's *Homer.*" *Journal of Aesthetics and Art Criticism* 22 (1963): 25–28.

Corse, Taylor. "Heaven's 'Last Best Work': Pope's *Epistle to a Lady.*" *SEL* 27 (1987): 413–25.

Cunningham, Joseph S. *Pope: The Rape of the Lock.* London: Arnold, 1961.

Damrosch, Leopold, Jr. *The Imaginative World of Alexander Pope.* Berkeley: U of California P, 1987.

D'Angelo, Frank J. "Imitation and Style." *College Composition and Communication* 24 (1973): 283–90.

Derrida, Jacques. "Plato's Pharmacy." *Dissemination.* Trans. Barbara Johnson. Chicago: U of Chicago P, 1981. 61–171.

Devonshire, Duke of (Andrew Cavendish). "Chiswick House: Polishing a Family Jewel." *Architectural Digest* Aug. 1989: 28, 34, 38.

Dixon, Peter, ed. *Alexander Pope: Writers and Their Background.* Athens: Ohio UP, 1972.

———. "'Talking upon Paper': Pope and Eighteenth Century Conversation." *English Studies* 46 (1965): 36–44.

———. *The World of Pope's Satires: An Introduction to the* Epistles *and* Imitations of Horace. London: Methuen, 1968.

Doody, Margaret Anne. *The Daring Muse: Augustan Poetry Reconsidered.* Cambridge: Cambridge UP, 1985.

———. "Swift among the Women." *Yearbook of English Studies* 18 (1988): 68–92.

Douglas, Mary. *Purity and Danger: An Analysis of the Concepts of Pollution and Taboo.* London: Routledge, 1966.

Downie, J. A. "1688: Pope and the Rhetoric of Jacobitism." Fairer, *New Contexts* 9–24.

Dryden, John. "Discourse concerning the Original and Progress of Satire." *Poems 1693–1696.* Vol. 4 of *Works.* Ed. A. B. Chambers, William Frost, and Vinton A. Dearing. Berkeley: U of California P, 1974. 3–90.

————. *The Poems and Fables of John Dryden*. Ed. James Kinsley. Oxford: Oxford UP, 1970.

————. Preface to *Annus Mirabilis*. *Works* 1: 49–56.

————. *The Works of John Dryden*. Ed. Edward Niles Hooker and H. T. Swedenberg, Jr. 20 vols. Berkeley: U of California P, 1956–89.

Dunlop, Ian. "Cannons, Middlesex: A Conjectural Reconstruction." *Country Life* Dec. 1949: 1950–54.

Easthope, Anthony. *Poetry as Discourse*. London: Methuen, 1983.

Edwards, Thomas R., Jr. *This Dark Estate: A Reading of Pope*. Berkeley: U of California P, 1963.

Ehrenpreis, Irvin. "The Cistern and the Fountain." *Pope: A Collection of Critical Essays*. Ed. J. V. Guerinot. Englewood Cliffs: Prentice, 1972. 111–23.

————. "The Style of Sound: The Literary Value of Pope's Versification." *Literary Meaning and Augustan Values*. Charlottesville: UP of Virginia, 1974. 232–46.

Eliot, T. S. Introduction. *Selected Poems*. By Ezra Pound. 1928. London: Faber, 1928. vii–xxv.

————. *Selected Prose of T. S. Eliot*. Ed. Frank Kermode. New York: Harcourt, 1975.

Elliot, Robert C. *The Power of Satire: Magic, Ritual, Art*. Princeton: Princeton UP, 1960.

Empson, William. "Wit in the *Essay on Criticism*." Mack, *Essential Articles* 198–216.

Erskine-Hill, Howard. "Alexander Pope: The Political Poet in His Time." *Modern Essays on Eighteenth-Century Literature*. Ed. Leopold Damrosch, Jr. New York: Oxford UP, 1988. 123–40.

————. "Literature and the Jacobite Cause: Was There a Rhetoric of Jacobitism?" *Ideology and Conspiracy: Aspects of Jacobitism, 1689–1759*. Ed. Eveline Cruickshanks. Edinburgh: Donald, 1982. 49–69.

————. *Pope: The Dunciad*. London: Arnold, 1972.

————. *The Social Milieu of Alexander Pope: Lives, Example, and the Poetic Response*. New Haven: Yale UP, 1975.

Erskine-Hill, Howard, and Anne Smith, eds. *The Art of Alexander Pope*. New York: Barnes, 1979.

Fabricant, Carole. "Pope's Moral, Political, and Cultural Combat." *Eighteenth Century: Theory and Interpretation* 29 (1988): 165–87.

Fairer, David. *Pope: New Contexts*. New York: Wheatsheaf-Harvester, 1990.

————. *Pope's Imagination*. Manchester: Manchester UP, 1984.

Ferguson, Rebecca. *The Unbalanced Mind: Pope and the Rule of Passion*. Brighton: Harvester, 1986.

Foster, Gretchen M. *Pope versus Dryden: A Controversy in Letters to the* Gentleman's Magazine, *1789–1791*. English Literary Studies Monograph Series 44. Victoria: U of British Columbia, 1989.

Fowler, Alastair. "Country House Poems: The Politics of a Genre." *Seventeenth Century* 1 (1986): 1–14.

Fox, Christopher. *Locke and the Scriblerians: Identity and Consciousness in Early Eighteenth-Century Britain*. Berkeley: U of California P, 1988.

Fraser, George. "Pope and Homer." *Augustan Worlds: Essays in Honour of A. R. Humphreys*. Ed. J. C. Hilson, M. M. B. Jones, and J. R. Watson. Leicester, Eng.: Leicester UP, 1978. 119–30.

Freud, Sigmund. "The 'Uncanny.'" *The Standard Edition of the Complete Psychological Works of Sigmund Freud*. Trans. and ed. James Strachey et al. 24 vols. London: Hogarth, 1953–74. 17: 210–56.

Frye, Northrop. *Anatomy of Criticism*. Princeton: Princeton UP, 1957.

———. *Fearful Symmetry: A Study of William Blake*. Princeton: Princeton UP, 1947.

Fuchs, Jacob. *Reading Pope's Imitations of Horace*. Lewisburg: Bucknell UP, 1989.

Girard, Rene. *Violence and the Sacred*. Trans. Patrick Gregory. Baltimore: Johns Hopkins UP, 1977.

Girouard, Mark. *Life in the English Country House*. Harmondsworth, Eng.: Penguin, 1980.

Goad, Caroline. *Horace in the English Literature of the Eighteenth Century*. New Haven: Yale UP, 1918.

Goldstein, Malcolm. *Pope and the Augustan Stage*. Stanford: Stanford UP, 1958.

Gordon, I. R. F. *A Preface to Pope*. Preface Books. London: Longman, 1976.

Griffin, Dustin H. *Alexander Pope: The Poet in the Poems*. Princeton: Princeton UP, 1978.

Griffith, Reginald H. *Alexander Pope: A Bibliography*. 2 vols. Austin: U of Texas P, 1922–27.

———. "Pope on the Art of Gardening." *Texas University Department of English Studies in English* 31 (1952): 52–56.

Guerinot, Joseph V. *Pamphlet Attacks on Alexander Pope, 1711–1744: A Descriptive Bibliography*. New York: New York UP, 1969.

Hakluyt, Richard. *A Discourse on Western Planting, Written in the Year 1584*. Ed. Charles Deane. Cambridge: Wilson, 1877.

Halsband, Robert. *The Life of Lady Mary Wortley Montagu*. Oxford: Clarendon–Oxford UP, 1956.

———. *The Rape of the Lock and Its Illustrations, 1714–1896*. Oxford: Clarendon–Oxford UP, 1980.

Hammond, Brean S. *Pope*. Brighton: Harvester New Readings, 1986.

———. *Pope and Bolingbroke: A Study of Friendship and Influence*. Columbia: U of Missouri P, 1984.

Hervey, John. *Lord Hervey and His Friends*. Ed. Earl of Ilchester. London: Murray, 1950.

Hill, Christopher. *The Century of Revolution: 1603–1714*. New York: Norton, 1961.

Horace. *Satires, Epistles, and Ars Poetica*. Trans. H. Rushton Fairclough. Loeb Classical Library. London: Heinemann, 1926.

———. *The Works of Horace*. Trans. Christopher Smart. 2 vols. London: Newberry, 1756.

Hotch, Ripley. "Pope Surveys His Kingdom: *An Essay on Criticism*." *Studies in English Literature* 13 (1973): 474–87.

Hunt, John Dixon. "Emblem and Expressionism in the Eighteenth-Century Landscape Garden." *Eighteenth-Century Studies* 4 (1971): 294–317.

———, ed. The Rape of the Lock: A Casebook. London: Macmillan, 1968.

Hunter, G. K. "The 'Romanticism' of Pope's Horace." *Essays in Criticism* 10 (1960): 390–404.

Hunter, J. Paul. "Fielding and the Modern Reader: The Problem of Temporal Transition." *Henry Fielding in His Time and Ours*. Los Angeles: William Andrews Clark Memorial Library, 1987. 1–28.

Ingram, Allan. *Intricate Laughter in the Satire of Swift and Pope*. New York: St. Martin's, 1986.

Irigaray, Luce. *Speculum of the Other Woman*. Trans. Gillian C. Gill. Ithaca: Cornell UP, 1985.

Jackson, Wallace. *Vision and Re-vision in Alexander Pope*. Detroit: Wayne State UP, 1983.

Jackson-Stops, Gervase, ed. *The Treasure Houses of Britain: Five Hundred Years of Private Patronage and Art Collecting*. New Haven: Yale UP, 1985.

Jackson-Stops, Gervase, and James Pipkin. *The English Country House: A Grand Tour*. Boston: Little, 1985.

Johnson, Samuel. *Life of Pope. Lives of the English Poets*. Ed. George Birkbeck Hill. Vol. 3. Oxford: Clarendon–Oxford UP, 1905. New York: Octagon, 1967. 82–276.

Jones, Emrys. "Pope and Dulness: The Chatterton Lecture Delivered on an English Poet: 13 November 1968." *Publications of the British Academy* (1969): 232–63.

Jones, John A. "The Analogy of Eighteenth-Century Music and Poetry: Bach and Pope." *Centennial Review* 21 (1977): 211–35.

———. *Pope's Couplet Art*. Athens: Ohio UP, 1969.

Jones, Wendy L. *Talking on Paper: Alexander Pope's Letters*. English Literary Studies Monograph Series 50. Victoria: U of British Columbia, 1990.

Jordan, Winthrop P. *The White Man's Burden: Historical Origins of Racism in the United States*. New York: Oxford UP, 1974.

Kallich, Martin I. *Heaven's First Law: Rhetoric and Order in Pope's* Essay on Man. De Kalb: Northern Illinois UP, 1967.

Kamuf, Peggy. *Fictions of Feminine Desire: Disclosures of Heloise*. Lincoln: U of Nebraska P, 1982.

Kelsall, Malcolm. "Augustus and Pope." *Huntington Library Quarterly* 39 (1976): 117–31.

Kenner, Hugh. *The Counterfeiters: An Historical Comedy*. Bloomington: Indiana UP, 1968.

Kernan, Alvin B. *The Cankered Muse: Satire of the English Renaissance*. New Haven: Yale UP, 1959.

———. *The Plot of Satire*. New Haven: Yale UP, 1966.

Kinsley, William. *Contexts 2:* The Rape of the Lock. Hamden: Archon, 1979.

Knight, Douglas. *Pope and the Heroic Tradition: A Critical Study of His* Iliad. New Haven: Yale UP, 1951.

———. "Pope as a Student of Homer." *Comparative Literature* 4 (1952): 75–82.

Kowalk, Wolfgang. *Alexander Pope: An Annotated Bibliography of Twentieth-Century Criticism, 1900–1979.* Frankfurt am Main: Lang, 1981.

Landa, Louis A. "Pope's Belinda, the General Emporie of the World, and the Wondrous Worm." *South Atlantic Quarterly* 70 (1971): 215–35.

Landry, Donna. *The Muses of Resistance: Laboring-Class Women's Poetry in Britain, 1739–1796.* Cambridge: Cambridge UP, 1990.

Lauritzen, Peter, and Reinhart Wolf. *Villas of the Veneto.* New York: Abrams, 1988.

Leranbaum, Miriam. *Alexander Pope's "Opus Magnum," 1729–44.* Oxford: Clarendon–Oxford UP, 1977.

Lindley, David, ed. *De puluerea coniuratione [The Gunpowder Plot].* Trans. Robin Sowerby. Leeds: Leeds Studies in English, 1987.

Lipking, Lawrence. *Abandoned Women and Poetic Tradition.* Chicago: U of Chicago P, 1988.

Locke, John. *An Essay concerning Human Understanding.* Ed. Peter H. Nidditch. Oxford: Clarendon–Oxford UP, 1975.

Lopez, Cecilia L. *Alexander Pope: An Annotated Bibliography, 1945–1967.* Gainesville: U of Florida P, 1970.

Lovejoy, Arthur O. *The Great Chain of Being.* Cambridge: Harvard UP, 1936.

———. "'Nature' as Aesthetic Norm." *Essays in the History of Ideas.* Baltimore: Johns Hopkins UP, 1948. 69–77.

Lumsden, Susan. "A Palladian Journey in Vicenza." *New York Times* 13 Aug. 1989, sec. 5: 8–9.

Mack, Maynard. *Alexander Pope: A Life.* New York: Norton, 1985.

———. *"Collected in Himself": Essays Critical, Biographical, and Bibliographical on Pope and Some of His Contemporaries.* Newark: U of Delaware P, 1982.

———, ed. *Essential Articles for the Study of Alexander Pope.* Rev. and enl. Hamden: Archon, 1968.

———. *The Garden and the City: Retirement and Politics in the Later Poetry of Pope, 1731–1743.* Toronto: U of Toronto P, 1969.

———, ed. *The Last and Greatest Art: Some Unpublished Poetical Manuscripts of Alexander Pope.* Newark: U of Delaware P, 1984.

———. "On Reading Pope." *College English* 7 (1946): 263–73.

———. "A Poet in His Landscape: Pope at Twickenham." *From Sensibility to Romanticism: Essays Presented to Frederick A. Pottle.* Ed. Frederick W. Hilles and Harold Bloom. New York: Oxford UP, 1965.

———. "'Wit and Poetry and Pope': Some Observations on His Imagery." *Pope and His Contemporaries: Essays Presented to George Sherburn.* Ed. James Clifford and Louis A. Landa. Oxford: Clarendon–Oxford UP, 1949. 20–40.

———. *The World of Alexander Pope.* New Haven: Yale UP, 1988.

Mack, Maynard, and James A. Winn, eds. *Pope: Recent Essays by Several Hands.* Hamden: Archon, 1980.

Maclean, Ian. *The Renaissance Notion of Woman*. New York: Cambridge UP, 1980.

Maresca, Thomas E. *Pope's Horatian Poems*. Columbus: Ohio State UP, 1966.

Martin, Peter. *Pursuing Innocent Pleasures: The Gardening World of Alexander Pope*. Hamden: Archon–Shoe String, 1984.

Mason, H. A. *To Homer through Pope: An Introduction to Homer's* Iliad *and Pope's Translation*. London: Chatto, 1972.

McCrea, Brian. *Addison and Steele Are Dead: The English Department, Its Canon, and the Professionalization of Literary Criticism*. Newark: U of Delaware P, 1990.

Mell, Donald C., Jr. *English Poetry, 1660–1800*. Information Guide Series 40. Detroit: Gale, 1982.

Modleski, Tania. "Feminism and the Power of Interpretation: Some Critical Readings." *Feminist Studies/Critical Studies*. Ed. Teresa de Lauretis. Bloomington: Indiana UP, 1986. 121–38.

Montagu, Lady Mary Wortley. *The Complete Letters*. Ed. Robert Halsband. 3 vols. Clarendon–Oxford UP, 1965–67.

———. *Essays and Poems and* Simplicity, a Comedy. Ed. Robert Halsband and Isobel Grundy. Oxford: Clarendon–Oxford UP, 1977.

Morreall, John. *The Philosophy of Laughter and Humor*. Albany: State U of New York P, 1987.

Morris, David B. *Alexander Pope: The Genius of Sense*. Cambridge: Harvard UP, 1984.

———, ed. Spec. issue on Pope. *Eighteenth Century: Theory and Interpretation* 29 (1988): 97–224.

Mudrick, Marvin. *Mudrick Transcribed: Classes and Talks*. Ed. Lance Kaplan. Santa Barbara: U of California P, 1989.

Murphy, James J. "The Modern Value of Roman Methods of Teaching Writing, with Answers to Twelve Current Fallacies." *Writing on the Edge* 1 (1989): 28–37.

———. "Roman Writing Instruction as Described by Quintilian." *A Short History of Writing Instruction from Ancient Greece to Twentieth-Century America*. Ed. James J. Murphy. Davis: Hermagoras, 1990. 19–76.

Nason, Richard. *A Modern Dunciad*. New York: Smith, 1978.

National Geographic Atlas of the World. 5th ed. Washington: National Geographic Soc., 1981.

Nicolson, Colin. *Pope: Essays for the Tercentenary*. Aberdeen: Aberdeen UP, 1988.

Nicolson, Marjorie H., and G. S. Rousseau. *"This Long Disease, My Life": Alexander Pope and the Sciences*. Princeton: Princeton UP, 1968.

Nicolson, Nigel. *The National Trust Book of Great Houses of Britain*. Boston: Godine, 1978.

Nokes, David, and Janet Barron. *An Annotated Critical Bibliography of Augustan Poetry*. Hertfordshire: Wheatsheaf-Harvester; New York: St. Martin's, 1989.

Nussbaum, Felicity. *The Brink of All We Hate: English Satires on Women, 1660–1750*. Lexington: UP of Kentucky, 1984.

 ————. "Pope's 'To a Lady' and the Eighteenth-Century Woman." *Philological Quarterly* 54 (1975): 444–56.

Nuttall, A. D. *Pope's* Essay on Man. London: Allen, 1984.

Oldham, John. *The Works of Mr. John Oldham, Together with His Remains.* London, 1684.

Parkin, Rebecca Price. *The Poetic Workmanship of Alexander Pope.* Minneapolis: U of Minnesota P, 1955.

Paulson, Ronald. *The Fictions of Satire.* Baltimore: Johns Hopkins UP, 1967.

Plowden, G. F. C. *Pope on Classic Ground.* Athens: Ohio UP, 1983.

Pocock, J. G. A. *The Machiavellian Moment.* Princeton: Princeton UP, 1975.

————. *Virtue, Commerce, and History.* Cambridge: Cambridge UP, 1985.

Pohli, Carol Virginia. "The Point Where Sense and Dulness Meet: What Pope Knows about Knowing and about Women." *Eighteenth-Century Studies* 19 (1985–86): 206–34.

Pollak, Ellen. *The Poetics of Sexual Myth: Gender and Ideology in the Verse of Swift and Pope.* Chicago: U of Chicago P, 1985.

————. "Pope and Sexual Difference: Woman as Part and Counterpart in the 'Epistle to a Lady.'" *SEL* 24 (1984): 461–81.

Pope, Alexander. *Alexander Pope: Selected Poetry and Prose.* Ed. Robin Sowerby. London: Routledge, 1988.

————. *The Art of Sinking in Poetry [Peri Bathous].* Ed. Edna Leake Steeves. 1952. New York: Russell, 1968.

————. *The Correspondence of Alexander Pope.* Ed. George Sherburn. 5 vols. Oxford: Clarendon–Oxford UP, 1956.

————. *The Dunciad Variorum. With the Prolegomena of Scriblerus.* 1729. Facsimile. Leeds: Scolar, 1966.

————. *Literary Criticism of Alexander Pope.* Ed. and introd. Bertrand A. Goldgar. Regents Critics Series. Lincoln: U of Nebraska P, 1965.

————. *Memoirs of the Extraordinary Life, Works, and Discoveries of Martinus Scriblerus.* Ed. Charles Kerby-Miller. 1950. New York: Oxford UP, 1988.

————. *The Poems of Alexander Pope: A One-Volume Edition of the Twickenham Text with Selected Annotations.* Ed. John Butt. London: Methuen; New Haven: Yale UP, 1963.

————. *Poetry and Prose of Alexander Pope.* Ed. Aubrey Williams. Riverside edition. Boston: Houghton, 1969.

————. *Pope: Poems and Prose.* Ed. Douglas Grant. New York: Penguin, 1985.

————. *Pope's "Epistle to Bathurst": A Critical Reading with an Edition of the Manuscripts.* Ed. Earl R. Wasserman. Baltimore: Johns Hopkins UP, 1960.

————. "Pope's *Pastorals.*" Ed. and commentary by Maynard Mack. *Scriblerian* 12 (1980): 85–161.

————. *Pope's* Windsor-Forest, *1712: A Study of the Washington University Holograph.* Ed. Robert M. Schmitz. St. Louis: Washington UP, 1952.

————. *The Prose Works of Alexander Pope, 1711–20.* Vol. 1: *The Earlier Works, 1711–1720.* Ed. Norman Ault. Oxford: Blackwell, 1936. Vol. 2: *The Major*

Works, 1725.1744. Ed. Rosemary Cowler. Hamden: Archon–Shoe String, 1986.

——. *The Rape of the Lock*. Ed. Geoffrey Tillotson. 3rd ed. London:Methuen, 1971.

——. *Selected Prose of Alexander Pope*. Ed. Paul Hammond. Cambridge: Cambridge UP, 1987.

——. *The Twickenham Edition of the Works of Alexander Pope*. Ed. John Butt et al. 11 vols. London: Methuen; New Haven: Yale UP, 1939–69.

——. *The Works of Alexander Pope*. Ed. Elwin Whitwell and W. J. Courthope. 10 vols. London: Murray, 1871–79.

Pound, Ezra. "Marianne Moore and Mina Loy." *Selected Prose, 1909–1965*. Ed. W. Cookson. London: New Directions, 1973. 424–25.

Price, Martin, ed. *The Restoration and the Eighteenth Century*. New York: Oxford UP, 1973.

Rawson, C. J., ed. *Pope, Swift, and Their Circle*. Spec. issue of *Yearbook of English Studies* 18 (1988): x + 1–366.

Rayman, Jan, and Eran Zaidel. "Rhyming and the Right Hemisphere." *Brain and Language* 40.1 (1991): 89–105.

Richards, J. M. *The National Trust Book of English Architecture*. New York: Norton, 1981.

Ricoeur, Paul. *Freud and Philosophy: An Essay on Interpretation*. New Haven: Yale UP, 1970.

Rogers, Pat. *An Introduction to Pope*. London: Methuen, 1975.

——. "Pope and the Social Scene." Dixon, *Alexander Pope* 101–42.

Rosoman, T. S. "The Decoration and Use of the Principal Apartments of Chiswick House, 1727–70." *Burlington Magazine* Oct. 1985: 663–77.

Rosslyn, Felicity. *Alexander Pope: A Literary Life*. New York: St. Martin's, 1990.

Rothman, Irving N. "The Quincunx in Pope's Moral Aesthetics." *Philological Quarterly* 55 (1976): 374–88.

Rousseau, G. S. "On Reading Pope." Dixon, *Alexander Pope* 1–59.

——, ed. *Twentieth Century Interpretations of* The Rape of the Lock: *A Collection of Critical Essays*. Englewood Cliffs: Prentice, 1969.

Rousseau, G. S., and Pat Rogers, eds. *The Enduring Legacy: Alexander Pope Tercentenary Essays*. Cambridge: Cambridge UP, 1988.

Rudat, Wolfgang E. H. "Sex-Role Reversal and Miltonic Theology in Pope's *Rape of the Lock*." *Journal of Evolutionary Psychology* 8 (1987): 48–62.

Rumbold, Valerie. *Women's Place in Pope's World*. Cambridge Studies in Eighteenth-Century English Literature and Thought 2. Cambridge: Cambridge UP, 1989.

Salvaggio, Ruth. *Enlightened Absence: Neoclassical Configurations of the Feminine*. Urbana: U of Illinois P, 1988.

Sambrook, James. *The Eighteenth Century: The Intellectual and Cultural Context of English Literature, 1700–1789*. London: Longman, 1986.

——. "Pope and the Visual Arts." Dixon, *Alexander Pope* 143–71.

Schleifer, Ronald, ed. *The Poststructuralist Pope*. Spec. issue of *New Orleans Review* 15.4 (1988): 1–85.

Sedgwick, Eve Kosofsky. *Between Men: English Literature and Male Homosocial Desire*. New York: Columbia UP, 1985.

Seidel, Michael. *Satiric Inheritance: Rabelais to Sterne*. Princeton: Princeton UP, 1979.

Shankman, Steven. *Pope's Iliad: Homer in the Age of Passion*. Princeton: Princeton UP, 1983.

Sherburn, George. *The Early Career of Alexander Pope*. Oxford: Clarendon–Oxford UP, 1934.

———. "Pope at Work." *Essays in the Eighteenth Century Presented to David Nichol Smith in Honour of His Seventieth Birthday*. Ed. James Sutherland and F. P. Wilson. Oxford: Clarendon–Oxford UP, 1945. 49–64.

Sitter, John E. *Argument of Augustan Wit*. Cambridge: Cambridge UP, 1991.

———. *The Poetry of Pope's* Dunciad. Minneapolis: U of Minnesota P, 1971.

Smith, Molly. "The Mythical Implications in Pope's 'Epistle to a Lady.' " *SEL* 27 (1987): 427–36.

Spacks, Patricia Meyer. *An Argument of Images: The Poetry of Alexander Pope*. Cambridge: Harvard UP, 1971.

———. "Some Reflections on Satire." *Genre* 1 (1968): 13–20.

Spence, Joseph. *Observations, Anecdotes, and Characters of Books and Men*. Ed. James Osborn. 2 vols. Oxford: Clarendon–Oxford UP, 1966.

Spitzer, Leo. *Classical and Christian Ideas of World Harmony*. Baltimore: Johns Hopkins UP, 1963.

Stack, Frank. *Pope and Horace: Studies in Imitation*. Cambridge: Cambridge UP, 1985.

Stone, Lawrence. *The Family, Sex, and Marriage in England, 1500–1800*. New York: Harper, 1977.

Sullivan, Dale L. "Attitudes toward Imitation: Classical Culture and the Modern Temper." *Rhetoric Review* 8 (1989): 5–21.

Summerson, John. "The Classical Country House in Eighteenth-Century England." *Journal of the Royal Society of Arts* 107 (1959): 539–87.

Swift, Jonathan. *The Correspondence of Jonathan Swift*. Ed. Harold Williams. 5 vols. Oxford: Clarendon–Oxford UP, 1963–65.

———. *Gulliver's Travels*. Ed. Peter Dixon and John Chalker. Harmondsworth, Eng.: Penguin, 1967.

———. *The Poems of Jonathan Swift*. Ed. Harold Williams. 3 vols. Oxford: Clarendon–Oxford UP, 1958.

———. *The Prose Works of Jonathan Swift*. Ed. Herbert Davis. 14 vols. Oxford: Blackwell, 1939–68.

———. *A Tale of a Tub*. Ed. A. C. Guthkelch and D. Nichol Smith. 2nd ed. Oxford: Clarendon–Oxford UP, 1958.

Sypher, Wylie, ed. *Enlightenment England*. New York: Norton, 1962.

Temple, C. M., et al. "Ten Pen Men: Rhyming Skills in Two Children with Callosal Agenesis." *Brain and Language* 37.4 (1989): 548–64.

Terence. *The Comedies.* Trans. Betty Radice. London: Penguin, 1976.

Theobald, Lewis. *Shakespeare Restored.* 1726. New York: AMS, 1970.

Tillotson, Geoffrey. *On the Poetry of Pope.* 2nd ed. Oxford: Clarendon–Oxford UP, 1950.

———. "Pope." *English Poetry: Select Bibliographical Guides.* Ed. A. E. Dyson. London: Oxford UP, 1971. 128–43.

Tillotson, Geoffrey, Paul Fussell, and Marshall Waingrow, eds. *Eighteenth-Century English Literature.* New York: Harcourt, 1969.

Tobin, James Edward. *Alexander Pope: A List of Critical Studies Published from 1895 to 1944.* New York: Cosmopolitan Science and Art, 1945.

Trimbur, John. "Consensus and Difference in Collaborative Learning." *College English* 51 (1989): 602–16.

Vander Meulen, David L. *Pope's* Dunciad *of 1728: A History and Facsimile.* Charlottesville: UP of Virginia, 1991.

———. *Where Angels Fear to Tread: Descriptive Bibliography and Alexander Pope.* Washington: Library of Congress, 1988.

Warton, Joseph. *An Essay on the Genius and Writings of Pope.* 1756; 1782. Facs. 4th ed. 2 vols. New York: Garland, 1970.

Wasserman, Earl R. *The Subtler Language.* Baltimore: Johns Hopkins UP, 1959.

Weinbrot, Howard. *Alexander Pope and the Traditions of Formal Verse Satire.* Princeton: Princeton UP, 1982.

———. "Recent Studies in the Restoration and Eighteenth Century." *SEL* 25 (1985): 692–94.

White, Douglas H. *Pope and the Context of Controversy: The Manipulation of Ideas in* An Essay on Man. Chicago: U of Chicago P, 1970.

Williams, Anne. *Prophetic Strain: The Greater Lyric in the Eighteenth Century.* Chicago: U of Chicago P, 1984.

Williams, Aubrey L. *Pope's* Dunciad: *A Study of Its Meaning.* London: Methuen, 1955.

Wilson, Penelope. "Feminism and the Augustans: Some Readings and Problems." *Critical Quarterly* 28 (1986): 80–92.

Wimsatt, W. K. *The Verbal Icon.* Knoxville: UP of Kentucky, 1954.

———. "What to Say about a Poem." *Hateful Contraries: Studies in Literature and Criticism.* Lexington: UP of Kentucky, 1965. 215–42.

Winn, James. "Writing in the Margins of Mack: Continuing Problems in the Biography of Pope." *Scriblerian* 21 (1988): 6.

Wood, Allen G. *Literary Satire and Theory: A Study of Horace, Boileau, and Pope.* New York: Garland, 1985.

Woodman, Thomas. *Politeness and Poetry in the Age of Pope.* London: Associated UP, 1989.

Woolf, Virginia. *To the Lighthouse.* 1927. New York: Harcourt, 1955.

Wundram, Manfred, Thomas Pape, and Paolo Marton. *Andrea Palladio (1508–1580): Architect between the Renaissance and Baroque.* Cologne: Taschen, n.d.

Yearsley, Ann. *Poems on Various Subjects.* London: Robinson, 1787.

INDEX OF NAMES

INDEX OF WORKS BY POPE